FINDING GOD'S WILL

In the Decisions of Life

Help for those striving to
find and follow God's will

by

MARK HYSKELL

Christian Faith
PUBLISHING

To: Terry & Billie,
You Are Loved!
Mark

ISBN 978-1-64569-921-7 (paperback)
ISBN 978-1-64569-923-1 (hardcover)
ISBN 978-1-64569-922-4 (digital)

Christian Faith Publishing, Inc.
832 Park Avenue
Meadville, PA 16335
www.christianfaithpublishing.com

Printed in the United States of America

"Nowhere have I seen a book just like it, and seldom have I seen one any more faithful to the corpus of the Scriptures. Without reservation I commend this excellent study in the finding of God's will."

Dr. Paige Patterson
Past President, Southwestern Baptist Theological Seminary
Fort Worth, Texas

"Lots of folks have explored the concept of 'how to know' the will of God. Mark Hyskell has written in these pages from the overflow of his life's journey about his quest of FINDING GOD'S WILL for himself. He relates to every man's struggle. His skills in conveying clear Biblical principles supported by great illustrations, powerful quotations from giants of the faith, and personal honesty and insights provide practical principles that are readily applicable. This is the kind of book every Christian would benefit from reading to gain understanding about doing God's will."

Nick Garland
Pastor, First Baptist Church
Broken Arrow, Oklahoma

"Mark D. Hyskell's Finding God's Will is a powerfully insightful look into Christ's call to total surrender. With its down to earth illustrations and practical life applications, this is a must read for anyone seeking to know what it means to truly follow Christ and discern His voice."

Brad Vickrey
Pastor, First Baptist Church
Forgan, Oklahoma

"This is more than a book about finding God's will for your life. It is a book about a vibrant personal relationship with Jesus Christ. It is written like a conversation between close friends that is deeply vulnerable and personal."

Mike Stowe
Bible Teacher and Church Leader, First Baptist Church
Broken Arrow, Oklahoma

"I really enjoyed reading Finding God's Will because the Lord clearly spoke to my heart through the scriptural truths in its pages. I wish you could publish the book for the whole world because it is so needed, especially for all our young people. This book clearly expounds the principles of finding and following God's will. Thank you for this book!"

Marvin Azuelo Verde
Pastor, Barangay 2 Community Church (SBC)
Team Leader, Champions for Christ
Philippines

"Mark has presented a book that is well written and illustrated and shows his passion for the subject. It can be a foundational tool used to assist people in acquiring a thorough understanding of God's will from a person who has learned it through life experiences. It is an especially good book for new Christians to read and digest. God's will is a complex subject and many of the complexities are addressed herein."

Danny McCartney
Bible Teacher and Church Leader
Jacksonville, Florida

"Having never personally read another book on this exact subject, I can truthfully say this book is nothing short of life-changing. The practical wisdom alone is worth the price of admission. This book not only speaks to such a crucial element of Christian life which is finding and following God's will, but could easily double as a guide for how to stay close to the Lord. It is a simple, yet profound, examination of the Christian life and what finding God's will looks like on a daily basis. I highly recommend making this book a constant in your reading rotation."

David Hyskell
Worship Leader and Music Major at Southwestern
Fort Worth, Texas

"Thank you Pastor Mark for reminding us what true Biblical discipleship looks like. Your book reminds me of what a balanced, Christ-centered life should look like in the midst of a spiritually confused culture. God's most powerful tool on earth is a believer yielded and obedient to the Holy Spirit and this book shares many principles that lead us to live out that life of power and purpose for Christ."

Keith Morgan
Chaplain, Resurrection House and Learning Skills Institute
Chickasha, Oklahoma

"Spot on! Spoke to me in volumes! Finding God's Will, In The Decisions of Life is a remarkable tool for anyone in their life journey. The practical elements of this book are priceless and it is dosed with vitamins of discipleship. A MUST Read!"

Dr. Stephen Peeples
Pastor, Roopville Road Baptist Church
Carrollton, Georgia

"As I read Finding God's Will, I was greatly motivated, inspired, and challenged in my walk with Christ. As a Pastor and Guidance Advocate, these truths inspired me to further develop my love relationship with Christ and understand my identity in Him as I follow His will and stand against the schemes of the enemy. I was motivated toward spiritual maturity, awakened to spiritual traps, and determined to enjoy more intimate communication with my Lord. I highly recommend this book."

Richard Sayco
Pastor, Chelsea Southern Baptist Church
Guidance Advocate, SBC Learning Center, Inc.
Philippines

DEDICATION

I want to dedicate this book to my beloved Christian family in the Philippines. Thank you to Rudy and Ever Tabudlong and their precious family, all our pastors and wives, our youth, our EHCS staff, and our whole north mission base family who have loved me unconditionally through all our mission work together and give their whole heart to support us in every task. Thank you to Pastor Gauran (in heaven), Melly Damasco and Joy Damasco Viernes and their precious family, all our pastors and wives, our youth, our SBCLC staff, and our whole south mission base family who have also loved me unconditionally and have worked tirelessly to support our conferences and make everything work. Thank you to all my Champions for Christ through the years that have not only loved me as "Daddy Mark" but have exceeded my expectations in loving and serving Christ. You all have been one of God's greatest blessings to my life and have truly brought overflowing joy to my heart. The grace of Christ flows through all of you and I am truly blessed beyond measure! I love you all!

CONTENTS

ACKNOWLEDGMENTS

I would like to acknowledge the help and support of numerous people who have had a part in my life journey. My wife Gretchen of forty-five years, my daughter Mary and her husband Todd and my beautiful granddaughter Rachel, and my son David and his wife April have always loved me and supported me with unconditional love through every joyful victory and every crushing loss. I would like to thank my dad who is now with the Lord, Dr. Joseph F. Hyskell, pastor, missionary, and author, for a lifetime of teaching and standing uncompromisingly on God's Word, and my mom, who is now with the Lord, Dixie Hyskell, who has been the greatest prayer warrior and encourager in my life.

I would like to especially thank Dr. Paige Patterson, who not only helped me with the content of this book but has been a great friend and mentor for many years. You will notice a few dated references in his foreword as we began this project years ago, but he has graciously given me current permission to use it. I would like to thank my dear friends Danny McCartney, ThM, Dallas Theological Seminary, for always being ready to dig through scripture with me and help with any project or anything else I need and his loving wife Diane for always loving me. I want to thank the late Dr. W. A. Criswell, pastor of FBC Dallas, Texas, for being a loving and supportive pastor/teacher to me and many others at Criswell College. I want to acknowledge the invaluable input in my life from the professors and leaders from Luther Rice Seminary, The Criswell College, and Dallas Theological Seminary. I also thank my ministry brothers Nick Garland, Stephen Peeples, Danny McCartney, David Hyskell, Brad Vickrey, Mike Stowe, Keith Morgan, Richard Sayco, and Marvin Verde, who have read, given input, and written recommendations for this book.

Thank you to all of my young people through the years, and all those who find themselves mentioned in this book that have been part of my journey. Thank you to all my sons and daughters in ministry who have been a joyful blessing of God. Thank you to each of the church families I have served over these years for your valuable input in my life even if difficult at times.

FOREWORD

*F*inding God's will in the decisions of life ought to be a major concern for every genuine believer in the Lord Jesus Christ. The very fact that we call Him Lord is enough to confirm that finding His will in every situation ought to be paramount for anyone who wishes in his heart of hearts to please God. But as important as such subject matter is, the monographs which have been penned on this subject are few in number and for the most part, insignificant in terms of genuine practical assistance for the person who wills to know God's will.

Mark D. Hyskell, a gracious young pastor in Mesquite, Texas, has certainly written a treatise on the subject of finding God's will that is an exception to the usually ineffective treatments of the subject. I am unalterably convinced that one of the reasons for the success of Pastor Hyskell's assessment here is that what he has written is actually in a sense biographical. This is the way that Mark Hyskell has come to find and experience the will of God in his own life and ministry. Those who know him generally express some amazement about the versatility of this pastor. In addition to being a pastor with a heart for lost people, Pastor Hyskell is also a consistent expositor of the Word of God, a devoted husband and father, an approachable shepherd, and a man of principle, which is doubtless borne out of seeking the face of God.

Finding God's Will advances no mystical formula and parades no novel shortcut for ascertaining the will of God. The emphasis is placed where it ought to be. The great themes that impinge upon this subject namely the Lordship of Christ, Prayer, The place of the Bible, the importance of knowing God, being obedient to Him, experiencing spiritual cleansing, and waiting for God's perfect timing are all expounded herein.

The pastor further tells us how to evaluate the opened and closed doors of life and how to have a genuine shalom in one's heart as he walks through the challenges of life.

Along the way, Pastor Hyskell demonstrates familiarity with much of the pertinent literature which evangelicals have produced across the years in attempting to ascertain the answer to such pressing questions as the ones he addresses. He has faithfully provided credit for material he has used without in any way marring the flow of the discussion.

There are actually two reasons why this book will be particularly helpful to any Christian who would enter its pages. First, the book is superbly illustrated. Although illustration alone is insufficient, books on subjects such as these are books that need to be cogently illustrated. People identify with what has transpired in the lives of others, and here they will be able to find themselves more often than not standing beside the characters who emerge from the pages of the book. The second reason for great value in this book lies in the way that Pastor Hyskell pulls together the relevant information from the Bible itself in order to focus on the subject of finding and doing the will of God. Nowhere have I seen a book just like it, and seldom have I seen one any more faithful to the corpus of the Scriptures. Without reservation I commend this excellent study in the finding of God's will.

Dr. Paige Patterson
Past President
Southwestern Baptist Theological Seminary

PREFACE

*T*his book has an interestingly unique advantage that will happen only once in a lifetime. It has been written by a young, passionate pastor in his thirties and also by a more seasoned and mature pastor in his sixties and they are both me. I actually wrote this manuscript in my thirties while a pastor in the Dallas area. It was 1991–1992, and I simply wanted to help those seriously trying to find God's will. After sending it to a few publishers with no positive response, I laid it aside. I assumed that either God had wanted me to record these principles and thoughts for myself, my family, and my ministry family, or His time for wider influence had not come. Many years later I began to assume it was an exercise to sharpen my skills as a pastor in helping others and nothing more. So it has laid for over twenty years in its cheap coffin (box).

Now in my sixties, and some twenty-five years after writing it, the Lord has once again prompted my heart and given me a great desire to pull it out of the file, update, supplement, and refine it to help others. I can now recognize that the Lord had many things to teach me in order to fulfill His design for this book. How the Lord might use it, I don't know yet, but I am excited He has in His time brought it up again.

I want to say at the outset that I am only adding my small and humble supplement while gratefully acknowledging the enormous and ongoing influence of the classics the Lord has used in such a mighty way. Books like *The Pursuit of God* by A. W. Tozer, *Knowing God* by J. I. Packer, *Streams in the Desert* by Mrs. Charles E. Cowman, *Experiencing God* by Blackaby, Blackaby, and King and many, many others by godly servants that have deeply impacted several generations of Christians, including myself. To be honest, there is some hesitance to offer my supplement in light of these enduring classics, but I must be obedient to the Lord's prompting. Also, I am struck by some similarities in pursuing God's will, as recorded by some of these great authors and what the Lord laid on my heart all those years ago. It is further confirmation of the Holy Spirit leading all of us through scriptural principles that are timeless. These scriptural concepts I will share are certainly not original with me and have been communicated through the pens and lives of many of God's great servants through the centuries. What is unique, and I pray also helpful, is the way God brought them to bear in my journey with Christ and in that sense, the book is autobiographical. My prayer is that some thought or truth from my own journey, and these scriptural principles, would be enlightening to those striving to follow Christ and fulfill His purpose for their lives.

This book does not dive into the deep theological depths of some of the previous classics, or present an extensive defense of the Word of God such as the outstanding volume, *The New Evidence That Demands A Verdict* by Josh McDowell. You would be well served to read some of the classics in the bibliography of this book. However, this volume humbly offers a practical outline and personal testimony of how the Lord spoke to my heart through His Word and led me to find His will in the decisions of life. I have consciously tried to share these truths in a way that avoids large words or complicated reasoning, which could be an impediment to some of my Christian family in third world environments. My prayer is that you will be encouraged and drawn closer to the Lord in your love relationship with Him and be prompted to study some of the outstanding books I have referenced.

Here's what I know for sure: in Christ you can be an overcomer and find His will and fulfill His great plan for your life. It will never happen through your strength of will or gutting it out; in fact, that path will always end in failure as I know from personal experience. It is Christ in you! It is His almighty power resident within you! It is the power of the Holy Spirit flowing through you! I hope some word or thought or scene from my life or someone else's life will be an encouragement to you and help you in finding God's will and following it to honor Him. With Christ as the central focus of your life and His power within you, I can guarantee that you can find it and follow it and make a big impact in this world. That is the truth!

Mark D. Hyskell

INTRODUCTION

*A*re you frustrated, hurting, angry, guilty, doubting, ready to give up, desperate, emotional, trying to hold on, trying to figure things out, wondering why, seeking, searching for answers? Do any of these painful words describe cruel, nagging feelings deep in the recesses of your soul? Feelings you won't let anybody else know about? Feelings you keep hidden? Feelings you have masked with the protective exterior of joy and peace because you were afraid someone would realize you are weak and confused? Feelings that seem to prove you don't trust fully in God's providential control of your life? Feelings that make you feel you will be disappointing God if you even admit to them?

Perhaps now or at some time in your life, you have been eagerly searching for the will of God and felt totally unable to find it. As you continued to look with no results, you felt like you were on a greased sliding board to nowhere and even more frustrated. Perhaps you even began to question your direction in life, wondering if somehow you accidentally slipped onto the "broad way" that leads to destruction. While in this condition, your joy seemed to be devoured by a monstrous pair of jaws (discouragement and depression) nipping at your heart every day. You began to even feel you had been placed on the shelf and forgotten. You remembered those terrible actions from your past and began to assume the valley in which you now seem to be hopelessly trapped is your deserved consequence. Maybe you wondered if you should just give up and accept the present dilemma as your constant companion for life. Perhaps it was some kind of ball and chain to which you were sentenced from some heavenly court case based on your past sins.

If you have ever felt the sting of these thoughts or are now battling with them, you are not alone. Though it seems you are in a struggle nobody else is facing, the feelings of despair, emotional pain, and the inability to nail down God's will for your life are shared by thousands. In fact, many of the spiritual leaders of our nation, both past and present, have been battered by the unwelcome guests of doubt and discouragement. Perhaps more people than we would ever imagine are struggling with finding God's will and the stinging discouragement and depression that accompanies that search at times. As a pastor for many years, I can assure you that this struggle extends to every segment and strata of our society and is prevalent also among the body of Christ.

Through this struggle, be assured that God is faithful to teach us about His will and how to follow it if we genuinely focus on Him in our search. Regardless of the picture you may have in your mind, which is conditioned by our culture, our loving Father wants us to find His will and plan, and be blessed as we live it, just as any loving parent would.

The greatest treasure book of information about finding God's will and then diligently following it is the incomparable Word of God. There is no other book like it in history because, "All Scripture is given by inspiration of God," and it is literally "God breathed" (2 Tim. 3:16). When we realize everything we are searching for flows out of our intimate love relationship with the Lord, then His authoritative Word will be, "a lamp to my feet and a light to my path" (Psalm 119:105). His Spirit inspired Word will direct, convict, teach, inspire, and soothe our troubled hearts like no other medicine. I have experienced difficult times when the Psalms have comforted me beyond words. It was as though God was literally laying His hand on my shoulder and calming the raging storm. In those precious moments, it becomes a love letter of comfort, principle, and direction instead of a list of religious rules.

It is a tragic mistake, with painful consequences, to leave God's Word out of one's daily walk. I'm not talking about some legalistic, daily duty that you perform to check off a box in your spiritual checklist and feel better about your walk with Christ. Nor am I suggesting that if you miss your daily duty you are on the spiritual naughty list and riddled with guilt. Actually, the enemy uses that tactic to bring guilt that pushes you even farther away and makes it seem hopeless. Don't fall for that trap. This divine roadmap to life, as part of your intimate communication with the Lord, is not an option for those sincerely seeking God's direction. Yet, it has become one of the most overlooked and ignored of the entire spiritual arsenal with which God has blessed us. In many instances, it has become a book on the shelf, a book the pastor uses on Sundays, and a dust collector on the coffee table.

Suppose you decided to visit some beautiful, faraway city. You carefully planned the date with great anticipation and made all the preparations to go, except you overlooked getting a map, or nowadays loading GPS on your smart phone. Would anyone in their right mind simply get into the car and start down a randomly chosen road hoping to get there? Would you play "Guess the right road" at each intersection to discover the right direction? Would you just go with whatever direction "feels" right at the time? No! Yet so many get into the car of life, carelessly drive down the highway of time, and foolishly hope they arrive at the desired location. The confirmation and direction of God's Word, in truth and principle in any important decision we make, is vital.

We also learn of God's wonderful direction through obedience, which is empowered and birthed out of our loving relationship with Him. Many times, finding God's will seems like looking through a maze because we have not even taken the beginning steps of loving and grateful obedience. We have no spiritual point of reference. Our flesh tends to rebel at the elementary ABCs of God's direction because we have often taken a legalistic, religious rules approach that is duty-oriented and prideful. The frustrating outcome is that we are completely unable to understand or recognize the (spiritual) college level English literature of God's will because we have no preparation learned from the prerequisites. When we have not taken those beginning steps of loving obedience, self is still in control and we don't comprehend the step-by-step process of obedience and growth into maturity. It is a proven principle that obedience which flows out of our loving relationship with Christ will lead to further direction and more loving obedience as He grows us and grooms us to take His next step.

It is also vitally important to remember that God's will may be obscured by willful disobedience and allowing the flesh to control our lives. The question that confronts us is, "Am I following Christ which flows out of my intimate relationship with Him, or am I following my own desires?" Just as the dangerous fogs of San Francisco Bay set in and make vision difficult or impossible, so the dangerous fogs of fleshly control and willful disobedience set in and make spiritual vision difficult without a daily, sometimes hourly, time of confession and cleansing. As part of our intimate, daily walk with Christ, a time of spiritual examination and spiritual cleansing is vital, as communicated by 1 John 1:8–9.

One area often overlooked and even ignored in finding God's will is the inner leading of the Holy Spirit. Just as we would call and get directions from a friend about the best way to get to our desired location, so the precious Holy Spirit of God gives us inner direction. Many times in this race car life, we are so overwhelmed by the sound of the loud engines, the break neck speed of the race, and the voices yelling at us that we totally miss the still, small voice of God speaking to our hearts. In our loud, race car culture, in many respects we've lost the ability (or the desire) to be quiet and listen to the prodding of God in our soul. God is speaking, but who is really listening? Who is making the effort and taking the time to actually be quiet and listen in our day? Many of us would make excuses that we don't have time to be quiet and listen. Could it be with that overused excuse we are listening to the voice of our own desires rather than God's?

God also leads us through opened and closed doors. This part of God's leading can be especially dangerous. The precarious aspect is that we can easily make anything into an open or closed door depending on our fleshly wants and desires. I will confess I have been the creator of some opened and closed doors. How do we avoid this excruciating detour of creating our own opened and closed doors? One way is by using the other avenues of God's leading in conjunction with this one, as we will discuss and I will illustrate from my own life. Just as we would be foolish to use one verse of God's Word out of context to prove our point, so we can be very misguided as we take an isolated incident in our lives and instantly build a complete picture of God's desire with no further prayer and confirmation. If we try to bake a wonderfully delicious cake but use just one isolated ingredient, the results would have little similarity to the intended dessert. The resulting taste could be quite bitter regardless of the external appeal. God definitely uses opened and closed doors. The painful problem is, sometimes, we do too. Whose interpretation of opened and closed doors are we using? This is a question we will answer and illustrate.

As we seek to know God's will, our intimate walk with Christ and the love and grace that flows out of that walk will result in a heart that desires to do things God's way. Our gratitude and commitment to the Lord will be to follow His direction, regardless of where it might lead. It will be His strength and life flowing through us, and the desires of His heart will become the desires of our heart. Please understand that God does not mightily lead those who are playing religious games while following their own fleshly desires. That is self-deception and empty religion. God is looking for men and women who will love Him and be empowered by His Spirit to follow His direction and experience His supernatural power and blessings. God is looking for those who want to leave the frustration and dead end of religious duty and enter into His empowerment and freedom, flowing from an intimate love relationship with Him. He desires to use you and me to impact this world, to make a statement, and to leave a lasting impression for Christ.

The pertinent questions for us are, "Are we serious about surrender to Him so that we can move beyond legalistic religious duty to loving gratitude, and will we walk in a love relationship with Him regardless of the accompanying circumstances in order to fulfill His plan and purpose?" Without an affirmative answer to these questions, the empowerment and fulfillment God so strongly desires for us will be missed because we are following our own plan and purpose whether intentionally or unintentionally.

If we are being spiritually honest, it becomes painfully evident why so many people are desperately miserable and unable to find the will of God and His fulfillment. They want the will of God and His blessings upon them, but "they want it on their own terms." They want all of God's abundant blessings, but are resistant and fearful of sacrifice and service. They find it difficult to hear the Master speaking about denying yourself, taking up your cross and following Him. Therefore, they are conned by the enemy's weapon of fear into missing the most rewarding and fulfilling life through the unequaled love and divine power of Christ.

> "We come to the Master either in loving submission, placing Him on the throne of our lives, or following our own chosen path, keeping ourselves on the throne."

It's God's way or our way. His way is life and fulfillment. Our way is self and regret. By reading this book, you are showing a desire in your heart to take the steps to follow the most rewarding, loving, and fulfilling way possible. His way!

I

Preparations For Knowing God's Will

1. Knowing Him
2. Knowing Obedience
3. Knowing Cleansing
4. Knowing Timing

Chapter 1

Knowing Him

Dead End!

*H*ave you ever driven down a road searching for the street that would lead you to an exciting party already in progress?

You are late and probably speeding. You are growing more impatient with each passing minute. Suddenly, you look up and see a sign that reads, "Dead End." You are shocked, disgusted, and angry at all the precious time wasted. You hurriedly turn around and speed back the other direction to get off the "dead end." You begin again to look for the right street which will lead to the exciting time with your friends at the party.

This is a heart-rending picture of the spiritual lives of multitudes in our generation. Masses are desperately groping for the right street that will lead them to the excitement and fulfillment for which they yearn, but they are headed down a "dead end" street. Why are they speeding like a sleek race car down a "dead end" street? The answer is simple, though it has become shrouded in our increasingly secular culture.

> "*A*ny road that hasn't begun with a total life commitment to Jesus Christ and being born again through His gracious gift of redemption leads to a 'dead end.'"

Actually, it's worse than a "dead end." Without a total life commitment to Jesus Christ as personal Lord and Savior which results in spiritual birth, the road ends in eternal pain and suffering. That is where I was headed which I will describe in more detail.

It is a painful reality that many people, especially in America, believe they are Christians without anything but empty words and a self-proclaimed label to back it up. If you asked them, "Are you a Christian?" their response would be a resounding yes. They would strongly insist they are religious people. They would begin to list various reasons for this assumption. They may explain that their father or grandfather was a preacher or deacon. They might share of their saintly mother who faithfully took them to Sunday school and church every Sunday morning. Some would tell you how they went forward and joined a church. They may give a touching description of how they were baptized by the preacher. Others may speak of involvement in various ministries of the church. Others might even speak of their daily prayers. The sad story is they are traveling a "dead end" street which leads to destruction and they don't realize it, just as I didn't. It is all the more dangerous because they adamantly insist their religious path is the right path. One of the great preachers of yesteryear, C. H. Spurgeon, spoke of those who claim Christianity, while their lives deny it. In his touching book, *Lectures To My Students*, he explains,

> "Thousands are congratulating themselves,
> and even blessing God that they are devout wor-
> shippers, when at the same time they are living in
> an unregenerate Christless state, having the form
> of godliness, but denying the power thereof" (1).

My Own Misconception

Actually, this is the testimony of my own life. I pray my misconception will shed some bright light on this critical point and highlight the truth. I explained in a previous book:

"I had prayed the sinner's prayer, been baptized by immersion, became a member of a church, had gone to Sunday school and church every time the doors were open, went to Vacation Bible School, prayer meetings on Wednesday nights, and had tried my best to live like a Christian. If you would have asked me if I were a Christian I would have immediately said yes and pointed to the things I had done. I probably would have been a little insulted if you had asked.

My problem was that I was following a religious system and placing my trust in the things I had done and was continuing to do.

I finally realized that something was very wrong in my heart. I heard about being a new creation in Christ, but it was just nice words to me at the time. It was religious speech. I cried out to God asking what was wrong with me. I was churning inside. The Holy Spirit spoke to my heart and revealed that I was a Christian in name only. I realized that I had never been changed on the inside. I had gone through the motions of being a Christian. Even though I had assumed all those years that I was saved because of the prayer and other religious actions, I was just acting out a role.

When the Holy Spirit convicted my heart and revealed my need to move beyond religion and into a personal relationship with Christ, I responded with everything that was in me. I was tired of the empty words and the emptiness in my soul. I erupted in prayer and poured my heart out to God. I had heard the words before, but now they made sense. I knew I had sinned. 'For all have sinned and fall short of the glory of God' (Romans 3:23). I knew what would happen if I continued in that direction. It was clear to me as I wept in that little room by myself that Christ was changing me from the inside out. 'For the wages of sin is death, but the gift of God is eternal life in Christ Jesus our Lord' (Romans 6:23). I realized God's incredible love for me and the price that Jesus paid. 'For God so loved the world [that is you and me] that He gave His only begotten Son, that whoever believes [trusts in, relies completely upon, clings to] in Him should not perish but have everlasting life' (John 3:16).

I remember surrendering everything to Christ that day and making a blank check commitment of my life to Him. I turned away from my works-based, messed-up life and turned it all over to Him. I asked Him to come into my life as my personal Savior and Lord. I thanked Him for dying on the cross and shedding His blood for my sins. I praised Him that He rose from the dead. I thanked Him for coming to live within me. This was a genuine surrender from the bottom of my heart. That was the moment I was changed on the inside. I remember the next day being surprised at how my motives and desires had changed. Though I had a bunch of growing to do, I had been changed and I knew it.

If you find yourself where I was and sense the Holy Spirit prompting your heart now, just give it all to Him. This is your moment. You don't have to be in a church service to do it.

Move from the religious system into a real, personal relationship with Christ. Surrender your heart and life to Him.

Don't worry about what others may think even if you have been in church or called yourself a Christian. Your salvation and eternal life is infinitely more important than embarrassment or what others might think. Just pour your heart out to God and surrender your life to Him right now. There is no exact formula of words, but if you need a little help you could pray, 'Dear Lord, I know I am a sinner, and I can't save myself. I thank You that You died on the cross to pay for my sins, that You were buried and rose again. I turn away from this direction my life is headed and surrender my heart and life to You. Please forgive me of my sins and save me and come into my life as my Lord and Savior. In Jesus name I pray. Amen!'

Remember, just saying those words will not save you. That was my mistake early in life. There is no exact formula of words, and your trust cannot be in the words; it must be completely in the Lord Jesus. The real inner change comes when the Holy Spirit is convicting your heart of your need and you genuinely surrender your life to Jesus. When you change direction and make that complete surrender of your life to Jesus, you will become a new creation in Christ. Your life will be changed forever, and we will meet someday" (2).

Spurgeon speaks of completely trusting everything into Christ's hands, when he writes,

"Come and commit your cause and your case to those once-pierced hands which are now glorified with the signet rings of royal power and honor. No suit ever failed which was left with this great Advocate" (3).

The Great Lie

Through a spiritual deception that sounds good on the surface, some in America have bought into and even vigorously promoted the lie that if you are just a good person and do your best in life, you will be saved and go to heaven.

> "It is the belief that if your good works outweigh your bad works at the end of life that God will allow you into heaven based on the tipping of the scales toward good works."

As you just saw in my testimony that was the misconception I was living under. To the thinking of many, Christianity has become nothing more than a system of religious ethics, a compilation of things you do, and things you don't do. The true theme of Christianity has been veiled. In his wonderful book, *Grace*, Dr. Lewis Sperry Chafer writes,

> "Through false emphasis by many religious leaders, Christianity has become in the estimation of a large part of the public no more than an ethical system. The revealed fact, however, is that the supreme feature of the Christian faith is that supernatural, saving, transforming work of God, which is made possible through the infinite sacrifice of Christ and which, in sovereign Grace, is freely bestowed on all who believe" (4).

A Dangerous Game

There is a sport that has grabbed the attention of many thrill seekers through the years. It is the sport of bungee jumping. Normally sane people get on a bridge, or some high structure, and attach a long elastic cord (mega rubber bands) to their feet and also to the structure. After building up enough courage (if courage is the correct term), they jump. They of course have made sure the other end of their bungee cord has been firmly anchored to the bridge or whatever edifice from which they are jumping. As they are plunging down through the air toward the ground, at just the right distance the cord reaches its full length before disaster strikes (before there is a human pancake). The elastic cord snatches them from sure disaster and jerks them back up into the air.

Great numbers of people today are doing spiritual bungee cord jumping. They are leaping off the bridge of life looking for intense excitement. They are pushing the limits of danger with what they think is a perfectly safe cord. They have made sure the cord is firmly tied to their feet and anchored to the edifice securely, but they haven't thoroughly checked the material and strength of the cord itself which they are trusting to save them. The horrible tragedy of massive proportions is they are jumping off the bridge with a lifeline unable to hold their weight or snatch them to safety.

"The cord of human goodness and good works will surely snap and leave its jumper facing certain death."

Satan is the great liar, the father of lies. This lie that human goodness gets one to heaven and brings salvation is one of his most prized lies. As I have spoken to hundreds of people over the years and asked them why they think they are saved and going to heaven, the most common response has been because of human goodness and good works. They give me responses like, "I've been a good person. I've tried to be honest. I haven't really hurt anyone. I've tried to help other people." Some offer even more religious responses like, "I've always gone to church, I believe in Jesus," or "I was baptized." Though their responses sound adequate, and even noble to those unfamiliar with the clear mandates of Scripture, those who know God's Word concerning salvation by grace alone through faith alone realize they are tragically inadequate.

The Truth Says...

The true truth found in the Word of God clearly communicates something diametrically opposed to this dangerous misconception. Jesus said in John 14:6, "I am the way, the truth, and the life. No one comes to the Father except through Me." In our American culture, where we are expected to accept every truth claim as equally valid, some would complain the Bible is a very narrow book. Don't be misled by the demanding, polytheistic voices of secular culture that try to shame you for believing Scripture. The inescapable truth of Scripture is, when it comes to salvation, it is narrowed all the way down to one way, as Jesus Himself is speaking in this verse. If you say you believe in Jesus Christ and that the Word of God is true, this is the clarion call of the Lord in which you believe. Our God does not play games or lead us astray by complicated theological formulas. He made it exceedingly plain about this matter of salvation, so no one who is genuinely seeking could miss it.

> "Spiritual salvation only comes one way as the Holy Spirit convicts our hearts, we repent of our sins, and make a total faith commitment to Jesus Christ as Lord and Savior which results in spiritual birth which Jesus referred to in John 3 as being 'born again.'"

It is not through a commitment to human goodness or acceptance of every truth claim as valid. It is not even a commitment to religious diligence which is what I was trying to do. Remember also that Jesus was speaking to one of the most religious leaders of His day when He said, "You must be born again!" Spiritual salvation comes only through a real, life-changing, spiritual birth as we repent and make a total commitment to Jesus Christ and receive His gift of grace (unmerited and unearned favor).

A Hijacked Concept

At the very beginning of this book, I want to lay the foundation to help you have a clear understanding of a scriptural principle that has been hijacked by the enemy and his world system. You will learn of several other scriptural principles that have also been hijacked and distorted such as religion's negative spin on obedience to the Lord in chapter 2, and the contrast of what genuine spiritual obedience to Christ really looks like. However, at this initial stage, I want to share about the concept of "total commitment" to which I just referred.

I use the terms "total commitment" and also "blank check commitment" when I refer to a scripturally-based salvation commitment to Jesus Christ as Lord and Savior. The call for this kind of commitment in Scripture will be addressed and expounded numerous times throughout this book, but here I would like to share from my own life how this concept was distorted, and maybe that will help you relate to it also.

Years ago, whenever I would hear the terms "total commitment" or "blank check commitment" in reference to following Christ, there was one main response, and that was fear. That fear ran wild through my imagination as the enemy manipulated and fueled my thoughts. The fear-fueled distortions led me down several different roads of thought and none of them were good. The fear of giving up control was compounded by the fear of the resulting unknown. The fear of the unknown led to thoughts of dark jungles and painful sacrifice, and you can probably imagine the continuing downward spiral. Fear feeds on fear and produces more fear.

Of all these fear distortions, there was one in particular that was one of my biggest misconceptions, and I think one of the biggest misconceptions in our contemporary culture that keeps people away from a "total commitment" to Christ. I had a great fear of failure. Let me try to explain the struggle going on in my heart. As I contemplated making a total commitment to Christ, here are some things I kept insisting to myself:

"There is no way I can keep that commitment the rest of my life! I can make a total commitment of my life now, but I can't keep it up! I know me and I know that will be impossible over the long haul! There is absolutely no chance I can sustain that kind of lifestyle! I don't have the strength of will to do it! I will end up being a hypocrite and failure! I may start well, but knowing me I will not end well! I have failed before as I have tried hard to keep commitments! I am weak and I know it! I will blow it! I know I will blow it! My fear is after I make that commitment I will dishonor Christ and let Him down! I cannot make a total commitment to Christ because I know I cannot keep it! My resolve will weaken in the heat of temptation! My strength will fail!"

> "The misconception/fear I struggled under was believing that if I made a genuine, total commitment to Christ, I would have to keep that commitment through the sheer strength of my own will. That's all I knew at the time."

I would have to sustain that devotion over a lifetime with grit, sweat, determination, and even blood. I would have to beat my will into religious submission and live a perfect, boring life. I would be in a daily fight, with me. I just knew from past experiences, I couldn't sustain that by the mere strength of my own will. I was right in that regard!

Here is what I want you to hear clearly and retain in your mind when you think about a total commitment to Christ.

The enemy had cunningly taken Christ's call of total commitment and had led me, and I think many others, to a false conclusion rooted in fear. This fear was a weapon of the enemy to keep me away from true freedom in Christ and His indwelling power.

> " *T*he truth is, it is impossible for anyone to live a life of supernatural power sustained for a lifetime in the strength of their own will. Here's the great news! You don't have to!"

This is not something you can do or even have the ability to do by your own grit and determination. When we answer the call of Christ and make a total commitment to Him which results in being born again, the Holy Spirit of God comes to live within us. It is the indwelling power of the Holy Spirit of God by which you then live your life for Christ. It is no longer your strength; it is His strength! Your feeble determination has failed before because His supernatural power was not flowing through you. It is His life being manifested through your life. Paul made this exceedingly clear when he said, "I have been crucified with Christ; *it is no longer I who live, but Christ lives in me;* and the life which I now live in the flesh I live by faith in the Son of God, who loved me and gave Himself for me" (Gal. 2:20, author's italics).

Now, and I mean right now, you can reject those unfounded fears and live in the truth of the indwelling power of the Holy Spirit as your source. The truth is when I made a blank check commitment of my life to Jesus Christ, it was by far the greatest and most freeing decision I've ever made. I don't walk in my strength, I live in His strength. My resources are unlimited in Him. My focus and dependence are on Christ, and His power flows through me. With that foundational concept firmly planted in our minds to allay unfounded fears, let's continue.

The Problem

Many people are groping and clawing in an attempt to find God's will, when tragically some of them don't even know God. Knowing God is the key! Really knowing God, not just knowing about God, answers a multitude of questions. In his excellent book, *Knowing God*, J. I. Packer explains,

> "Once you become aware that the main business that you are here for is to know God, most of life's problems fall into place of their own accord" (5).

Some have never surrendered their lives to the only One who can change them on the inside and show them the way. Some in our Christian culture might ask, "Is it absolutely necessary to make a total commitment to Christ?" Let's look at what Jesus said is necessary to be His disciple and you can see for yourself.

In Matthew 16:24, Jesus said, "If anyone desires to come after Me, let him deny himself, and take up his cross, and follow Me." Jesus made it very simple as to the commitment it takes to be His disciple. That commitment is "everything." The blinding problem for many is they have been artfully deceived into thinking they can make a partial commitment as so many attempt to do in our contemporary culture. Between the cultural conditioning of our day and a lack of actual scriptural knowledge of what Jesus proclaimed, they have developed an incomplete personal belief. They believe they can "receive" Jesus as much or as little as they desire. They believe they can give a part of themselves to Jesus. Their misguided assumption is they can commit what they want, when they want, and the way they want, on a kind of religious installment plan. Jesus did not mince words. He said you must deny yourself and take up your cross and follow Me. He called for total commitment. Numerous scriptures that confirm this call will be shared in the following pages.

Perhaps that total life commitment would be more clearly understood in thinking of the commitment between a groom and his bride at their wedding. When the groom is passionately committing his life to his bride and promising to cling to her alone, no matter what life brings, it would be ludicrous to think of the bride pledging part of her life to the groom while keeping several boyfriends on the side. It would be the equivalent of the bride exclaiming, "Yes, my love, I commit my Sundays completely to you, though I have various commitments to others through the week." Deep down we know that kind of commitment doesn't make spiritual sense and certainly cannot be what Christ was defining here.

Jesus explained that His disciples must deny self. We live in an age that is possibly farther removed from that truth than any other in history. Our incredible progression in almost every field and unparalleled resources seem to have dulled our spiritual senses. We not only know little about denying self, we glory in selfishness when the flesh is in control. We live to get, not to give. We live to enjoy, not to bring enjoyment. We live to buy more things, not to deny self. Too often we live to be served and not to serve.

Jesus said the first principle to be grasped in the life of someone who is serious about following Him is to deny self. We must deny serving self as our priority in order to serve Him as our priority.

> " *J*esus was saying that loving and serving Him was to be our priority in life instead of our self-determined desires."

Jesus then spoke of taking up one's cross. This thought pushes yet further against the too prevalent self-priority of our culture. Though Jesus accomplished many things at the cross we may not realize this side of heaven, He primarily did one thing while hanging above Golgotha: He died to sacrifice His life for others. The cross is a symbol of death. The cross is the ultimate symbol of sacrifice. Dr. Chuck Swindoll shared a touching story of willingness to sacrifice that touched my heart. He writes,

> "This reminds me of the six-year-old girl who became deathly ill with a dread disease. To survive, she needed a blood transfusion from someone who had previously conquered the same illness. The situation was complicated by her rare

blood type. Her nine-year-old brother qualified as a donor, but everyone was hesitant to ask him since he was just a lad. Finally they agreed to have the doctor pose the question.

The attending physician tactfully asked the boy if he was willing to be brave and donate blood for his sister. Though he didn't understand much about such things, the boy agreed without hesitation: 'Sure, I'll give my blood for my sister.'

He lay down beside his sister and smiled at her as they pricked his arm with the needle. Then he closed his eyes and lay silently on the bed as the pint of blood was taken.

Soon thereafter the physician came in to thank the little fellow. The boy, with quivering lips and tears running down his cheeks, asked, 'Doctor, when do I die?' At that moment the doctor realized that the naïve little boy thought that by giving his blood, he was giving up his life. Quickly he reassured the lad that he was not going to die, but amazed at his courage, the doctor asked, 'Why were you willing to risk your life for her?'

'Because she is my sister…and I love her,' was the boy's simple but significant reply" (6).

That is the beauty of true love. Love is willing to sacrifice for the beloved. Jesus spoke of dying to self. Our life of self on the throne must die the death on the cross to truly live in the freedom of Christ. Our life is a trophy of grace to be lived in love and gratitude for the One who gave us real life through His grace.

Jesus says that after we have followed His formula of denying self and dying to self, then the path is truly opened to follow Him according to His plan wherever He leads. The barrier of enthroned self is then dethroned. The unfortunate reality in our day is some desire to claim they are following Jesus without following His formula in this scripture. People try to learn about doing the things of Christianity and following Christ without going through the path Jesus outlined and it ends up in failure and frustration. They attempt to follow Jesus in discipleship without first denying and dying to self. According to His clear statement on discipleship, this is putting the proverbial cart before the horse. We may try this approach, but our attempt will be superficial at best, and never fulfilling. It is safe to say that the Lord's formula is the only one that truly works, and a clear reason why so many are unable to experience the resurrection power of Christ. Denial, death, and "then authentic discipleship."

The Solution

The solution to this problem is obvious if we look at it through the lens of our Lord's own words. We must follow the words of Jesus and make a total commitment to Him. Not a partial commitment, not a half-hearted commitment, not a commitment with strings attached, but a total, blank check commitment of our life to Jesus Christ as Lord and Savior. Then we will begin to see the wonderful plan and purpose of God begin to unfold before us and we will begin to live in true freedom and the power of Christ. The fog will begin to lift and we will start to understand the direction God is leading us. Then our heart will begin to be drawn toward His purpose, and it will become our heart's desire. The relevant question that must be answered is, "How do I make a total commitment to Jesus Christ as Lord and Savior?"

How Do I Make a Total Commitment to Christ?

Though I shared some of this in my own personal testimony previously, let me set the table here to facilitate a clear spiritual understanding. With any question in life, we should always turn to the incomparable Word of God.

We must first come to the realization we are lost spiritually (even if we have been religious), and that we've never made a total commitment to Jesus Christ as Lord and Savior, meaning we've never been "born again." Without this realization and admittance, we can proceed no further. It takes being painfully honest with one's self as we genuinely seek real truth before the convicting power of the Holy Spirit of God. When the Holy Spirit is touching/convicting our hearts with our lost condition and need for salvation, we must respond humbly and honestly, even if we have claimed to be a Christian for years, or even if we have been leaders in the church.

We must acknowledge the fact that we are sinners before a Holy God. Romans 3:23 tells us, "For all have sinned and fall short of the glory of God." No matter how good a person we may think we are, we are all in the same category as sinners that come up short of God's standard according to His Word. We are sinners in need of a Savior. The big lie of human goodness alone being able to win salvation has led many souls down the path to destruction. Concerning this point, God's Word is very clear. We are all sinners, we have missed the mark, and we cannot save ourselves.

We must accept the Scriptural truth that Romans 6:23 reveals, "For the wages of sin is death." We will receive spiritual death as our future and just judgment unless there is an applied payment made on our behalf. There is no way around it. Death will always be the future without that redeeming payment of Christ on our behalf. Though culture and pride emphatically deny such a thought, it is the truth from God's immutable Word.

Romans 6:23 goes on to say, "But the gift of God is eternal life in Christ Jesus our Lord." We have been offered the unspeakable gift of salvation through the sacrificial death of Jesus Christ on the cross. The complete and perfect redeeming payment has been made for us. Our sin debt has been paid. In accounting terms, He placed our sins into His account and placed His righteousness into our account. We can have spiritual life, eternal life because of that payment. God loves us so much that He made the payment for us: "For God so loved the world that He gave His only begotten Son, that whoever believes in Him should not perish but have everlasting life" (John 3:16).

"What an astonishing truth! The very payment that God's justice requires because of our sin and rebellion, He pays!"

Through the sacrificial death, burial, and resurrection of Jesus Christ, we can have eternal life. Through the blood of the perfect Lamb of God that payment has been fully paid for you and me. When Christ cried out, "It is finished!" the original Greek word is very interesting. The single Greek word translated, "It is finished" was found written across many ancient receipts meaning, "Paid In Full!" My debt before God has been paid in full.

The remaining step is to repent and receive this payment on our behalf as we respond to the conviction of the Holy Spirit. We do this by faith through yielding and commitment. There is absolutely nothing we can do to earn our salvation. We must simply receive it by faith through the grace (the unmerited favor) of God. Ephesians 2:8–9 says, "For by grace you have been saved through faith, and that not of yourselves, it is the gift of God, *not of works, lest anyone should boast*" (author's italics). By faith as the Holy Spirit convicts and prompts our hearts, we gratefully yield and commit our lives to Jesus Christ as our personal Lord and Savior. Paul spoke of this confession when he explained "that if you confess with your mouth the Lord Jesus and believe in your heart that God has raised Him from the dead, you will be saved. For with the heart one believes unto righteousness, and with the mouth confession is made unto salvation" (Romans 10:9–10).

This confession is not merely an intellectual acknowledgment, but a deep and genuine statement from the heart that He is your Lord, the risen Christ. We repent and turn to Him in surrender. We receive His redeeming blood as the full payment for our sins before a Holy and Just God. We receive the righteousness of Jesus Christ as He took our unrighteousness upon Himself on the cross. We move from lost without hope, to saved with absolute, eternal security. We give our life to the One who has paid the price for it: Jesus. First

Corinthians 6:20 states, "For you were bought at a price; therefore glorify God in your body and in your spirit, which are God's." Out of an overwhelming gratitude for the unspeakable grace of our Lord, it is our joy to glorify Him Who paid the price for our salvation. The correct interpretation according to the inspired words of Scripture can be nothing less than total commitment. It is ludicrous to think we could receive this total, complete payment from Christ on the cross by reluctantly deciding to give a portion of ourselves to Him while retaining self's control. This is nothing more than destructive, dangerous, contemporary rationalization.

If you never made a total commitment of your life to Christ, you can certainly do it right now as the Holy Spirit is revealing these truths to your heart. As I said before, there is no exact formula of words because this surrender comes from your heart. If you would like some help with this prayer of commitment you could pray this: "Dear Lord Jesus, I thank You for dying on the cross in my place. I thank You for shedding Your blood to make the full and complete payment for my sins. I realize that I am a sinner with no way of saving myself and that I am spiritually lost without You. I choose to turn away from my life of sin and self-control, and I ask You to come into my life as my personal Lord and Savior. With all my heart I receive your perfect and complete payment for my sin debt. I give You my life and make a total commitment to Your ownership. Please live Your life through me. Thank You for saving me and coming into my heart as You promised. With your strength and power flowing through me I will live the rest of my life to love and serve You. In Jesus name I pray, Amen!"

Praise the Lord! Now that you have made a total commitment of your life to Jesus Christ as Lord and Savior, He will begin to work in you in a powerful way. It is His power that will now be at work in your life and not your own strength. Remember, when you commit your life to Christ and He comes to live in you, you don't get more will power, you get His power. Christ in you! Here is that truth as Paul describes it: "I have been crucified with Christ; *it is no longer I who live, but Christ lives in me;* and the life which I now live in the flesh I live by faith in the Son of God, who loved me and gave Himself for me" (Gal. 2:20, author's italics). As you keep your focus on Christ and are yielded to Him, He empowers you. You are no longer living under condemnation but under grace. Your penalty has been paid by Christ and you are free to live for Him by His power within you. That is true freedom! You also need to be aware of the devil's devices and realize that total commitment which brings about spiritual birth does not mean instant perfection. Will a Christian that has made a total commitment to Christ and been born again make mistakes? Yes! When you are tempted and your focus gets pulled away from Christ and onto the flesh, do not let the enemy deceive you into thinking you are lost again. I will discuss your security in Christ more, later ("Secure in Christ," chapter 6), but when you sin, the good news is we have a wonderful way of confessing and dealing with those sins, as we will see in chapter 3, "Knowing Cleansing."

Conclusion

Here is the loving concern in my heart for anyone who has been struggling like I was with a flawed spiritual concept. None of this is preacher talk. It may seem very straight forward and terse, but I assure you it is the concerned heart of one who was misguided and lost for those who are misguided and lost. I want you to be truly okay. I am simply striving to clearly proclaim the bedrock scriptural truths that have set me and many others free and will set you free.

"Struggling for ten lifetimes to know the will of God for one's life will never accomplish that goal without first knowing Him."

The struggle is most definitely in vain until we have made a total commitment to Jesus Christ as our personal Lord and Savior which results in spiritual birth and sight.

The devil will do everything to convince you otherwise and to lead you in all other possible directions, even religious directions of diligence. In fact, if you are hearing a voice inside right now telling you all this is not true, that is the voice of the enemy trying to keep you in bondage and lead you away from the only truth that will set you free. That voice will tell you that you will be in bondage to a bunch of rules if you truly follow Christ. The scriptural reality is that without Christ you are already in bondage. The truth is your true freedom awaits as you reject that voice. Break free from that lie by responding in faith and living in the truth. Here is the "true truth" as Jesus was speaking to His disciples: "I have come that they may have life, and that they may have it more abundantly" (John 10:10b). The fact that faces you is simply this. If you are serious about finding God's will for your life, it must begin with a total commitment of your life to the Lord which results in being born again and gives you spiritual sight and indwelling power. Nothing less will bring success!

Final Question to Ponder:
Do I really "know" Jesus or do I just know about Him?

Chapter 2

Knowing Obedience

Lessons from Training

*T*here was an interesting movie many years ago called, Karate Kid. I studied the martial arts when I was younger and this movie caught my attention. In this movie as I remember it, a young teenaged boy and his mother have moved to a new town. As he is adjusting to a new school and making new friends, he is confronted by a group of bullies who want to make his life miserable. These teenage bullies are more than the normal, schoolyard variety because they are experienced in karate and the martial arts. They also have a ruthless and cruel karate instructor that teaches them how to hate people and win at any cost.

During the beginning weeks, these bullies beat the new kid several times. He comes home with black eyes and unexplained cuts and bruises. This continuing hatred and abuse causes him to be totally frustrated and ready to give up. It is about that same time when he meets a kind, old, Asian man in his neighborhood who is a repairman. They begin a friendship and in the process of spending time together, he learns the old gentleman is also a master at karate. The teenage boy is excited and immediately pleads with the old man to teach him the art of karate. The old man refuses at first, but after the kid continues his passionate requests, he reluctantly consents to teaching him on the condition the boy will do everything he is told during training, no matter what.

As they begin the training regimen to prepare the kid to defend himself against the bullies, the training itself takes on an unconventional approach. The old man takes the teenaged boy out to the yard and shows him a lot of old cars. He instructs the boy to wax one of the old cars. He carefully explains how it is to be done. He is to use both hands. He is to put the wax on with one hand and to wipe it off with the other. He is instructed to use the exact strokes the old karate master has shown him, "wax on, wax off," he says as he demonstrates with the circling motions. The boy is disappointed and frustrated, but he concedes and does it, as he has promised to do whatever is asked.

In another training session, the teenager is excited they will now get down to business and start learning various ancient martial arts techniques. To his surprise and dismay, the old man simply leads him out to a long wooden fence and carefully instructs the youth how to take each stroke as he stains it. "Up and down," he said as he demonstrates the proper stroke with each hand. The teen can hardly believe it, but again he reluctantly obeys, realizing he has made a solemn promise to follow the old man's training instructions. Though very tedious and seemingly meaningless, he finally perseveres and finishes staining the fence.

Now that he is done with what he considers ridiculous nonsense, he feels sure they will begin to learn the techniques he has been eagerly anticipating in the mystical world of karate. When he returns for another lesson, again he is disappointed and dismayed at the training request. The old man left a sign on the door asking him to paint the whole house. The kid is astounded at this continuing treatment. The kid's resentment is boiling as he begins to paint. He is just about to give up hope he would ever learn the karate that had so excited him earlier and gave him hope to be able to defend himself against the bullies.

Finally, when the old man returns, he has all he can take of this seeming nonsense and begins to yell at the old gentleman about the total waste of time. He screams that the old man had promised to teach him karate, and yet all he has done is use him to fix things around the house.

The sage old man asks him about the strokes he learned and then begins with lightning speed to throw karate punches at the teenager. As each punch is thrown at his head and then his body, the boy reacted out of trained reflex. Each punch is met with the exact stroke needed to block it which had been born out of countless repetitive strokes from the previous days.

After an intense flurry of blows, the stoic old man immediately stops. The boy stands there stunned at what he has just done. Where did those moves come from? How had he acquired this arsenal of trained reflexes? How could he possibly have defended himself like that?

As they stand there considering what has just happened, the kid begins to realize the answers to his probing questions. Each of those thousands of strokes of waxing, staining, and painting had a specific meaning and wise intention. Even though he thought it was meaningless at the time and had no comprehension of any strategic intention, the master had been teaching him the essentials of the very thing the boy desired the most. The boy now understands that the key to this amazing accomplishment in his life is trusting obedience to the master's commands. The master's love sees the bigger picture. Every blow is blocked with the exact stroke learned from daily, trusting obedience. Without being obedient in the beginning training sessions with boring instructions, he could never have progressed to the finely tuned reflex actions he now possessed. There is no shortcut. There is no quick fix. There is no instant expertise. He could not have achieved these new moves without trusting obedience in the former stages of training. The Master's love knows exactly what is needed and pushes him beyond his comfort zone to equip him for victory. Unconventional? Yes! Frustrating? Yes! Effective? Absolutely!

To be honest, I can now look back at my own life and see the same kind of wise love applied. I didn't see it at the time. I certainly didn't like it, but I am so grateful now that the Father's love saw the big picture and pushed me beyond my comfort zone. I believe with all my heart this is one of the key reasons people are unable to progress in their spiritual life. It is a scriptural principle of faithfulness recorded in the parable of the talents which stated, "Well done good and faithful servant; *you have been faithful over a few things*, I will make you ruler over many things" (Matt. 25:23, author's italics). Some are unable to find God's full purpose and will for their lives simply because they have never submitted to trusting obedience in the beginning training sessions that have a specific meaning and wise intention. They have never been obedient to follow God's will through the less exciting beginning lessons, and the daily faithfulness, and therefore they cannot progress toward graduation when the ABCs have not been faithfully learned.

The Motive behind Obedience

It is crucially important as we begin to speak about obedience that I lay a foundation for understanding obedience in the proper context. This is another scriptural concept that has been cunningly distorted. Let me draw a contrast that will accurately portray the difference between the distorted religious perspective of obedience and what obedience to Christ really looks like.

Distorted Obedience

There is an obedience born out of legalism and duty such as was seen in the lives of the Pharisees and Saul of Tarsus himself that is actually spiritually destructive and leads to pride, arrogance, blindness, and eventually death. It leads away from God and not toward God. This legalistic obedience is spiritually dead. It feeds on manmade structure and rigid dogmatism. It is born out of self-will and pride and is a favorite tool of the enemy because he knows how irresistible it is for the flesh to become intoxicated with self. It is toxic and hateful to anyone not under its heavy bondage and it reeks with self-righteous arrogance. It is performed out of the drudgery of legalistic duty. It is meticulously performed to the letter of the law out of a pride that feeds on enthroning self. This obedience loves to be seen and praised by men. Ironically, this obedience blindly believes it is performing its task to honor God, when it is actually dishonoring Him in the worst way. This obedience is a ball and chain with all its extensive rules and is a prison to the soul. It becomes life-consuming as we see Paul speaking of his former life when he stated, "Circumcised the eighth day, of the stock of Israel, of the tribe of Benjamin, a Hebrew of the Hebrews; concerning the law, a Pharisee; *concerning zeal, persecuting the church; concerning the righteousness which is in the law, blameless"* (Phil. 3:5–6, author's italics).

It is a spiritual trap that causes serious blindness. It does not honor God and was vehemently rebuked by Christ Himself when He exclaimed, "Woe to you, scribes and Pharisees, hypocrites! For you are like whitewashed tombs which indeed appear beautiful outwardly, but inside are full of dead men's bones and all uncleanness" (Matt. 23:27). It tends to have the outward appearance of religious purity and piety while being full of inward corruption and spiritual darkness. It becomes one of the most damning kinds of blindness which is proven by the fact that it led them to hatefully call for the crucifixion of the very Son of God, while they were convinced they were doing a great service for God. Keller refers to this pharisaic mentality as the "elder brother spirit" which he develops extensively in his book, *The Prodigal God*. Though most treatments concerning the parable of the prodigal son focus mainly on the younger brother's disrespectful departure, the ruinous life which ends in the hog pen, and then the humble return to the father, Keller's book focuses more on the elder brother. He vividly describes the elder brother's angry, begrudging compliance which revealed a hard heart that was just as lost and separated from his loving Father as his younger brother. He wrote,

> "Another sign of those with an 'elder brother' spirit is joyless, fear-based compliance. The older son boasts of his obedience to his father, but lets his underlying motivation and attitude slip out when he says, 'All these years I've been slaving for you.' To be sure, being faithful to any commitment involves a certain amount of dutifulness.

Often we don't feel like doing what we ought to do, but we do it anyway, for the sake of integrity. But the elder brother shows that his obedience to his father is nothing but duty all the way down. There is no joy or love, no reward in just seeing his father pleased" (1).

"Behavioral compliance to rules without heart-change will be superficial and fleeting" (2).

I am articulating a clear distinction between two different kinds of obedience because of the distortion that has been foisted on it. This kind of dead, destructive obedience is the opposite of what I am referring to in genuinely following Christ.

> "The spiritual disciplines in our lives can only be true to the heart of Christ when they are motivated and carried out by loving devotion and not legal duty."

True Obedience in Christ

There is another obedience born out of love and grace. It is an obedience that flows from a heart overwhelmed by gratitude and awe at the unspeakable grace gift of forgiveness on the cross. This obedience is also seen in the life of the Apostle Paul after his salvation experience on the road to Damascus. It is spiritually transforming and leads to humility, gratitude, true spiritual sight, and eternal life. It leads to God and not away from God. This loving obedience is spiritually alive and vibrant. It feeds on the love and power of Christ within. It is born out of a realization that "without Him I can do nothing." It is prayerful and loving to others who have not experienced the forgiveness of grace. It is performed out of love and joy and deep gratitude. It is fueled with passion fed by overwhelming grace. This obedience doesn't care if it is seen and praised by men and actually tries to avoid man's praise. It is just lost in the wonder of a love beyond words.

This obedience is a blessing to one's life and reveals the true spiritual freedom in the soul. It is also life-consuming as we see in Paul's life when he proclaimed, "But what things were gain to me, these I have counted loss for Christ. Yet indeed *I also count all things loss for the excellence of the knowledge of Christ Jesus my Lord,* for whom I have suffered the loss of all things, *and count them as rubbish, that I may gain Christ*" (Phil. 3:7–8, author's italics). It is a spiritual blessing that leads to further spiritual blessing. It honors God and the heart of Christ who lovingly set the standard for loving obedience at the cross. It has the outward appearance of grace which is fed by an inner core of grace. It becomes one of the most impacting kinds of spiritual life which led Stephen to pray while he was being stoned to death: "Lord, do not charge them with this sin" (Acts 7:60). This kind of life-giving and grace-filled obedience is what I am referring to throughout these pages. Though the enemy has manipulated contemporary culture to put a very negative spin on obedience to God, this grace-inspired obedience is love responding to love.

> "*O*bedience because of grace is very different from obedience because of grit. Is yours obedient grace from the heart or obedient grit from the will?"

So if you attempt to carry out what you think are your religious duties in the strength of your own will power, you will fail sooner or later (for most of us sooner). If out of a legalistic sense of duty you meticulously check off each item on your list of religious rules, it will lead toward frustration, failure, and a sense of guilt when you miss one (which you will). If you are performing religious, spiritual habits you think others expect in order to be an accepted part of a group, it will be empty and you will try to hide those items wherein you don't measure up. However, if you put your focus on Christ and His matchless love, your devotion will bubble up in your life like an artesian spring. This focus is much different from the focus of religion. Keller explains,

> "Religion operates on the principle of 'I obey—therefore I am accepted by God.' The basic operating principle of the gospel is 'I am accepted by God through the work of Jesus Christ—therefore I obey" (3).

I love that crystal clear distinction. If your focus is on Christ and His power and strength in your life, a sense of loving gratitude will make it a great joy to serve Him. When you focus on Him and realize it is His life flowing through you, your joy spills out. As Paul explained, "I have been crucified with Christ; *it is no longer I who live, but Christ lives in me*; and the life which I now live in the flesh I live by faith in the Son of God, who loved me and gave Himself for me" (Gal. 2:20, author's italics). Live free out of love for Christ, not in bondage out of legalism. Please don't be fooled any longer by the clever scheme to distort obedience. When I speak of obedience in these pages, let this be the accurate picture in your mind, not the negative and harsh punitive spin of the culture. Remember, it is love responding to love.

Obedience Under Fire

When some endure the waxing, staining, and painting in their spiritual walk, they insist there is no good reason for the things they are enduring. Sometimes rebellion and anger is evident in their thinking and responses. They see no progress in a simple life of faithfulness to God and in the small duties they've been assigned. They bristle at what they consider menial labor for the Lord. They respond to the day-by-day faithfulness that God uses, just as the Karate Kid did to his waxing, painting, and staining. I don't like it! I don't see any sense in it! This is not what I was anticipating! This is not exciting! This is not what I signed up for! This is not getting me any closer to my desired accomplishment! Why are you doing this!? I am tired of following your instructions! When these responses begin to fill your mind, resentment builds, and giving up is not far behind.

Obedience: Beginning Steps

Just as a father cannot entrust the overwhelming power of a 12 gauge shotgun into the hands of his two-year-old son, so God cannot entrust overwhelming divine power into the hands of His children that have not even begun to learn loving submission and obedience to His plan. It would be like giving more and more to a spoiled child that would inevitably cause havoc to those around him and lead to his own destruction. In twenty-first century America, we have witnessed the deterioration of the basics of spiritual growth and health, such as feeding upon God's Word, intimacy through prayer, and serving in the body of Christ which is His church, not to mention sharing the good news of the gospel and the Great Commission. These are literally some of the ABCs of growing in Christ and finding and following God's will. Their lack is crippling millions of people who are seeking God's will for their lives on their own terms.

Feeding on God's Word

Again, remember the genuine motives of spiritual obedience we discussed previously. We don't feed on God's Word because it is some rule requirement to check off the list. We do feed on God's Word because it is one of the absolute joys that flows out of our intimate relationship and love for God, so we are spiritually nourished and strong. This is not something I have to do. This is something I get to do. This is something that my heart yearns to do. As the Psalmist exclaimed, "Oh, how I love Your law! It is my meditation all the day...therefore I love Your commandments more than gold, yes, than fine gold" (Psalm 119:97, 127)! Do you get the difference?

> "When your love relationship with Christ is intimate and growing, your time spent in His Word will be a treasure hunt and not a religious duty."

We are all very committed to eating food each day. In fact, it seems many of us are overcommitted. Before our next meal time rolls around, some of us are looking into sacks of greasy chips and devouring the rest of the ice cream. It is tragic we are so overcommitted to eating our physical food (which is so temporary) and yet so lacking in joyful commitment to our spiritual food from the Word of God (which nourishes us for life).

The Bible is much like the stolen treasure map in the pirate movies. Somebody has it in his possession and somebody else is desperately looking for it. It contains directions to treasures that people dream about and for which everyone yearns. Yet for most of us, there are numerous treasure maps lying unused around the house. It is the treasure of all treasures. It is the actual Word of God to us. It is the book of unspeakable promises. It is the book of heart-touching encouragement and comfort. It is the book of the past. It is the book of the future. It is the book of wonderful heroes. It is the book of love. It is the book with the answers. It is the book that corrects us and gives true direction in life. With all of this treasure available, it is tragic that so many completely ignore it.

It is ludicrous to imagine that a person will find God's will and the answers they are desperately seeking if they never spend any time in the answer book of life. God didn't speak His living Word for it to lay around ignored. God didn't intend that His Word of truth and direction should gather dust on someone's coffee table. God didn't supernaturally bring together all the individual parts of His Word over many centuries with many different human authors only to hear some intellectual who is spiritually blind (1 Cor. 2:14) say it is either a fairy tale that is a complete fabrication or outdated and not usable for contemporary people. Nothing could be further from the truth! Great knowledge in academics certainly does not guarantee great wisdom. God lovingly gave this great treasure to us and He intended that His Word be lovingly, diligently studied in order for people to find and follow His will.

The Word of God is as current as man's problems. Untold numbers of people that need answers to life's questions have found God's Word to be the source of help for which they are looking. Many of the great heroes of history, even of American history, have known and admitted their reliance on and firm belief in the Word of God. Abraham Lincoln said,

> "It is the duty of nations as well as of men to own their dependence upon the overruling power of God...and to recognize the sublime truth, announced in the Holy Scriptures and proven by all history: that those nations only are blessed whose God is the Lord" (4).

Samuel Adams stated,

> "The rights of the colonists as Christians... may be best understood by reading and carefully studying the institution of The Great Law Giver and Head of the Christian church, which are to be found clearly written and promulgated in the New Testament" (5).

Historical accounts are replete with leaders that staked their careers and their very lives on the Word of God.

Are you in dire straits? Have your days been filled with crying and pleading for God to give you direction, while at the same time you've been ignoring the direction He has provided? Have you overlooked what is right under your nose because of the misguided concepts of the day that you can't find answers in God's Word? Is a little (hissing) voice whispering in your ear that you won't find what you need in God's Word? You need to understand that the road leading away from confidence in God's Word is a fictitious road full of misdirection and heartache. In fact, it is a finger print of the enemy to cast all kinds of clever dispersions against the Word of God. The teachings and principles of God's Word are exactly what you need, and they are the "true truth" in a world of misdirection and redefining of truth. Dig into the dazzling treasure chest and pull out your answers. Start to study God's living Word and ask Him to reveal what He wants to teach you each day.

Intimacy in Prayer

Another of the ABCs of Christianity is prayer. This is, if it is possible, an even more sorely neglected blessing than is the Word of God. It is almost inconceivable that such a high privilege would be so apathetically forgotten or neglected. Some of the blame for this tragedy lies at the minister's doorstep. According to some surveys, the sad fact is few ministers spend more than a few minutes daily in intimate communication with the Father. No wonder there is such a terrible famine of prayer. If the pastor's life doesn't show the incredible value of prayer, it can only have a negative impact on those he serves whether intentional or not.

In his classic book, *Why Revival Tarries*, Leonard Ravenhill points to some of the reasons why there is such a serious lack of prayer today. He says,

> "Poverty-stricken as the Church is today in many things, she is most stricken here, in the place of prayer. We have many organizers, but few agonizers; many players and payers, few prayers; many singers, few clingers; lots of pastors, few wrestlers; many fears, few tears; much fashion, little passion; many interferers, few intercessors; many writers, but few fighters.
> Failing here, we fail everywhere" (6).

This is a vivid and accurate assessment of the prayer life in much of American Christianity. We need to heed the words of this great preacher, "Failing here, we fail everywhere." It's not always easy or convenient to keep a car serviced and in good working condition, but it is essential if the car is to keep running and performing well. Prayer is not always an easy ministry, but it is essential if we are to receive God's direction and answers in order to fulfill His purpose. The Scripture plainly states, "Ye have not because ye ask not," as R. A. Torrey explains,

> "Prayer is God's appointed way for obtaining things, and the great secret of all lack in our experience, in our life and in our work is neglect of prayer. James brings this out very forcibly in chapter 4 and verse 2 of his epistle: 'Ye have not because ye ask not.' These words contain the secret of the poverty and powerlessness of the average Christian—neglect of prayer. Many a Christian is asking, 'Why is it I make so little progress in my Christian life?' 'Neglect of prayer,' God answers. 'You have not because you ask not'" (7).

If this is such a drastic need in our lives and it is, why do we neglect it so apathetically? Many reasons are given and of course the enemy plays a part in all of them. Some say, "I just don't seem to have the time." Others explain, "I guess I'm just lazy." Some claim, "I don't feel that it does me that much good." Whatever the various excuses are, they are all effective blinders on our eyes to keep us from all the wonderful things of God and from Him speaking clearly and personally to our hearts.

How would you know what your boss expected if you never took time to ask? How would you be able to discuss your concerns about your job if you never spoke? How would you find out what your performance evaluation was if you never asked? How could you receive encouragement after a mistake if you never spent time with your boss? How could you discover his direction and intentions for you if you never inquired? How could he lead you in the right direction if the only interaction was "Hi," "Thanks for the job," and "Bye"? If you do realize that it is essential to communicate with your earthly bosses, how much more important is it for us to communicate with our Lord and Master Jesus Christ?

Again, as with God's Word, prayer is not something I have to do. That is the attitude of the spiritually-blind culture. If there is genuine love, it is something my heart yearns for and desires to do.

> "Though we can certainly be in communication with Him through the day in bits and pieces and we should, His desire is also for heart-to-heart communication in your quiet place."

We develop and grow our relationship with the Lord through our prayer time together. It is unfortunate that many people pray just to use the Lord for their own selfish wants and desires. They come to the Lord only when there is a tragedy or a consuming need. They essentially take the Lord off-the-shelf when they need Him and put Him back as soon as the need is met or has passed. No wonder they have a failing prayer life. Our prayer life will truly begin to flourish as we learn to love the Lord through our communication time with Him. We will enjoy that intimate relationship with the Lord as we come to Him just because we enjoy spending time with Him. We will learn just to love and worship the Lord with no ulterior motives. Our heart will sing to Him out of the depths of our soul. We will cherish the time we are privileged to spend with Him each day. As we progress in this intimacy we will also learn that we will feel a certain spiritual longing begin to set in when we don't spend time in His presence. The Lord will shower blessings and answers upon us as we draw near to Him. His desire is to enjoy intimacy with His children and speak to their hearts.

Remember that the road away from confidence in a true prayer life is one of danger, frustration, and unanswered questions.

Loving and Building One Another Up

As the little, rebellious four-year-old heads out the door of the house and yells in anger, with his chubby little fist raised in the air, "I'm leaving this place!" we think to ourselves, "Boy has he got alot to learn!" He has no idea how foolish and dangerous that statement is. He has no idea how much he really needs his family. He doesn't understand the protection, comfort, nourishment, help, and wisdom he enjoys from being part of the family. He doesn't yet realize that isolating himself from his family will have very painful consequences.

In the same way many Christians have left the family of the body of Christ. They've left the very group for which Jesus died to make them a part. They've left a family that is essential to their growth. They've ignored the Word of God which instructs us to use our gifts to build up the body of Christ. They've left a ministry in which God has told us we are to bear one another's burdens and share one another's joys. They are neglecting the use of the unique spiritual gifts with which God has blessed them in order to edify and build up the family. They are refusing to be faithful in the ABCs of the Christian walk. How can we possibly think it is acceptable to demand answers from the Lord when we have rebelled against His plan for the spiritual family in which He has placed us? The church is His plan in this New Testament age, according to Scripture.

Jesus shared some very emotional words with His followers just before He would be led away to His crucifixion. They were very strong words that were in fact a command. He knew full well the trials they were about to face and the needs they would have in the persecution and chaos that would follow. Of all the things Jesus could have told them to do in preparation He simply said, "A new commandment I give to you, that you love one another; as I have loved you, that you also love one another. By this all will know that you are My disciples, if you have love for one another" (John 13:34–35).

Out of His love and concern for them, through the difficult time to come, the commandment He gave them was to love one another. F. F. Bruce eloquently states,

> "He is about to leave them, but He will bequeath spiritual treasures to them before He does so; His love, His joy (John 15:11) and His peace" (John 14:27) (8).

He knew they would desperately need each other. He knew their intimate and sacrificial love for each other would carry them through the following days. He also knew their genuine love for each other would be the key distinguishing characteristic of their testimony to the world as His genuine followers. That deep need for genuine love among His followers in the body of Christ is as needed today as ever and it is still a testimony of the genuine followers of Christ. It is a loving command from the Master because He knows that we need each other. He wired us that way.

Let me share a few of the statements emotionally thrown at me through the years. I've heard many times the statement, "I don't have to be in the church to be a Christian." Yes, just as that four-year-old didn't have to stay in that house to be a member of the family, so a born-again Christian doesn't have to be involved in the church to be a part of the family. However, it is also true that a born-again Christian needs to be involved in the church to be an obedient, productive, and functioning member of the family using the gifts that God has provided. This is, of course, with the understanding that there are legitimate reasons why some sweet Christians can't be involved, such as terrible illnesses, bed confinement, remoteness of their locations, inability of missionaries to reach certain tribes, Alzheimer's/Dementia, and many other valid reasons. However, other than providential hindrances that are unavoidable, God's desire and design is for us to be faithful to the body of Christ—the Church.

Some have also said, "I don't have to be in church to love the Lord." Again, with providential hindrances this is true, but for many people this sounds suspiciously like nothing more than an excuse for other underlying reasons including unfaithfulness. Let me lovingly explain how without knowing it, these people have actually contradicted themselves. The Bible teaches that the Church is The Body of Christ. As Paul is talking to the Corinthian Christians about how they are all different parts of the same body, he states, "And if one member suffers, all the members suffer with it; or if one member is honored, all the members rejoice with it. Now *you are the body of Christ*, and members individually" (1 Cor. 12:26–27, author's italics). How can a Christian love Christ and manifest no loving commitment to His body? The two are inseparably connected. If we truly love Christ, we will also love the organism which is His body and the various parts of the body that are part of us.

The Scriptures also speak clearly about each Christian's function within the body of Christ. The individual Christian is referred to as a part of the body. One is an arm. Another is a leg. Still another is a finger. Some are ears and some are mouths (unfortunately it seems there is an overabundance of this part).

> "*If* every born again Christian is a part of the body, wouldn't it seem reasonable that God would want them performing their functions together for the good of the whole?"

If they are a finger, would God approve of them having nothing to do with the hand or the arm? If they were a toe, could they please God by having nothing to do with the foot or the ankle? God has clearly given each Christian a function/ gift within the body of Christ. To rebel against or ignore the church body except in cases of providential hindrance is to leave yourself isolated without the fellowship and growth of the body and abstaining from your God-given ministry that is so needed by the rest of the body.

Let me address one other reason that has caused some to leave the church in our day. I have sweet friends who know the Lord, but have experienced an emotional hurt from someone in the church that was so deep that it caused them to leave not only their fellowship, but also the church. I certainly empathize with them and understand their deep hurt from many personal experiences as a leader and pastor. I assure you I have felt it also and wanted to walk away! You would find it hard to believe some of the hatred and venom that has been pointed my direction. I want you to know I get it. In fact, one of the most difficult parts of my hurts from others in the church is when they hurt my wife, my daughter, and my son in a deep way also.

New Understanding from Old Hurts

Allow me to share a few thoughts that may help you with gaining a different perspective. I have come to understand a few things through my hurtful experiences.

There are no perfect churches because we are all imperfect people who make mistakes. I am not making excuses for hateful and mean actions because they are wrong and dishonor Christ. I am in no way discounting your genuine pain as I have felt it myself. My point is that anywhere I go there will be imperfect people that are hopefully trying to move forward from an old way of life and of acting in ways that dishonor Christ. However, whether they are trying to grow spiritually and move forward or not, if my first response is to run each time there is a difficulty from an immature person, then I will spend my life running which will not solve my problem or fulfill God's purpose.

With that said, there are some churches that are more loving and welcoming and full of life and striving to follow Christ, and some that tend to be more rigid, cold, and spiritually dead, following a religious routine. If you feel the Lord is leading you away from a dead church, then by all means go somewhere else as you follow God's leading. Follow the Lord's direction to a fellowship where you can sense the genuine love of Christ, hear the whole counsel of the Word of God, and use your gifts to build up the family. However, if you catch yourself using a difficult situation as justification to completely drop out, then you would do well to reevaluate your real motives. That is not Christ's desire for you and doesn't honor His gifting and calling in your life.

Above all, I have learned that my commitment is to love and serve Christ as my top priority where He has placed me. There have been times I have wanted to just run and leave it all behind, but if I am being honest in my heart, I know my top priority is to love Him and use the gifts He has given me for His honor and glory to impact lives in the body.

> "*Y*our real love and highest devotion is to Christ. The question is, 'Where has He placed you?'"

If He hasn't led you and placed you there, then leave and find wherever He is leading you to fulfill His purpose. If He has led you and placed you there, then serve Him above everything else, even when your feelings are hurt. If loving and serving Christ is my top priority, then I will stay where He has placed me until He gives me release and direction to another spiritual family.

A strong commitment to the church is important to our worship, fellowship, and growth. Our worship together as a family can be one of the most exciting and uplifting times of our week. I truly look forward to the special hours I can spend with my Christian brothers and sisters as we worship and sing to the Lord. Another element of the Christian walk that can't be duplicated outside the body of Christ is the personal fellowship of a particular group of people. This is one of the spiritual and emotional highs for the child of God. We need each other, and it is a great joy to be together in the bond of God's love. The church is also important to our spiritual growth. God has graciously gifted some within the body of Christ to be pastors and some to be teachers. Though spiritual nourishment every day is essential, it is important to be under the study of God's Word by those whom God has specifically gifted. What a joy it is to hear a dedicated Bible Study teacher share the truths of God's Word.

How refreshing it is to hear the Word of God preached in the power of the Holy Spirit by a great pastor who loves Christ. This is undeniably needful in the life of a Christian. It is the way God has wired us within the body of Christ.

One of the reasons people are desperately searching for God's will and having little success is that they have denied or neglected some of the ABCs of God's will which are growth principles for every Christian. If God has seen that we lack the maturity to follow His preliminary commands, can we really expect Him to open up the sky and shower miraculous directions upon us to take us to the next level? If God has seen our apathy in kindergarten, do we seriously expect Him to place us in graduate school? If we have not made it through boot camp, should God thrust us into the Green Berets? God knows best and wants to see a loving submission and willingness to be obedient in the small directions before the big ones will be assigned. This usually takes time, which is the painful downfall of many. I pray that we would all have the heart of the prophet Isaiah as he saw the Lord on the throne high and lifted up. As the Lord asked, "Whom shall I send, and who will go for Us?" Isaiah answered, "Here am I! Send me" (Isaiah 6:8). This classic response of surrender ripples through the pond of time all the way to our shores today. Whether the call is small and seemingly stationary, or huge and supernaturally demanding, may our hearts respond, "Here am I! Send me."

God wants us to be faithful where we are. He wants to see that character which is only revealed when things don't seem to be progressing at all. I had an old pastor tell me years ago, "You show who you really are by what you do when no one is looking."

God is looking for a few good men and women and young people who love Him and who will be yielded to pay the price of total obedience to His direction, even if it seems like no direction. So allow me to share one final note about persevering obedience. As I was in the office one day going through my mail, I read this short but powerful testimony:

> "It was a miserable time of ministry. Something just didn't seem to be working. After

64

several years of rather unsuccessful ministry, it might have seemed as though he wasn't really designed for preaching. Nonetheless, he stuck it out in the pastorate and sought another place of ministry in a different part of the country. This time he tried Fullerton, California. Good thing he did; otherwise, the world might have missed out on the ministry of Charles Swindoll" (9).

It is encouraging to me that one of the most gifted writers and pastors of our time went through a period that was termed, "rather unsuccessful." This also has personal application to my life as Dr. Swindoll became president at Dallas Theological Seminary while I was doing some graduate work there, and I admire him greatly. Determined obedience to God flowing out of loving devotion has once again proven its value. Dr. Swindoll's current ministry could be accurately termed, "supernaturally successful."

Final Question to Ponder:
Is my obedience flowing out of my love relationship
with Christ or out of religious duty?

Chapter 3

Knowing Cleansing

Watching for Kinks

*M*any times I have uncoiled and pulled my long water hose out to wash the car. I usually have someone turn the faucet on and wait at the end of the hose. I have the car prepared to wash, the soap ready to mix, the bucket ready to use and my rags handy. On some of those occasions where I was ready and waiting to start cleaning my filthy vehicle, which had the words, "wash me" written in the dirt on the back window, there was a hold up because I didn't have any water coming out of the hose. As I looked along the hose to see what the problem was, I would find a kink. I would quickly straighten out the hose and the water would begin to flow freely. The same thing happened several times, and then I finally learned to keep a close eye out for the kinks when rolling out the hose. I started to look for them ahead of time. My learned habit is to be ever watchful to keep the hose free of kinks.

God has made it clear to me in many instances that there were obstructions in my life that were hindering the free flow of His power and direction. There have been times when I have had everything prepared to the best of my ability, but there was still a problem some-where along the line. There was a spiritual kink in my life, a disobedi-ence, an anger or rebellion of some form. It was a problem that would not allow me to progress any further until the kink was straightened out. I sensed it was something that God, in His wonderful love and nurture wouldn't allow me to hold on to. I have grown to understand this as "Conviction Grace":

"Conviction Grace"

When my heart is troubled, something's wrong I know
And I search for an answer, to my Lord I go
Then I quickly remember, and it pains my soul
That I said something hateful, flesh was in control
Though that pain isn't easy, what I know for sure
Is the heart that has sent it for my good is pure
It is sent by my Father, it's His grace to me
It's His grace of conviction, sent to keep me free
Conviction grace from my Father
Conviction grace because He cares
Conviction grace for my freedom
Conviction grace breaks the snares
Conviction grace, don't reject it
Conviction grace, from above
Conviction grace, His sweet favor
Conviction grace, His pure love (1).

It is very important to understand this action by the Father, especially in light of the overtly cynical and negative reactions of our contemporary culture toward conviction. The culture leads us to a faulty understanding which in turn leads us to a faulty conclusion.

> "*I*t is His 'love' that convicts and constrains me as I am conformed to the image of Christ."

This conviction that is cunningly disguised by the enemy as the punishing whip of a harsh and ruthless tyrant is actually the opposite. It is, in fact, the perfect love of my perfect Father that constrains me.

That loving constraint actually protects me, corrects me, redirects me, and rescues me. When you really think about it, that kind of love is also our motivation as imperfect parents with an imperfect, though deep love toward our children. Out of love we want to protect and direct our kids into the path that will provide the greatest health and benefit to them in the long run. How much more would it be true of our perfect Father with a perfect love?

> "The highest form of love from a parent to their beloved child is not to always tell them what they want to hear to shield them from any discomfort, but to tell them the true truth of God's Word that they need to hear to shield them from ruin."

When you have truly committed your life to Christ and the Lord lovingly convicts you of sin, it is one of those things you can either obediently deal with, and move forward in freedom and growth, or continue to be stilted and stagnated by not living up to being a new creation in Christ. When you hold onto things you know dishonor Christ, the Holy Spirit within you will convict you.

I believe this culturally promoted (enemy initiated) disconnect concerning conviction is one of the reasons many people are unable to find God's direction. It is because they have spiritual kinks that haven't been straightened out due to a faulty concept based in fear and cynicism. They haven't yet learned the extravagant love of the prodigal son's Father who is watching the road and waiting with open arms. They haven't learned consistent spiritual cleansing in their lives on a daily basis. This obviously overlaps with the preceding chapter on obedience. Unless one learns loving obedience to the promptings and conviction of their loving Father, there will not be the enjoyment of the forgiveness and cleansing we have through Christ. When we are willing to submit to God's direction through loving obedience and confession, then we will be able to thank Him for the forgiveness and cleansing according to His precious promise in 1 John 1:9.

Without submissive obedience to God's nurturing direction and cleansing, we will struggle under a load of unconfessed sin and make ourselves more of a target for the enemy.

Spiritual Soap

The question is, "How do I get rid of the kinks?" God has graciously given us a wonderful promise to live by in first John 1:9: "If we confess our sins, He is faithful and just to forgive us our sins and to cleanse us from all unrighteousness." What an incredible promise!

Without slogging through the theological underpinnings of scriptural confession which most would likely choose not to endure, I will be brief concerning the "need" for confession. I will try to help make it clear for you by making a brief explanatory statement and then share study notes from a couple of respected Bible sources.

There is the need for genuine confession "at salvation" as it pertains to the new birth (being born again as Jesus referred to in John 3) and then there is the need for genuine confession "after salvation" as it pertains to paternal intimacy and sanctification as illustrated in chapter 6 between my son and myself.

The ESV Study Bible note on First John 1:9 explains,

> "Christians must confess (their) sins, initially to receive salvation and then to maintain fellowship with God and with one another (vs. 3)" (2).

The MacArthur Study Bible note on First John 1:9 confirms,

> "Continual confession of sin is an indication of genuine salvation... Confession of sin characterizes genuine Christians, and God continually cleanses those who are confessing (cf. v. 7)" (3).

Knowing cleansing and a renewed intimacy after His loving conviction prompts our hearts is critical to understanding God's direction, and therefore, to recognizing God's will. Always be aware that the enemy is striving to drive any kind of wedge (kinks/unconfessed sins) between you and our loving Father to keep you from true freedom and power as you walk in God's will. His stealthy strategy that sometimes flies under our radar is to use guilt and fear that create estrangement and separation. When we stay in close, intimate fellowship with our Master, we will have little trouble in discerning His direction for our lives, even when it means waiting on His timing.

I want to be very clear at the outset of this section on scriptural confession and cleansing that it is a deeply serious matter concerning a genuine heart thirsting after intimacy with their Lord and not some religious card played to take care of one sin and move on to the next. Insincere, manipulative motives have absolutely no place to hide from the eyes of omniscience. Insincere motives will get no further than Jonah did running.

A daily walk of loving fellowship with Jesus Christ is a lifestyle that is becoming more the exception among Christians than the rule. In many cases, it is fast becoming the lowest priority in the typical life of extreme busyness. Many are allowing the rush of life to control every waking moment and abandoning the most important time of the day, which is our quality, quiet time with God. Many would respond, "I talk to God all day long." That's great, but I'm speaking about giving Him some quality, intimate time lovingly set aside just for Him. Just think for a moment how it would make you feel if you wanted to spend some intimate, quality time with your spouse or best friend and they were constantly doing other things or even walking away while you were attempting to share special moments from your heart. It is even more convicting when you think about the fact you are speaking to the One who died for you, the King of Kings and Lord of Lords. As we think about keeping the kinks out of our spiritual lives, let's investigate a few of the kinks that seem to be especially problematic in our culture.

Going Our Own Direction

In Richard Lee's excellent book, *Issues Of The Heart*, he shares an interesting story in chapter 4 ("How to Know God's Perfect Will"):

> "The story is told about an Eastern newspaper man who went to visit a town in the old West. As he rode into town on the stagecoach, he noticed that there were targets drawn on the sides of the buildings and hitching posts and that someone had shot the bullseye out of each target. Not a single target missed, and every target had nothing shot out but the bullseye.
>
> 'Wow!' he thought to himself, 'The man who did this must be the best shot in the West. I'll interview him and get a great story for my paper back East.' So he asked around town who this man was who shot out the bullseyes. The townspeople referred him to the town drunk.
>
> 'How in the world did you shoot out every bullseye?' he asked the drunk. 'Oh, it wasn't all that hard,' said the drunk. 'You see, I just shoot first and draw the targets later'" (4)!

Many have a kink in their spiritual life because of this very practice. We shoot first and draw the target around the shot to make it look like we have hit the bulls-eye. We proceed with our own game plan instead of listening to the coach. We make our own blueprints instead of talking to the Master architect. We even make our own test instead of getting the authentic one from our teacher. We create our own map without an intimate knowledge of the road. Herein is one of the most disruptive and misguided practices of our spiritual life: "We do our own thing and ask God to bless it!" Blackaby, Blackaby, and King address this as one of the key issues in their book, Experiencing God:

"He does not invite us to set magnificent goals and then pray that He will help us achieve them. He already has His own agenda when He approaches us. His desire is to get us from where we are to where He is working" (5).

This core truth permeates their book. Find out where God is working and then join Him in His work.

The key to real success in life is finding and following God's plan. Going our own direction will always lead to pain, heartache, and away from God's blessing and empowerment. Even though it looks good on the surface, it is a dead end road. Yes, it is evident from scripture that there are many times when the right road is more difficult. Yes, there are many times when God's plan calls for sacrifice and inconvenience, but it will always prove to be the very best plan to follow because He loves us. As we lovingly follow His plan, all the resources of heaven go before us to accomplish His purpose.

If this has been a kink in your own life, there is great news. You can confess it to God as a sin of self will and know His cleansing and forgiveness. Our precious Lord Jesus loves you more than anybody else, and He will take over, direct your life, empower you, and put you exactly where you need to be if you will simply confess it to Him.

Following Our Own Wisdom

" *E* very time man follows his own wisdom without God's wisdom, man is revealing his lack of true wisdom."

Man's wisdom, because of his finite mind, will lead him to believe in such things as the "theory" of evolution instead of the truth of creation, and in logical explanations which adamantly deny miracles, and in truth based upon his physical senses alone. Man is destined to end up on a dead end road when following his own, very limited wisdom. This is another of the often seen kinks in our lives.

Seeking True Wisdom

When we begin to consider what true wisdom is and how to avoid the spiritual kinks in life, wouldn't it make sense to investigate the Holy Spirit inspired Word of God? Wouldn't it also make sense to study some of the books of the inspired Word of God that specifically deal with wisdom? Further, wouldn't it make sense to seriously contemplate that inspired wisdom literature written by one of the wisest men of all time? Solomon was a king that God greatly blessed with exceptional wisdom as he wrote most of the Proverbs, some Psalms, Ecclesiastes, and Song of Solomon. Scripture says, "And God gave Solomon wisdom and exceedingly great understanding, and largeness of heart like the sand on the seashore. Thus Solomon's wisdom excelled the wisdom of all the men of the East and all the wisdom of Egypt" (1 Kings 4:29–30). Though, later in his life, Solomon allowed the flesh to be in control, and he experienced some terrible failures, this wisdom literature inspired by the Holy Spirit of God is exceptionally valuable concerning the foundations of wisdom.

Proverbs is one of those exceptionally valuable books concerning true wisdom. One of the core truths seen throughout this book is the correlation between "the fear of the Lord" and "wisdom." MacArthur comments,

> "The two major themes which are interwoven and overlapping throughout Proverbs are wisdom and folly. Wisdom, which includes knowledge, understanding, instruction, discretion, and obedience, is built on the fear of the Lord and the Word of God. Folly is everything opposite to wisdom" (6).

If true wisdom from God's inspired Word is repetitiously correlated to "the fear of the Lord," then it would be wise for us to understand and live out that truth. When some have heard this phrase, "the fear of the Lord," they have immediately reacted and jumped to a verse in the New Testament attempting to deny its veracity in the current age. This New Testament verse states, "There is no fear in love; but perfect love casts out fear, because fear involves torment. But he who fears has not been made perfect in love" (1 John 4:18). There is no contradiction between the two and we need to understand the distinction between them to live in true wisdom.

This section of Scripture immediately before 1 John 4:18 is expounding the incredible love of God and how that incredible love being manifested in our own lives proves that we are born of God: "Beloved, let us love one another, for love is of God; and everyone who loves is born of God and knows God" (1 John 4:7). Again, "God is love, and he who abides in love abides in God, and God in him" (1 John 4:16). The truth of God's love manifested in our lives which reveals our salvation means that we will stand with absolute boldness in the Day of Judgment because Christ has already taken our judgment: "Love has been perfected among us in this: that we may have boldness in the day of judgment..." (1 John 4:17). Then in verse 18 we see there is no fear of judgment because the perfect love of God abiding in us casts out that fear and further explains that fear involves torment. In those of us who have been truly born-again there is no fear of the Day of Judgment, and there is no abiding torment because the divine love of Christ that has invaded our hearts has completely cast that fear out. Christ was our perfect sacrifice. He endured the judgment for us. He took all our sin upon Himself. My redemption price is paid in full. No more fear of judgment. Hallelujah! An ESV Study Bible note gives great clarity concerning 1 John 4:18 when it explains,

> "No fear in love does not rule out the presence and constructive effect of 'the fear of the Lord' that is 'the beginning of knowledge' (Prov. 1:7). Here John speaks of fear of final judgment

(cf. 1 John 4:17). God's perfect love for believers casts out the fear of wrath and eternal punishment" (7).

The "fear of the Lord" that is inextricably tied to wisdom in the Proverbs is a different scriptural concept that is not only still active, but very needful. This fear which is distinguished in Proverbs as the beginning of wisdom is not a dreadful, tormenting fear of judgment as we have already noted because Christ has taken our judgment. This "wisdom fear" is more identified with characteristics like reverence, awe, admiration, submission, respect, worship, veneration, and honor. MacArthur's study note on Proverbs 1:7 states,

> "This reverential awe and admiring, submissive fear is foundational for all spiritual knowledge and wisdom (cf. 2:4–6; 9:10; 15:33; Job 28:28; Ps. 111:10; Eccl. 12:13)" (8).

This "wisdom fear" of reverential awe, honor, and submission flows freely out of the loving heart of one who has been born again and has caught a glimpse of the infinite cost of Christ on the cross. Far from being considered a spiritual impediment, it is the joy and honor of the child of God. When we discount or ignore this truth principle in scripture we show a lack of wisdom and do a disservice to our children. When there is not a proper fear (awesome, reverential, and submissive respect for God), the temptation gate of our fleshly inclinations is wide open and the enemy is happy to walk right through it. One of the reasons for the troubling lack of respect in our secular society is that some parents who had no spiritual role models have raised a generation according to hedonistic cultural values. The result is inevitable. With very little if any loving, scriptural discipline, the lack of respect for their parents and authority is painfully evident. Even with no malicious intent, this has an unintentional, but very devastating effect upon their spiritual lives.

"When there is very little respect or proper fear for authority, then the pendulum tends to swing wildly toward following one's own opinions and directions. Self-will reigns. This inescapably leads away from loving submission to the Lord."

A proper fear and respect for the Lord is the beginning of true wisdom, according to numerous verses in Proverbs. Without true spiritual wisdom from the Lord, we are following our own fleshly course. This becomes a subtle kink in a person's spiritual life, even though the contemporary culture praises it.

We also discover in Proverbs that the knowledge of the Holy is understanding. How do we attain a knowledge of the Holy? Through God's Holy Word! Most of us are so busy that we have forgotten the most important guide for our lives and the key to understanding. J. I. Packer in his great book, *Knowing God* explains,

> "Wisdom is divinely wrought in those, and those only, who apply themselves to God's revelation. 'Thou through thy commandments hast made me wiser than mine enemies,' declares the psalmist, 'I have more understanding than all my teachers:' why?—'for thy testimonies are my meditation' (Ps. 119:99 f.). So Paul admonishes the Colossians: 'Let the word of Christ dwell in you richly in all wisdom' (Col. 3:16). How are we men of the twentieth century to do this? By soaking ourselves in the Scriptures… Again, it is to be feared that many today who profess to be Christ's never learn wisdom, through failure to attend sufficiently to God's written Word" (9).

When we fail to have a proper fear of the Lord through an inadequate intake of God's Holy Word, we fail to give ourselves the chance to know God's will for our lives and we have another kink in the spiritual hose of life. There is still good news; you can simply confess this lack as sinful neglect and know the cleansing and forgiveness of God in your life as you sincerely move in an obedient direction to soak up spiritual wisdom.

The focus of this section is to encourage you to stay close to God through daily fellowship and cleansing. If you truly know Christ, your relationship with Him can never be taken away, but the intimacy and empowerment of your fellowship can be hindered (see "A Heart of Purity" in chapter 6). Stay in close fellowship with the Lord on a daily basis by confessing anything not pleasing to Him. As you become more intimate in your love relationship with the Lord, you will find His will and more easily discern His direction. You will have a desire to follow His wisdom, not out of any religious duty, but out of love for His unspeakable grace. You will be freed from those nagging kinks in the hose of life that seem to keep you from having close fellowship and from knowing His will.

Final Question to Ponder:
Am I guarding my intimacy with Christ by quickly confessing sin or am I holding on to it?

Chapter 4

Knowing Timing

My Timing

When I was in sixth grade, I began to dream about the unspeakable joy of having my driver's license. I fantasized about the freedom I would have as I cruised around town. I thought about the places I could go and the sites I could see. I began to consider the possibility of enjoying it right then. I knew I could handle it properly. I knew I would be a wonderful and safe driver. In my mind there was not one good reason why I should not be able to drive.

I had an interesting experience about that time out on the farm. It may be somewhat shocking to those who grew up in the city, but in those days kids started working and running machinery at a young age. One day we were getting ready to go down the old dirt road from my grandparent's home to our farmhouse. We had been mowing with the old John Deere model B tractor on our farm in Kansas, and were finishing for the day. It was only a couple hundred yards from grandpa's driveway to ours, so I asked if I could drive the old tractor, solo. My dad was a bit hesitant, though I had mown pastures before. However, he allowed me to drive though he stayed close. Happy as a young boy could be, I took off down the old dirt road with great confidence and pride. As I drove down the few hundred yards of country road I said to myself and to everybody else (in my mind), "See, I told you I could do it."

I drove all the way down the road without a single problem and turned up into the driveway of our old farm house. I was still beaming over this accomplishment in my young mind when things began to go wrong. As I got to the end of the driveway, which was right beside the old farmhouse, I did what I normally did to stop the tractor when it had a bush hog on the back. I simply pulled on the hand clutch which usually brought the tractor to a stop out in the pasture. However, there was one very major problem in my life at that moment, the tractor did not stop. I was already in the back yard before I knew what was happening. I was still going full speed and wildly trying to steer away from the fences. With the first turn I ran under the clothesline and tore the smokestack off the tractor. With the next turn, I ran right over the top of the picnic table and flattened it to no more than 6 inches in height. Now came the real problem, there was nowhere else to go and I was headed for the car. As I rammed over the picnic table like the popular monster trucks of today, I was only a few feet from the car. I was really scared. To be honest, I was not so scared of the accident that was about to take place as I was the fearful wrath that would take hold of my little body after the accident was over. The thought that was racing through my mind at the moment was "dad is going to kill me!" (You would have to know Dad's temper and our rather violent upbringing to fully understand the terror.)

Just as the tractor bounded off the now flattened picnic table, only feet away from the car, dad jumped on the tractor, frantically did a couple things simultaneously jerking us to a stop and saved me and the car. In a moment, the tractor stood still and everyone breathed a sigh of relief. I had forgotten something very important when driving the old tractor. I not only had to disengage the hand clutch, but I had to do everything that Dad did as well, to stop the old machine. Even though I had the best intentions and the surest confidence in my abilities to handle the old green tractor, I was not fully prepared for the experience.

"The truth is the timing was not right! My timing was not His timing."

There are many times in our lives when we are absolutely sure we're ready for a particular experience when God sovereignly knows we are not. We become insistent that we are fully capable of taking the next step. When God does not seem to be opening a door, we begin to beg. After we have begged for a while and still do not see any open door, we begin to rationalize about moving ourselves in the desired direction. Finally, our self-willed flesh cannot stand it anymore and we move on our own. Tragically, this action puts us out of God's perfect timing for our lives. God uses waiting to teach us some lessons we could never learn otherwise. In the devotional classic, *Streams in the Desert*, Mrs. Charles Cowman asks,

> "Did you ever hear of anyone being much used for Christ who did not have some special waiting time, some complete upset of all his or her plans first; from St. Paul's being sent off into the desert of Arabia for three years, when he must have been boiling over with the glad tidings, down to the present day" (1)?

God loves us dearly! He wants better things for us than we even want for ourselves. He wants to do exceedingly, abundantly above what we can even ask or think. He wants to take us to heights that others have forfeited. He wants us to have everything that is good for us that will honor Him and fulfill His great plan and purpose for our lives. He wants to use us in special ways, with lasting effects upon our world and other precious lives. He wants the very best, and the very best can only be enjoyed within the bounds of His perfect timetable. He knows when we're prepared for the next step. He knows when it will *not* work. He knows the future, we do not know these things!

Blackaby, Blackaby, and King share some key words of wisdom on timing and our longing for God to do a great work through us. They explain the highest priority:

> "Many people long for God to do a sig-nificant work in their life. However, they try to

bypass the love relationship. The love relationship is why God created you. That is far more important to Him than what you do for Him. Anticipate that the first thing God will do in your life is to draw you into an intimate love relationship with Himself. When your relationship with God is as it should be, He will begin giving you assignments at His initiative. Whenever it seems that God is not doing anything fresh in your life, focus on the love relationship and stay there until God gives you a new assignment" (2).

Perhaps God's desire is for you to grow in your love relationship with Him as your highest priority before opening the door for the next mission. It has become apparent that patiently waiting on God's perfect timing in our contemporary culture is almost a lost discipline.

> "*O*bediently waiting on God's direction before going in any direction is a key to finding and following God's will."

We cannot know and be in the center of God's perfect will if we have forced our own "self-will" timetable. If you have jumped out of God's will because it was inconvenient or painful to wait and you want to get back on track, there's good news. Simply confess it as sin and commit yourself anew to love God supremely and to wait on and follow His timing. I am being transparent and honest with you in saying, this will not be easy and there will usually be a time of testing, but the peace and blessing that come when you get back on track with God's timing is incredible. You will find that the wait will turn out to be great!

We should be careful to heed the wisdom of God in Proverbs 3:5–6, which says, "Trust in the LORD with all your heart, and lean not on your own understanding; in all your ways acknowledge Him, and He shall direct your paths." When you apply these "wisdom principles" within the context of timing, it speaks loudly: "Trust the LORD with all your heart" can mean by way of application to trust the Lord with the timing of your life. If we jump into a new job, career, school, Ministry, relationship, house, car, credit card, or anything else without God's direction, we have failed to trust the Lord with all our heart. Also, "Lean not on your own understanding," can mean by way of application to refuse to follow your own timing. If we follow our own understanding as far as the timing of important decisions, we have short-circuited the wisdom of God's Word. "In all thy ways acknowledge Him," can mean by way of application to acknowledge and obey God's timing in the decisions of life. If we do not follow God's timing, then we are not acknowledging Him in all our ways. In order to find and follow God's will, we must follow His perfect timing and trust His heart. Trust God as you apply the "wisdom principles" from His Word.

God's "Timing Love"

My heart was greatly impacted when reading about God's "timing love" for His covenant people in Exodus 23. When He was speaking to Moses about leading them into the "promised land" and overcoming all their enemies He said, "I will cause the people ahead of you to feel terror and throw into confusion all the nations you come to. I will make all your enemies turn their backs to you in retreat. I will send the hornet in front of you, and it will drive the Hivites, Canaanites, and Hittites away from you. *I will not drive them out ahead of you in a single year; otherwise, the land would become desolate, and wild animals would multiply against you. I will drive them out little by little ahead of you until you have become numerous and take possession of the land*" (Exodus 23:27–30, HCSB, author's italics).

Isn't that wonderfully loving and encouraging! What a beautiful picture of the Lord's sensitive love. His timing is His loving! He would drive them out, "little by little" until they were fully able to take possession of the full victory He had already promised them.

What a loving Father to move them forward only as it was most beneficial to them. Could that be what our loving Father is doing in our lives? Could it be that He is moving us forward "little by little" until we are fully able to take possession of the full victory He has promised to us?

First Peter 5:6 exhorts us to "humble yourselves under the mighty hand of God, that He may exalt you in due time." Again we see God's timing in our lives lovingly demonstrated. We must humble ourselves under God's hand while trusting His "timing love." When we sincerely do this, He will place us in the exalted position at the appropriate time that He knows is best for us. It is easy to write and speak these words. It is much harder to obey them, but this is the key. Only when God sees that we *will* humbly trust Him, and His love, will He prepare us and then exalt us. Dr. Adrian Rogers shares an encouraging word of testimony about our trust in God's timing:

> "If you love Christ, if you long to please Him, remember this: God's delays are not God's denials. Many a Christian feels he is out in the wilderness; all he is doing is being led 'about,' in circles. I can remember years ago when I wanted instant progress. I desired it at an early age, but God has His own timetable.
>
> When I was nineteen years old and in college, one of my friends reported that he was going to see Dr. Robert G. Lee, for years the pastor of Bellevue Baptist Church. Every Baptist preacher boy virtually agreed that Dr. Lee was the greatest preacher since New Testament days. He was synonymous with powerful preaching that wafted you to heaven.
>
> I could not believe my ears when this friend came back and announced, 'I had a visit with Dr. R. G. Lee.' I asked him how he managed that (I have to admit I was a mite envious), and he said, 'I went to his secretary and asked if I could see

him.' Good grief, I could not imagine a pastor having a secretary—maybe the church having one but not the pastor. He went on, 'The secretary ushered me in.'

'What did you do?' I inquired. 'Oh, we talked a while. He asked about me, and then he had prayer for me.' I was amazed.

I was on the backside of the desert, going in circles out in the wilderness. I was bashful and timid. I didn't have the brass to walk in and visit with Dr. Lee. Years later Bellevue Baptist Church called me as their pastor. I became pastor of that same church!

Shortly after I had settled in as pastor, my secretary informed me, 'Dr. Lee is out here, and he'd like to see you.'

Maybe God is grooming you. He is not ready to thrust you into heavy responsibilities as yet. He has you in a holding pattern. Those circles are for a specific purpose" (3).

What a thought! What a gifted preacher and communicator. Our "circles" are for a specific purpose. Maybe like me you have rebelled at a few of those circles. If our loving Father has us traveling in some circles, we need to learn from the circles to move beyond the circles. That is really the bottom line in this issue of timing. It is simply a matter of trusting God with our timing and obeying His loving direction.

Final Question to Ponder:
Am I waiting on the Lord's timing out of trusting
love or pushing my own timeframe?

II

Provisions For Knowing God's Will

1. Opened and Closed Doors
2. Peace or Unrest in Your Heart
3. The Confirmation of God's Word
4. Putting the Three Keys Together

The Next Step

The first part of this book dealt with the preparations for knowing God's will. That is, the necessary preparations taken ahead of time, in order to be ready for the actual revealing of God's will. Our attention will now be turned to the actual elements of knowing God's will, i.e., those particular keys we watch and interact with to discern God's will. These keys are like the ingredients of the recipe which show us God's will; the pieces of the pie that when combined reveal God's will; the nuts and bolts of the machine that present God's will; the numbers that make the equation add up to the answer of God's will.

In viewing these pieces of the pie, it is vitally important to understand the inter-related nature of the pieces. To have the whole picture, you must have the whole pie. One piece will not do. Two will not do. It takes all three pieces to view the whole pie.

God has been patient with me over the years. He has shown me through some difficult experiences that there are some keys He wants me to look for as I seek to find and follow His will. At times I have learned my lessons the hard way (being stubborn) as I have stepped out of His will by not following these simple keys. Each time I walked those lonely roads, I have learned how important it is to stay closely attached to these keys. I have tried to make a point of learning where I went off-track and how to avoid the same mistake next time. I have tried to help my Christian family along the way to look for and follow these keys. That is my heart for you also. I believe it is for the purpose of helping my family and friends that God has allowed me the journey I have experienced: joy and heartbreak. This is the reason I wrote this book. I wanted to reach out to you with a helping hand of encouragement, that you might find and follow God's will and experience the wonderful joy and purpose it holds.

Again, let me stress the importance of these three elements being used in concert. It is a danger that I and many others have fallen into, to take one of these elements and manipulate it to make myself think I have found God's will. The flesh tends to manipulate circumstances and that is the danger when not combining all three (3) elements. In the same way Scripture can be taken out of context and manipulated to say something it actually does not say, so also, one of these three can be taken by itself to form a conclusion that can be totally faulty and not God's will at all. Again, trusting patience is involved as we are forced to wait on God's timing when all three elements come together and show us God's beautiful plan. I am certainly not claiming these are the only three (3) elements the Lord uses in our lives, but that they are the ones He has repeatedly used in my life to help me find and follow His will.

As you begin to study these keys or provisions for finding and following God's will, there is one more item of critical importance to enable you to have clear discernment. It is a matter of the heart. Blackaby, Blackaby, and King share this great truth from the life of George Mueller, a pastor in England that astounded his generation by his walk of faith and following God's will. His ministry of building orphanages in the nineteenth century which cared for and fed thousands of children, literally through his prayers of faith is inspiring. He literally "prayed in" millions of dollars. His faith is an enduring testimony to this day. Let's learn from this champion of faith. As Mueller explained how he prepared his heart to find God's will, it is very instructive for us. Mueller wrote,

> "I seek at the beginning to get my heart into such a state that it has no will of its own in regard to a given matter. Nine-tenths of the trouble with people generally is just here. Nine-tenths of the difficulties are overcome when our hearts are ready to do the knowledge of what His will is" (1).

That is truly a surrendered heart to the will of God. I love this simple yet profound truth from a heart of faith. Lord, my heart is yours and wants what You want. This simple truth from the life of this great man of faith impacted me so deeply that it is one of the first things that comes into my heart now as I begin to contemplate the Lord's direction. As you seek to find and follow God's will, let this be your heart of loving faith toward Him.

Chapter 5

Opened And Closed Doors

Dealing with Doors

*T*his is the most obvious key to knowing God's perfect will. Many times this will be the first key we recognize. When I speak of opened and closed doors in our lives, I am referring to things such as potential opportunities or directions that may open up or remain closed as we prayerfully seek the Lord's guidance and will. I have shared a personal illustration from my own life in chapter 8 to give you a clear picture of opened and closed doors at work in my life. Sometimes we will see a door we believe is opening and possibly at the same time one that is closing. This is part of what God uses to lead us in His direction. However, the danger is that our flesh desires to mold situations and manipulate possibilities into the open or closed doors of our own desires. At times, we do not walk through God's doors of direction. We kick down the closed doors and nail shut the open ones according to our preferred choices. We spend a lifetime earning our MM degree. We become masters of manipulation. Let me try to share some perspectives that may help avoid such dangerous manipulation which leads to failure.

Man-Made Doors

The first and most important lesson to learn with the doors of our lives is that we are incapable of opening and closing the right doors when we simply use our own understanding: "Trust in the LORD with all your heart, *and lean not on your own understanding*; In all your ways acknowledge Him, and He shall direct your paths" (Prov. 3:5–6, author's italics). The "protection truth" that is critical for us to understand from this verse is, if we are leaning on our own understanding instead of trusting His divine direction, we are directing our own paths and controlling the doors.

> "*The* only way we could be capable of opening and closing all the right doors would be if we had all knowledge and knew the future. We simply do not. He does!"

The historical record reveals that man has shown his fleshly inclination and incapacity to make all the right decisions since the Garden of Eden. Man has revealed his inability to do those things that please God when relying on his own strength and wisdom. Where do we find mankind today? Man has been slipping down the sliding board of spiritual decline and is on the verge of spiritual destruction because of the lack of proper direction and wisdom based on true truth from God's Word. Since the beginning of wrong decisions in the Garden of Eden, man has been in one sense constantly devolving. Some would strain to understand the picture of man devolving. Many would claim man has evolved and life has progressed to higher and higher forms. They would point to the amazing achievements of technology and science as proof. Although it is very true, man has achieved amazing breakthroughs in technology, science, and many other fields, and the new graduate students are furthering the work in these fields, is it also true that we have spiritually evolved and had amazing breakthroughs in the practice of the Lordship of Jesus Christ? The truth is while we see amazing advances in technology and science and other fields that are astounding, we also see a world that is growing much darker spiritually with a desire to walk away from God and follow our own fleshly will. That is the case in our country and even some in the church.

It is ironic that a country that inscribes "In God We Trust" on its money has had the highest court in the land rule against prayer to that very God of the Bible we claim to trust. It is further ironic and tragic that the same court would not protect the right to life for unborn babies that our God has created with their own specific purpose and design. Now the high court has taken a further step in the direction of following man's self will by redefining marriage. America in the twenty-first century is a country making its own decisions that are not only differing from God's will, but diametrically opposed to God's will. These self-made decisions are pulling us closer and closer toward a catastrophic judgment. We as the body of Christ need to take notice and avoid this destructive path, while also loving those and praying for those who are on it.

These humanistic decisions continue the decline spiritually which pushes us even further away from God's will revealed in God's Word. Some have decided that God did not create anything and that He doesn't control anything. Many have decided along with some of the most revered academics of our day that our ancestors were apes in a previous age. This line of secular reasoning permeates almost every TV show dealing with scientific discovery and is now presented as undisputed fact instead of as theory or supposition. Some of those academics have actually decided that God does not even exist and that the universe came into existence by one colossal explosion or other means that deny any God connection. These decisions and many others like them have shown that mankind has a startling inability to make correct decisions apart from the wisdom of God.

"In fact, once these decisions have been made by the academic elite, written in the textbooks of the day and taught to generations of students they are accepted as fact which deepens the spiritual darkness."

Looking for God's Doors

Realizing the terrible track record of man's self-made decisions, we would be wise to look to God for the doors of decision and direction. When sincerely looking for the doors God would lead us through, we can be confident of a couple things. First, God would never lead us in a direction that would contradict what He has clearly spoken in His Word. Second, God will lead us in a direction that will honor Him and bring glory to His name. With those principles in mind let's make some application as we seek to find God's will for our lives through doors.

Doors That Contradict God's Word

Contrary to some current lines of reasoning, God will absolutely not lead us in a direction that is contradictory to His Word. As you are watching for the Lord's direction through certain opening doors of opportunity or doors that are closed or closing, this is a vital truth to remember. Our contemporary culture has largely rejected scripture or are trying to redefine it for their own purposes. My heart has been saddened to watch various talk shows and news shows and to hear the claims some are making about following Christ that not only have no support in Scripture, but are clearly opposed by the truths and principles of Scripture.

I watched a talk show in amazement as a nude dancer insisted that she was simply a stripper for Jesus. My heart wants her to see the truth that will result in real love and purpose in her life instead of what is destructive. We have seen churches whose leadership and membership are made up of practicing homosexuals who claim that they love Jesus and that they are just as saved as any heterosexual Christian and even further that the Bible does not say anything in opposition to homosexuality. My heart wants them to thrive according to God's loving design and purpose for their lives. I have heard (professed) Christian married people spend an hour trying to explain how an extramarital sexual affair had saved their marriage and made it exciting and sizzling again. I have listened to Christian parents as they have claimed the leading of the Lord in allowing their kids to go to dangerous, ungodly functions and be active participants in committing illegal acts that sometimes end in tragedy. I sat in stunned silence as some have insisted God has led them into a job that requires them to do things that are completely immoral and against the principles of God's Word. These along with many others are man's decisions divorced from God's wisdom.

"*You* can ignore or reject the truths of God's Word, but what you can never do is change or escape them."

The tragic fact is that in our contemporary culture we have moved so far away from the truths of God's Word for so long that these crazy claims now seem pretty mainstream and acceptable to the secular worldview. Contemporary thinking has become so warped spiritually that this acceptability is now perceived as the noble position.

"*The* diabolical desensitization over a period of time has resulted in moving the immoral and bizarre into the accepted mainstream."

The list of these kinds of claims in the name of Christ and religious devotion could go on and on and I say with all sincerity that I want all of them to find real peace and purpose and find the truth, though they would likely insist they already have. It is of course their choice to live however they want to live, but it is not their choice to redefine God's Word, nor does that choice belong to any of us. I have dear friends, beloved family, and a host of others including many of my beloved people in the Philippines that continue to struggle with some of these issues and I love them all. Here is the critical truth that has become harder and harder to distinguish in our cultural fog as man pursues his own redefinitions.

We Cannot Redefine God's Word

"We cannot redefine the truths of God's Word in order to make them compatible with our desires or the desires of the culture. The redefinition does not change the true definition, it only masks it."

The redefinition mask is dangerous and even deadly. This mask is very skillfully made and engineered by the best mask maker in the world with thousands of years of experience. It is crafted to be beautiful and is adorned with many gems that are incredibly appealing to the eyes. It appears to have the same contours of the face except they have been improved upon and perfected to the secular eye. The mask adds an air of mystery, escape from the old and clandestine excitement. When a large group of people are titillated by the provocative mask and have begun to use it themselves, there is a great camaraderie that develops. They now share a common bond because of the appeal of the mask, and so they invite others to give it a try. Hence we see a brotherhood of the mask. When they look at the mask long enough, it becomes their reality. When new generations of the mask brotherhood see only the mask as they grow up, it is the only reality they know and anyone who doesn't believe in the mask or attempts to tell them it is just a mask is labeled as a bigot who is out of touch with reality and culture. The insidious cycle continues to grow as does the intensity of the response toward those who are not part of the mask brotherhood.

The insidious problem of the mask is that it covers up what is real. As it relates to the truths of God's Word, it disguises what is genuine. It hides the truth. It cunningly leads people away from what is real and keeps them enamored with what is counterfeit. It conceals what is truly life-giving and what will set the captives free. It is an external façade only. Its appearance may seem to be good, religious, and even angelic at times. This deception is clearly exposed in Scripture which states, "And no wonder! For Satan himself transforms himself into an angel of light" (2 Cor. 11:14). Appearances/masks can obviously be incredibly deceiving. As you seek to find God's will through opened and closed doors, be spiritually alert to believe and cling to His truth and not the mask.

I know there is a tendency to try and accommodate those we love who are caught up in the spiritually destructive counterfeits of the day because we love them. However, I would submit that if we try to redefine the truths of our sovereign God and His Word to appease them and the culture, we are not really loving them with a true love for their spiritual well-being as it is only the truth of God's Word and the indwelling power of Jesus Christ that will set them free.

As David Platt speaks about Christ calling us to a radical commitment and our tendency to try to creatively "spin" scripture to accommodate our own definition rather than face the actual reality of God's truth he explains,

> "And this is where we need to pause. Because we are starting to redefine Christianity. We are giving in to the dangerous temptation to take the Jesus of the Bible and twist Him into a version of Jesus we are more comfortable with" (1).

More pervasive now than when written a few years ago, it might be added that while we are quick to showcase examples in the world that are contradictory to God's Word, to be honest, those of us in the church who claim to be Christians have problems with contradictions to God's Word including the "elder brother spirit" that Keller unpacks in *The Prodigal God*.

"*G*od's Word is the immovable, spiritual bedrock of truth to build my life upon, not a small religious stone I can pick up and use for decoration or whatever sanctified sounding redefinition I desire. It is bedrock truth that is settled, 'Forever, O LORD, Your word is settled in heaven'" (Psalm 119:89).

Searching for doors God would open instead of those of our own making, we must be sure to understand that God would not lead us in a direction contrary to His revealed will for us. God is never the author of confusion. God will only lead in a direction that is in harmony with His Word. God's Word reveals His authority: "All Scripture is given by inspiration [God breathed] of God, and is profitable for doctrine, for reproof, for correction, for instruction in righteousness, that the man of God may be complete, thoroughly equipped for every good work" (2 Tim. 3:16–17).

"*F*or God to lead us in a direction that is against His Word would be the equivalent of a parent telling their child never to play in the street and then setting up the child's swing set in the middle of it."

It is ludicrous, it goes against the nature of true love, and it absolutely is not part of God's leading or direction for us.

Doors That Bring Honor to God

God is the only one who deserves glory and honor in and through our lives. He will lead us in directions that produce that deserved honor, and not in those that disgrace it. We can save ourselves much heartache and sometimes delay, by asking if the direction we are moving will bring honor to Christ. If we say we believe the Bible, this is the clear call of scripture that we cannot deny as Paul states, "Glorify God in your body and in your spirit, which are God's" (1 Cor. 6:20). Though some balk at the idea of employing this as criteria for decisions, it is a principle of Scripture for the redeemed that we ignore at our own peril and pain. Let's look at this scripture a little more as we seek to truly find and follow God's doors.

First Corinthians 6:19–20 clearly states, "Or do you not know that your body is the temple of the Holy Spirit who is in you, whom you have from God, and you are not your own? For you were bought at a price; therefore glorify God in your body and in your spirit, which are God's." One problem of twenty-first-century Christianity may be that many no longer seem to be aware of what the apostle Paul is asking. Perhaps the same "do you not know" question could be asked to many in the church today. Perhaps some of it is due to a lack of time in God's Word and internalizing His truths. We seem to have conveniently forgotten the fact that our body as a Christian is the temple of the Holy Spirit. Many seem to be unaware of the realization that the precious Holy Spirit actually resides within our bodies at the moment of and after salvation. It is apparent by contemporary culture and practice that we have discontinued any notion that we are not our own. With the encroachment of the culture into the church we flounder in the vast sea of forgetfulness when it comes to remembering the painful price paid for our redemption. Peter speaks about that price paid for our freedom when he says, "Knowing that you were not redeemed with corruptible things, like silver or gold, from your aimless conduct received by tradition from your fathers, *but with the precious blood of Christ*, as of a lamb without blemish and without spot" (1 Peter 1:18–19, author's italics). Many seem to have been subtly pulled into the humanism of the day which bristles at the fact that we belong to God. That scriptural concept is too often lost in the prevailing acceptance of a "live for yourself" lifestyle.

> "The self-centered and self-absorbed existence of many loses sight of the price of love's redemption at the cross and therefore of God's ownership."

The doors God would lead us through will be in perfect harmony with His Word and will bring honor and glory to Him. First Corinthians 10:31 states, "Therefore, whether you eat or drink, or whatever you do, do all to the glory of God." Again, God would not lead us in a direction that would contradict His Word. He would not lead us to do exactly what He has told us not to do. He leads us and expects us to do whatever we do to the glory of God through the power of the Holy Spirit in us. These verses, along with many others, show us that whatever doors God opens for us will be doors that will bring honor to Him. That is His Word and that is His plan.

Understanding these two principles, it would be wise to ask ourselves a couple of questions when looking at doors and directions. First, does this door of opportunity contradict the teaching of God's Word in any way? Second, can this door of opportunity bring honor and glory to God? If it goes against the principles of God's Word then it simply is not the direction God would lead us. If it will cause me to dishonor God and what He has communicated in His Word as His will for me, then it is not the direction in which God would lead me. We need to be clear on this issue as the aforementioned examples make shockingly evident. Please let these truths from God's Word be written with an indelible marker on your heart. This is not a question of whether your opinion/spin is that a certain direction would go against God's Word or wouldn't. Remember we are skillful at rationalization and the tendency of our flesh is to go with the flow. It is whether an honest exposition of God's Word in its divine context honestly reveals that it is or isn't. This is not a question of whether your opinion/spin is that a certain direction would bring dishonor to God or not, but it is whether an honest exposition of God's Word in its divine context reveals that it would or wouldn't. We are being dishonest with ourselves if we start with a fleshly desire and then attempt to find a proof text to support it.

Of course, this requires that we faithfully study God's Word to learn what it is teaching within the divine context and not what we are spinning from a presumed assumption. Paul wrote, "Be diligent to present yourself approved to God, a worker who does not need to be ashamed, *rightly dividing the word of truth*" (2 Tim. 2:15, author's italics). In the book of second Timothy the apostle Paul is writing his final, emotional letter to his son in ministry. In this verse you can feel the urgency and passion of the old warrior's words. He exhorts Timothy to be diligent or zealous as he presents himself as one who has been tested and approved to God, a diligent worker in his field who has no need to be ashamed because he has rightly divided or cut straight the word of truth. In trying to convey the concept of rightly dividing or cutting straight (perhaps a reference to cutting the material straight and true as Paul was a tent maker) the Word of God it may be helpful to share a couple of words used in reference to Biblical interpretation. They are unknown words to most, but they have obvious meanings that apply to our discussion. One is "exegesis" which Webster's defines as,

> "An explanation or critical interpretation of
> a text" (2).

The other is "eisegesis" which Webster's defines as,

> "The interpretation of a text (as of the Bible)
> by reading into it one's own ideas" (3).

We have too little of the first and way too much of the second!

We must hold to God's Word as the immutable standard of truth.

To do anything less would not only dishonor God, but would show that our love is not spiritually genuine for those we know and love who are headed to destruction without the truth of God's Word. Our own opinions and beliefs can be extremely unstable. Using our opinions and beliefs as the foundation for truth, leaves us vulnerable to the dangerous practice of rationalization and opens the door wide for infiltration by the enemy. We are capable of accommodating just about anything if our flesh is drawn to it. This danger is addressed by Dr. Francis Schaeffer when he wrote,

> "Here is the great Evangelical disaster—the failure of the evangelical world to stand for truth as truth. There is only one word for this—namely accommodation: the evangelical church has accommodated to the world spirit of the age. First, there has been accommodation on Scripture, so that many who call themselves evangelicals hold a weakened view of the Bible and no longer affirm the truth of all the Bible teaches—truth not only in religious matters but in the areas of science and history and morality" (4).

When it comes to something we really wish to do or approve, our self-serving powers of rationalization can almost always make us feel more comfortable with something that is contradictory to God's Word whether subtly or overtly. Please be aware that we can all be vulnerable to this misdirection. This should cause our devotion to the truths of God's Word, whether comforting or convicting, to be held even more tightly. Protect yourself by being careful not to inadvertently join the growing chorus of culture singing the praises of secular intellectual thought that undermines divine truth. To truly find God's truth concerning opened and closed doors is critical. Let's contemplate some of the dangers of rationalization and how to avoid them.

Doors of Rationalization

What is rationalization? My simple description for this discussion would be when we take something we know is questionable or wrong, and we use our own reasoning skills to talk ourselves or others into thinking it is acceptable or right. We use various methods to accomplish this, but the end result is we end up feeling better about something that is wrong or about something for which we at least had a spiritual red flag. We once again use our Master's Degree of Manipulation and convince ourselves with the greatest of skill. This is self-deception, and it will lead you away from God's will. Let's look at a few interesting examples that "could" have involved rationalization.

Adam's Apple

God had created a magnificent and beautiful place called, "the Garden of Eden." He had created a perfect environment which contained everything desired to meet every need. He lovingly fashioned Adam and Eve to enjoy this wonderful place. The luscious fruits, the sparkling water, the amazing colors, and the perfect climate made it a place of unspeakable joy and pleasure not to mention personal fellowship with their Creator. This was truly the most wonderful place that could be imagined.

God had provided many trees for fruit. A vast buffet of fruit was readily available on multitudes of trees hanging in easy reach. Just the array of colors and smells must have been incredible. God had given them free use of all the trees except for one. God had specifically commanded that they were not to eat of the fruit of one tree out of the vast array of luscious and tantalizing fruit. Tragically, Eve responded to the temptation of the serpent and ate the forbidden fruit.

Normally, most people (especially in this perfect environment) would not maliciously and violently rebel against God who had given them an abundance of everything. They would not point their fist up at the sky and tell God they were going to disobey whether He liked it or not. No, most people will maneuver through a process of intellectual rationalization. They will begin to question and probe and exaggerate as they try to make themselves feel better about something they know is wrong. Finally, with great reasoning skills, they talk themselves into doing it, even though a convicting little voice continues to say, "This is wrong, this is wrong!" (Sound familiar?)

As Eve ate this forbidden fruit, she was not maliciously and violently rebelling against what she knew was God's will. Though it definitely was rebellion, I believe it is likely she was internally listening to crafty words and rationalization. She was trying to make herself feel better about an action she knew was wrong, but trying to talk herself into believing it was somehow not wrong. She was struggling to talk herself into believing that somehow it was all right after a crafty enemy had introduced a cunning question about God's Word: "Has God indeed said, 'You shall not eat of every tree of the garden'" (Gen. 3:1)? Planting a subtle seed of doubt about God's Word is the fingerprint of the enemy. It still is! If you ever find you are struggling to talk yourself into doing something you have a spiritual red flag about, realize that the red flag is from the Holy Spirit giving you direction away from disobedience and a painful consequence. It is "conviction grace."

Then she offered the forbidden fruit to Adam. He also knew the truth and God's specific command, but he ate anyway. What happened? Again, he did not eat with fist raised to the sky in malicious rebellion. I believe it is likely he ate with a heart of rationalization.

> "*H*e did not allow God's Word to be his guide. He allowed the emotions and desires of the moment to guide him. Therein lies the deadly danger!"

When you allow the emotions and desires of the moment to be the priority guide of your decision you are on dangerous ground and falling into a trap that you will indeed regret. Let's apply our two-fold test principle to Adam and Eve's situation. First, let's ask the question "Is this action going to contradict God's Word; will this door of opportunity cause me to go against God's Word?" The answer of course is a resounding yes! God had clearly said, "But of the tree of the knowledge of good and evil you shall not eat, for in the day that you eat of it you shall surely die" (Gen. 2:17). The serpent had clearly fueled the rationalization process by telling Eve, "you will not surely die" (Gen. 3:4). Second, let's ask the question: "Will this action bring glory and honor to God; will I be able to serve and uplift the name of God through this door of opportunity?" The answer is a resounding, "No!" Anytime we rebel and go against God's Word, our actions are a testimony of dishonor. Any time we begin to question, or listen to questions that subtly deny or cast doubt on the Word of God, we are in danger of eating our own deadly fruit. Be assured the pain of the consequences will far outlast the pleasure of the taste.

Jonah's Journey

God had prepared a specific man for a specific mission. He had chosen Jonah to go to the wicked city of Nineveh and preach repentance. He had communicated clearly to Jonah about the call He had placed on his life. God said, "Arise, go to Nineveh, that great city, and cry out against it; for their wickedness has come up before Me" (Jonah 1:2). Although Jonah's response of disobedience after receiving this call seems to be one of overt rebellion, it is possible that rationalization was part of the mental process which led to it. Knowing the tendency of human nature when we do not want to do something, think through this possibility with me.

Jonah could well have made some great sounding arguments in his mind against such a door of opportunity. He could have reasoned that the people would never listen to him. He might have also reasoned there was no way for one person to reach such a vast city. He might have also tried to convince himself that the Assyrian's brutal reputation for slaughtering and raping other peoples did not deserve anything but judgment (as seems plausible later when he was very angry that they repented and God spared them from immediate judgment). As he began to run down to the ship and was still desperately trying to convince himself of some logical reason not to go, he could have conceived of it as an open door that he was able to secure passage and get a ticket on the vessel.

Most of the time when a person is running from God, they are struggling to convince themselves they have good reasons for doing so. They are doing mental gymnastics to convince themselves that what they are doing is all right, that they didn't hear God clearly or perhaps even that God had changed His mind. They are trying to feel better about what they know deep down is wrong and is against God's direction. This is classic rationalization.

Let's look for a moment at what could have been considered an open door by Jonah, and apply the twofold test principle. After all, Jonah was able to get a ticket on the ship. Rationalization would attempt to justify by saying, "If God had not wanted me to go on this journey, He would not have allowed me to get a ticket. He would have made it impossible to get on the ship because He is all-powerful and could have stopped me in numerous ways. Perhaps God sees I really don't want to do this and is changing my direction." Only God truly knew his heart and what he was thinking.

What we must be very careful about is creating our own open doors. The problem for most of us is we can rationalize and make an open door out of anything. We can fool even ourselves into believing that something is an open door when we are traveling in the opposite direction from which God has instructed. At times, we desire to do something so badly that we discover a way to accomplish it. At other times, we desire not to do something to the extent that we will find a way out of it. We sometimes do this even if it means manufacturing some doors along the way. Please remember this doesn't end well for us.

Again, let's ask ourselves the two spiritual safety questions as we place ourselves in Jonah's situation: "Will this action cause me to contradict or go against God's Word, and will this action allow me to bring honor and glory to God as I lovingly serve Him?" The answers are painfully obvious. God had said to go and Jonah was rebelling against God's call. Jonah's disobedient action was moving in a direction that would dishonor God. Please remember these two questions as they may save you from being in a very dark place. It may not be in the belly of a large fish, but our dark places can be just as lonely and difficult in other ways. For your safety, ask these two questions and then answer them honestly.

> "*R*emember, if I run away from truth now, I will certainly collide with it later."

Aaron's Amazement

Moses had ascended Mount Sinai to spend a prolonged time with God after the Israelites had been miraculously delivered out of bondage in Egypt. Israel was now encamped at the base of Mount Sinai. While on the mountain, Moses received many instructions from the Lord and even the two tablets of stone on which God Himself had written the Ten Commandments.

While Moses was on the mountain, the people became restless. After he had been gone for some weeks, they began to doubt whether he was even coming back. They gathered around Aaron their spiritual leader and said, "Come, make us a god who will go before us because this Moses, the man who brought us up from the land of Egypt—we don't know what has happened to him" (Exodus 32:1 HCSB)! There was no rebuke from the high priest. We have no evidence that he even confronted them about their blasphemous request and then refuse to be a part of it. Amazingly, Aaron's response was for them to all remove their golden earrings and bring them to him. In a stunning display of spiritual rebellion and capitulation to paganism, Aaron took all the gold, melted it in the fire and fashioned it with an engraving tool into a golden calf.

Moses was with God on the mountain while this rebellion was fomenting. God told Moses to immediately get down to "his people" because they had made an idol and were reveling in great sin. On his way down the mountain, when Moses got close to the camp and saw the blasphemous golden calf and the way the people were behaving with their rebellious party and dancing, he was enraged. He threw the stone tablets down, smashing them on the rocks. In righteous anger he destroyed the calf, chastised the people, and then turned to confront Aaron and demanded, "What did this people do to you that you have led them into [such] a grave sin" (Exodus 32:21 HCSB)? Aaron then begins his explanation, blaming the evil intent and demands of the people.

As he finishes his explanation to Moses who is livid at him he is still stumbling and stammering to explain how this rebellion and debauchery happened. His final statement is one of the most ludicrous rationalizations in Scripture. He explained his response to the request of the people for a god. "So I said to them, 'Whoever has gold, take it off,' and they gave [it] to me. When I threw it into the fire, out came this calf" (Exodus 32:24 HCSB)!

If I was in trouble and trying to rationalize my way out of this situation with a very angry Moses, I might say something like the following: "Moses, please calm down. You know how rebellious and stubborn these people are and how they are always wanting to do evil things that dishonor God. I get so tired of trying to keep them in line and out of trouble. After they saw that you had not come back down from the mountain in weeks, they came and ganged up on me and started demanding that I make them a god to go before them. They insisted they needed this god because Moses is gone and we have no idea what has happened to him. They pressured me to the point that I told them to take off their golden earrings and bring them to me. Though I didn't want to do any of this, I simply took the gold the people threw at my feet, tossed it into the fire and to my great amazement out came this calf. Bam! There it was! A golden calf idol!"

Though it may look ridiculous as we look back at it now, our creativity in attempting to slant something in a specific direction is remarkable. If we are being honest, we have probably rationalized and made some claims that rival those of our ancestors.

"*We* seem to have a built-in ability to rationalize things in the direction of our desires whether it is toying with the truth in our minds as with Adam and Eve, reading circumstances in our own preferred way, as may have happened with Jonah, or even making defensive claims that leave out part (a large part) of the truth, as with Aaron."

It is an ability that can cloud our minds, our directions, and our perspectives. With this in mind, it is very important to have a daily intimate walk with Christ, and to remain dependent on discernment from the Holy Spirit within us.

Conclusion

If the doors of decision we are contemplating are in line with God's Word, and will allow us the opportunity to bring glory to Him, then we can move ahead in the process.

We can then attempt to tie the remaining elements of knowing God's will together with the open and closed doors, all in an attitude of prayerful dependence. Again, we need to be careful not to view opened and closed doors as the only answer or as the last word. This is an important piece, but, only one piece of the pie as we seek to accurately discern God's will.

Final Question to Ponder:
Am I evaluating opened and closed doors for God's confirmation or am I manipulating them myself?

Chapter 6

Peace Or Unrest In Your Heart

Hearing Him

*T*here is another very important element in finding and following God's will. It is what I refer to as the inner communication of the Holy Spirit within us. Sometimes it is referred to as the still small voice of God in our lives, or the non-verbal leading of God in our spirits. It is the wonderful, contenting peace of God in our hearts and the uneasiness of God's warning in our minds—the spiritual voice of God speaking to our spirit in unmistakable terms. I believe it was the beloved pastor Dr. Adrian Rogers that used to say with that deep, booming voice when sharing about hearing the Lord speak to him, "I didn't hear an audible voice; it was much louder than that!" I concur that it is clear and powerful.

One of the special blessings for me as a young preacher at the Criswell College in Dallas in the early nineties was the opportunity to hear Dr. Criswell preach. One Sunday night as he was seated on the front pew before the evening service, I decided to walk up to him and ask him to sign my Criswell Study Bible. I said, "Hi Dr. C, how are you doing tonight?" He lovingly responded, "Well not as good as you are!" with a warm smile and an encouraging tone. After he signed my Bible he reached his hand up to the side of my face and lovingly said, "God bless you son!" That little gesture was a big blessing for a young minister and an encouragement of love from an older warrior of the faith. Later, as I was reading the delightful autobiography of Dr. Criswell, *Standing on the Promises*, I was gripped by a vivid illustration of the inner communication of the Holy Spirit. As Dr. Criswell was attempting to follow God's will for his life about where to attend college as a young man, he explains his predicament. He writes,

> "What a temptation it was that summer to pack my bags and head north to New England! I longed for the exhaustive libraries and demanding classes of those historic eastern universities, and on the surface it looked as though God had cleared the way. I was accepted at Brown and Yale. It was an easy drive to that little Quaker church from Providence or New Haven. Once again, I could pay my bills and pastor at the same time. Everything seemed perfect, but I couldn't shake my uneasy feelings about the decision. Now, looking back, I know for certain that my "uneasy feelings" were in fact the voice of God deep in my heart crying out a warning" (1).

What a wonderful illustration of the inner communication of the Holy Spirit of God in our lives. Everything seemed perfect. His doors of direction would obviously stand up to our twofold principle: "Will I be doing anything that would go against God's Word and can this direction give me the opportunity to bring honor and glory to God?" But there was still something missing. There was still something that was out of place. There was still a piece of the pie that was absent. Something did not feel quite right in his spirit. It was the voice of God's warning in his life. God was speaking to his spirit with a loving red flag in order to lead him in another direction. God was intentionally making him uneasy about those attractive doors. God was showing him His direction, through the precious, loving, inner communication of His Spirit.

Listening to the Heart

Listen to your heart. Follow your heart. Those are statements we have all heard. In the context of this book, we are talking about listening to the voice of God in the heart. One of our problems seems to be the inability to do just that. Whether that inability is derived from too much ambient noise in our lives, no time spent listening, diminished intimacy and fellowship, or other reasons you may think of in your own life, hearing His voice in your heart is a spiritual treasure that is critically important to finding and following God's will. Let's try to uncover a few reasons that may hinder us from hearing God's voice in our hearts.

A Crowded Heart

There are many times we seem too busy to listen to God's voice. We have crowded so many things into such a short period of time that we find ourselves without any time to be quiet and listen. An absence of listening to God in our lives will result in an absence of hearing His direction. Many of us find ourselves frantically running everywhere and going nowhere. It's easy to fall into that trap in our culture.

Running around Like a Chicken with Its Head Off

As a young boy growing up on a farm in Kansas, I have some very vivid memories. Some of those experiences can only be truly appreciated by those who have lived on a farm; but I believe they will relate the desired point to everyone. One of those memories had to do with chicken dinners. We really loved fried chicken like most farm folks. However, it wasn't the fried chicken that sticks in my mind, as good as it was; it was the live one that left an indelible memory.

As I grew up, my dad would tell me the stories of his work experience at the chicken processing plant in Kansas City. He had become so proficient at cleaning and drawing a chicken (that's getting the feathers off and the insides out for the uninitiated), that he could complete the whole process in about thirty or forty seconds. I remember challenging him and timing him once to see if he could still do it and he did. That was pretty amazing to me, but that is not really the image that comes to mind when I remember butchering chickens with my dad. There is another more grotesque and vivid memory that was forever captured in my young mind during those years.

When it came time to butcher some chickens, I immediately started to cringe inside, knowing what was about to happen. We would scramble around and catch the chickens and I would hand them to dad one by one. He would take each chicken and with a sharp knife quickly cut off the head. It was the next scene after this action that the video in my young mind remembers so well. Dad would simply toss the chicken's body to the side. To my amazement the chicken's body would flop wildly and in a few instances even get up on its feet and run around without its head for a short distance. This is not an exaggeration. I have seen a chicken actually running around the farm yard with no head. That picture will always remain in my mind.

There are two obvious, applicable principles that come to mind when I think about those chickens running around without their heads. First of all, they have absolutely no direction, and second, it isn't going to last very long. Without their heads the total direction system for their body was gone. They would run full speed into anything that might happen to be in the way. They of course had no way of seeing. Their body was involved in one, last, desperate run to destruction. Also, regardless of how fast and furious they were running at the moment, it was only a matter of short moments before the body would lie completely still. The body would lose its last reserve of blood and strength would be gone. The struggle would be over and the end of life complete.

Though this illustration from my childhood is admittedly uncouth, some of these principles come to mind when thinking about our cluttered hearts and lives. Many of us sometimes run around like a chicken with its head missing.

"We are so over-involved in good things that we have no energy to do the best things. We run around with no apparent direction because our close fellowship with the Father and hearing His voice have been pushed out by many other things."

There are always numerous things on our checklist that are important and we run at full speed trying to accomplish them all (though we never get them all done). Our spiritual direction system is not functioning properly. We cannot hear and discern God's will for our lives because we haven't even taken the time to listen to Him. We fail to give quality time to the most important One in our lives. The further tragedy is that we will not last long in this desperate flight. Our own strength will be drained until there is none left. We will find ourselves without strength, running in the wrong direction. We will be running through the motions of what we call life. We will have no quality compassion and emotion to direct to the Father who truly deserves the best from our hearts. We will find ourselves tired and empty with little or no energy to worship the One who loves us so much that He died to pay for our debt. Think about it for a moment. If we had an appointment with a world leader for which we had great respect that wanted to develop a personal relationship with us and provide for the biggest needs in our lives, would we miss the appointment?

There is good news if this is a picture of your life. All you need to do is repent of this lifestyle of sinful neglect and claim the forgiveness that God is waiting and desiring to give you. You can be forgiven and begin once again to give God your whole heart. You can keep those appointments and once again enjoy that intimate fellowship with Him each day. You can experience the inner communication of God in your heart and follow His perfect direction. You can prioritize your lifestyle in such a way that God can speak to your heart and you can hear Him clearly. If this is already your daily habit, then you are in a good place. However, most of us struggle with the crazy pace of contemporary life.

Ignoring the Heart

There are times we struggle with another problem of the heart. We ignore what we know is there. Perhaps it does not meet with our approval or maybe we are afraid to openly confront it. The inner communication of the Holy Spirit in our hearts is sometimes just ignored out of self-will or fear. I especially want to address the fear.

Tragic though it is, we sometimes have our own agendas set in concrete. This would be a great place to remember the practice of George Mueller (preparing his heart) that I mentioned at the beginning of Section II. We know where we desire to go and we fear that if we listen to what God seems to be speaking to our heart that everything is going to be turned upside down and move in a terrible direction. At least, that's the message of the malevolent voice of fear in our head. You've heard the scenario of the fear of every Christian young person who struggles with committing themselves completely to God's direction. They have the horrible fear that if they actually listen to their hearts and surrender to what God is saying, they will immediately be required to take a vow of celibacy, put on the robe of a monk, sell everything they have, carry nothing but a satchel, and travel to the deepest, darkest jungles of Africa in a dugout to work with the wild cannibals of an unknown tribe while eating rats and tree bark, painting their faces, piercing their ears and noses, and wearing their loincloths (or nothing) to assimilate while getting eaten alive by mosquitoes, wild animals, or their tribe members! Though the horrific details may differ for each of us, you get the picture. Though it is not intentional, this fear is an insult to a loving God. Isn't it interesting that we expect God to do the very worst things to us and make us absolutely miserable, when He loved us so much that He gave His only begotten Son so we could be set free?

> " *The* source of those fears is quite obvious as is its intention. It reeks of a slimy serpent in the Garden trying to keep you living in fear and away from your true purpose."

Though our loving Father may indeed call us to share His love with an unknown tribe somewhere, He will fill us with excitement and His power to go. Ask me or thousands of missionaries if they love what they are doing where God has sent them. I have been in a very remote village in the middle of nowhere in a third world jungle, and I can honestly tell you it was a thrill to be there and share the love of Christ as is every mission trip I take. The same can be echoed by many of my missionary brothers and sisters in Christ in difficult and dangerous places all over the world. It is the joy of our lives. My dad was a prime example of this joy. I never saw him more full of joy than when we were serving on the mission field. He began his mission work smuggling Bibles behind the Iron Curtain in the seventies and early eighties, and he wrote commentaries for the underground church there. In the mid-eighties, he pioneered the mission work in Southeast Asia that I continue to lead today. On one of our first mission trips together, I clearly recall being a little surprised to see him walking around and singing worship songs to himself constantly (not something that was a habit at home). He was absolutely full of the joy of the Lord and exactly where he was supposed to be. Do you realize that as you read this there are thousands of missionaries all over the planet in every environment you could imagine filled with joy and gratitude and the power of God for their call?

If there is one thing in this world we can bank on, it is the awesome love of God. He loves us more than anyone else ever could. He loves us so much that we can't even comprehend it. Our understanding of love is without the capacity to grasp what He feels toward us. Even though we don't understand the circumstances we find ourselves in at times, we can be absolutely assured that He loves us dearly.

> "*H*e, more than any earthly father, wants us to grow and become champions who live in His freedom rather than captives who live in bondage."

He goes to great lengths to lead us in a way that is best. "The steps of a good man are ordered by the LORD, and He delights in his way" (Psalm 37:23). When He grows us through the experience of flaming trials, He always has His hand on the thermostat. If we find ourselves in a place of service where we are called to give our lives for Christ's sake as countless missionaries have and still are doing as you read this, we can say with Paul, "For to me, to live is Christ, and to die is gain" (Phil. 1:21). At that moment we are immediately transported from this world to the indescribable home awaiting us and hear the Master say, "Well done thou good and faithful servant." He gives us the grace and strength we need for every situation exactly when we need it. He has proven His love like no other Father ever has. He has provided for us and protected us. He gave His own son to die a horrible sacrificial death for us. How can we look up into the lacerated face of love on the cross and doubt His love for us?

Here is the truth. The enemy is out to steal away your freedom, your joy, and your true purpose for which you were created. His tactics are many times lies and fear. If you ignore God's voice in your heart, you will live in bondage and fear and miss His joy and freedom. Step on through the fear by trusting faith into the joy and fulfillment of God's freedom and power.

God's Desire Planted in Our Hearts

There is another wonderful element of God's leadership and blessing in our lives which I just mentioned, which is His desire in our heart. When God does call us to a task, He places within us the deep desire to fulfill that task. Some might respond, "I sure don't have the desire to do the ministry I am involved in." I would lovingly

117

suggest that it would be wise for that person to take a serious look and honestly evaluate the supposed call to that ministry and/or the divine direction to remain.

In case you think I am sharing pie in the sky truths that are divorced from reality and that I don't experience some of the same kind of fears that you do, let me share an honest example from my life to correct that misperception. A few years ago the Lord called me to go into a disaster zone just days after super Typhoon Yolanda had devastated part of the Philippines. I want you to see my raw uncensored thoughts in a Facebook post just before I got on a plane to go. My post was called,

"When your faith is SLAPPED in the face.

It is one of the most devastated places on the planet right now. The typhoon in the Philippines was one of the most powerful ever recorded with tornado-force winds. There was a twenty to twenty-five-foot storm surge that covered virtually everything, leaving a path of destruction that looks otherworldly. Thousands are laying everywhere dead. Tens of thousands are starving and without water or any kind of medical help or shelter. There is looting, stealing, and desperation just to survive. To say that it is a terrible tragedy is a terrible understatement.

O. K. I feel terrible for those poor people, but that is halfway around the world. I will pray for them. Then the Lord gives me one of those, 'I am calling you to go' kind of moments. This is when faith is slapped in the face. To be honest, I just returned from two weeks in the Philippines and I am exhausted and my stomach is still messed up. I usually take a couple weeks just to get back to normal, but the day after I return the

Lord puts it in front of me to jump back on a plane quickly.

Not to return to my normal mission work there where I have a ministry family after thirteen years, but to something I have not known. This is when faith is slapped in the face. I am going to a place I have never been with people I have never known. This is a place that is devastated on such a scale that it dwarfs me. I don't know how we will get to the island. I don't know how we will be able to travel. I don't know if the pastors I will look for are dead or alive. I don't know where we will sleep. I don't know how we will get back out. I don't even know about food or water. This is when faith is slapped in the face (2).

After a long trip, I arrived at a neighboring island. I met one of my closest Filipino brothers at the airport after a disconcerting delay and we sat down in a coffee shop to discuss how to get to the devastated island. Rudy (my Filipino brother in Christ) began to tell me two things. First, he told me that all of my Filipino pastor brothers were telling me not to go into the disaster zone because of the dangers of being robbed by desperate people or worse. Second, he told me that when the jailers saw the storm surge flooding into the city that they opened all the prison doors so the prisoners didn't drown in their cells. So essentially, we were about to travel into a city that had been devastated beyond belief with large parts of it completely wiped away, dead people everywhere, thousands of desperate people with no food and water, and hundreds of criminals running loose.

I told you I would be honest about fears so here is my quote from that moment:

"As he began to speak, my heart sank and thoughts of fear began to circle around me like vultures" (3).

That is the honest truth as I genuinely wondered if we would make it back out. The sweat started to pour down my face. I find that it is easy for me to sit in a comfortable worship center in America and sing, "He makes me brave," but the full weight of trusting faith is felt when actually walking into a dangerous disaster zone. Here is the rest of the story.

Even in those heavy moments the call God planted in my heart was to go. As we both sat there with tears in our eyes, I looked at Rudy and said, "God sent us here, and I believe He will make a way." That step of faith through the fear brought about God's intervention minutes later. That is a vital truth I want you to store in your memory bank. Step through the fear, in an act of trusting faith. Amazingly, Rudy got a call from a pastor in the middle of the devastated city (we thought no one could even call out) and I saw a smile break out on his face. That sweet pastor told us to come on to the island and he would meet us and take us back to their concrete church structure for some shelter. After Rudy got off the phone, we both sat there and just laughed through the tears of joy. If I had ignored God's call in my heart because of the fear, I would never have experienced one of the most rewarding missions I have been on and the loving fellowship with Pastor Rayos and the New Life Baptist Church family and all the pastors and leaders and doctors in that area as we served together. The power of Christ in their lives was amazing, and they actually ministered to me in the midst of their tragedy.

"God planted that call and desire in my heart, and He provided to accomplish it. God's peace washed over me after that phone call at the airport and during that mission."

Even though there is great hesitation because of the risk or enormity of some tasks and the heartache during some challenges, God gives the desire with the accompanying peace. For those people that have been called as missionaries to Africa, they have a desire and urge to fulfill God's task for their lives. I met one this past week at a mission conference that shares the gospel with unreached tribes out in the jungles of foreign countries and he said with joy, "That is our thing!" I have known many missionaries through the years including some of my young people from our ministries that are now in difficult parts of the world and they would all tell you it is the passion of their hearts and there is no place they would rather be. As someone who has been called to work in a few difficult places in the world, I can honestly confirm that it is the greatest passion and joy of my heart to fulfill God's call in those places. My heart is filled with love for those people, and I can't wait to get back.

Speaking through the Tears

We should be very vigilant not to ignore what God is speaking to our hearts. I will never forget an experience as a young Bible college student. One day as we were in class the professor asked several of the students to give a brief testimony. Most of the young, energetic students shared about how God had placed a call on their lives. Several of us shared about how we had left home and everything we knew in order to come to school. We spoke of God's miraculous provision for our journey and schooling and how God was continuing to bless us. They were all very touching testimonies and I will always treasure those experiences, but there was one testimony in particular that really burned its picture into my young heart.

There was a sweet, older man that stood up to give his testimony. He was in his late fifties, I think, which doesn't seem very old to me now. He stood with tears in his eyes and began to tell how God had called him to ministry when he was a young man. He struggled for several minutes with his emotions as he tearfully shared how he had ignored the call God had placed upon his life and how he had gone into business for himself. God was clearly calling and speaking to his heart but he was ignoring His voice. With a tinge of guilt he recalled how he had become a very successful businessman with a good deal of money. From the world's point of view this man was the epitome of the American success story. However, he said that he always knew in his heart he was settling for second best. He was never fulfilled in his business life. He always had a little voice reminding him from time to time that he was missing his true purpose in life. He was never really happy or fulfilled.

> "*That* man looked at us young boys with tears rolling down his cheeks and pleaded with us to never forsake God's direction in our lives and to never ignore the voice of God in our hearts. He said, 'you will never be truly happy unless you are following God's will for your life.'"

I was stunned and permanently impacted! That simple, tearful testimony has clearly stayed in my heart all these years and that was about 35 years ago. It has had more impact on my heart than most of the class assignments with which I struggled. To this day I can hear him saying, "You will never be truly happy unless you are following God's will for your life." I saw the hurt and pain in that man's life that was the result of ignoring what God was speaking to his heart. I heard the deep regret and sorrow for a wasted life as my tears joined his. I also heard the repentance for a mistake, though I must also add that his obedience at that point inspired me. Whatever you do, don't refuse to listen to God's leading in your heart. Living with passion to love and honor Christ now will drastically cut down on regrets later. I will probably never see that brother again this side of heaven (he may already be there). However, that few minutes of heartfelt testimony impacted my young life as much or more than any seminary class. Those tearful words of truth are tattooed on my heart. Actually, that also confirms the truth that it is never too late to be obedient.

Preparing the Heart

It should be the desire of every Christian to have a prepared heart to which God can clearly speak. Of all the heart problems I have experienced in the ministry, let me share two that seem to be especially counterproductive. They are a heart of hatred and a heart of apathy.

A Heart of Hatred

A heart of hatred is unprepared for God to speak to it. A heart of hatred is a heart with sin. Hatred is the cancer of the soul. Dr. Richard Lee states,

> "A lack of forgiveness is a spiritual sickness. Its roots run deep, and its branches reach far into the hearts of men. If you are an unforgiving person, you are a spiritually sick person. The roots of anger, bitterness, jealousy, guilt, and hatred will torment your soul and twist your life out of control" (4).

People who allow themselves to be taken over by this disease of the soul are unable to receive the intercommunication of God. They have a hard heart. The devil seems to use hatred as one of his main battle strategies. He knows that a heart entertaining hatred is not prepared to hear the still small voice of God. He realizes that although he cannot have the soul of a true born-again Christian, he can certainly destroy his or her effectiveness as a witness through hatred. He can tease them into a state of blocked communication if he can successfully tempt them to hold on to malevolent hatred. An interesting thing about hatred; the one who is always hurt the most is the one who is hating, not the one to whom hatred is directed. Mark Twain is credited with this quote,

"Anger is an acid that can do more harm to
the vessel in which it is stored than to anything
on which it is poured" (5).

It is a spiritual cancer that eats away at the health of the soul. Like cancer, it continues to grow and becomes so invasive that it affects everything around it. Though we all struggle with anger, especially when we have been betrayed or have endured evil attacks against us or our families, or a host of other legitimate reasons, allowing it to grow and become a root of hatred or extreme bitterness lodged in our heart, is a huge mistake that becomes a spiritual tumor.

A Heart of Apathy

A heart of apathy is also unprepared for God to speak to it. This state of being unconcerned and uncommitted about Christ and the church and His plan and purpose for our lives seems to be one of the plagues of the twenty-first century. Many seem to be vitally concerned about everything else swirling around their busy lives, but not about following God's will. We are vitally concerned about and committed to a good education which we should be. We are concerned about money and we have to be. We are concerned about safety, health, status, happiness, clothes, cars, homes, furniture, security, justice, jails, judges, juries, laws, guns, government, and a host of other legitimate concerns, but where is the vital concern for God's will and direction?

The devil also uses apathy as one of his most prized weapons. Whether it is derived from doing too many things at once or from being culturally assimilated by the world, it matters not to him. His mission is accomplished either way. We cannot seriously believe we can be unconcerned and uncaring about the things of God and expect God to respond as if everything is spiritually on track. Deep down we really know better. Apathy is not only one of the devil's most useful weapons, it is one of the biggest heartaches of the committed pastor as a shepherd. The individual Christian will not grow, and the church which is the body of Christ will not grow as God intended as long as the curse of apathy is prevalent in the body of Christ. The apathetic heart is also a hard heart.

Peace and Purity

To have a prepared heart that is sensitive to God's voice, we need to have a heart that is filled with the peace of God, and a heart that is filled with the purity of God.

A Heart of Peace

Paul speaks about the, "peace that passes all understanding" in Philippians 4:6–7. I dearly love these two verses and have claimed them for my own many times. These verses instruct us to, "Be anxious for nothing, but in everything by prayer and supplication, with thanksgiving, let your requests be made known to God; *And the peace of God, which surpasses all understanding, will guard your hearts and minds through Christ Jesus*" (author's italics). What a magnificent admonition about attaining the peace of God in our hearts.

These wonderful verses first of all instruct us not to worry. A heart full of "worry noise" will find it hard to hear. We are concerned about many things and legitimately so. This verse tells us that we are to refuse to be anxiety ridden over anything. Why? We say we have a God that we trust who is in control. When do we move from legitimate concern to illegitimate worry? Though that is a difficult answer to nail down at times, let me share a couple of thoughts that may help. Concern says, "Lord here is my concern and though my heart is heavy, I am trusting it into Your hands." Worry says, "I am sick about this and I don't know what 'I' am going to do." Concern says, "Lord I am hurt and I don't know what to do, but I know that You do and I am trusting You to guide me." Worry says, "I am heartbroken and I am going to push forward. I will just do my best and see what happens. This may be the death of me."

Some would argue these verses are easy words to proclaim and hard words by which to live. I am not portraying it as easy; I am saying it is needful and a spiritual truth principle that God has given to us. If "easy" is your main criteria, you will miss your purpose. Let's keep it real.

> "Fleshly tendency is toward worry and all have been caught up in it. If fleshly man is in control, we will live in worry. However, when the spiritual man is being controlled through the power of the Holy Spirit, then we will live in dependence and faith."

I don't recall a single instance when Christ said, "If you follow Me, it will be a cakewalk." Indeed these verses are difficult to live by at times because of our habitual worry streak and tendency to trust only on our own limited abilities instead of being trustful and dependent on God's unlimited abilities. Do we really trust Him?

We are to pray about everything and leave it in God's all-powerful hands. In his delightful book, *Laugh Again*, Chuck Swindoll shares his daily practice when he says,

> "Let me be downright practical and tell you what I do. First I remind myself early in the morning and on several occasions during the day, 'God, You are at work, and You are in control. And, Lord God, You know this is happening. You were there at the beginning, and You will bring everything that occurs to a conclusion that results in Your greater glory in the end.' And then? Then (and only then!) I relax. From that point on, it really doesn't matter all that much what happens. It is in God's hands" (6).

"We like to say that we trust God, but do we really trust Him to the point of peace? Do we truly trust it into His hands, or do we claim that we do while secretly keeping it in our own hands?"

We are reminded in 1 Peter 5:7 that we are to cast all our cares upon Him because He cares for us. We are to believe and strongly hold on to the fact that He cares and that He can handle any situation better than we can. Our experience with peace or the lack of it will be dependent upon our believing and applying these truths. That means that we trust it into His hands.

Then we begin to understand that based on the obedient actions of Philippians 4:6, we will receive the promise of Philippians 4:7. Namely, we receive the peace of God. When we trust everything into God's loving hands and show Him we truly desire to follow His admonition to us, God will take over and administer His unspeakable peace. After we trust our request into His hands, we see in this verse that His peace will guard our hearts and minds through Christ Jesus. Here we see the word picture of an attentive Roman soldier standing guard over his charge. He will not sleep and will watch intently every moment. God's wonderful peace will stand guard over your heart. He will not sleep and He will watch intently every moment of every day. Moule explains,

> "What it means is that, 'in Christ Jesus',
> who is the one true spiritual Region of blessing,
> the peace of God shall protect the soul against its
> foes" (7).

Through a trusting heart in His love and sovereign control we can enjoy a peaceful heart. It would be a great assurance and reminder to put up on your mirror to see every morning, "You will keep him in perfect peace, whose mind is stayed on You, because he trusts in You" (Isa. 26:3).

A Heart Of Purity

A prepared heart should also be a pure heart. I noticed in my own life as a young Christian that when I was living in disobedience and holding on to some things that I knew dishonored the Lord that something wasn't right in my spiritual walk. Something was off. As I studied God's Word and especially David in the Psalms (the one who scripture says was a man after God's own heart), I came to understand that a heart that is entertaining, regarding, or cherishing sin is blocked from intimacy and spiritual communication. The sin that I held on to whether from pride, anger, et cetera, was causing a spiritual hindrance. Psalm 66:18 states, "If I regard iniquity in my heart, the Lord will not hear." The New International Version translates this verse as, "If I had cherished sin in my heart, the Lord would not have listened" as does the English Standard Version (which uses the word iniquity instead of sin). The word "regard" here has the idea of, "looking upon with favor." If we favor, hold on to, or cherish sin in our hearts instead of confessing it and forsaking it, we create a barrier to our intimate communication with God. If we tolerate a heart that delights in, cherishes, and flirts with sin, we will find ourselves without the spiritual direction we are seeking.

Interestingly, the Psalmist is praising the Lord for answering his prayer in these verses but is cautioning the congregation in verse 18 that if he had been cherishing sin in his heart he would not have received the answer. Commenting on Psalms 66:16–18, Dr. Ross states,

> "Here he addressed the congregation in praise to God (a declarative praise). He told them that God responded to his prayer (I cried out to Him) and God delivered him. However, it would not have happened that way if he had clung to sin (cf. Prov. 28:9; Isa. 59:2)" (8).

The Nelson Study Bible comments on verse 18,

> "Iniquity: Among the things that can block effective prayer is ongoing sin in a believer's life" (9).

Though some would try to deny it, please know that there is a loving discipline from a loving Father when we are cherishing or holding on to sin. To deny this loving discipline in whatever form our loving Father employs to rescue us from the painful consequences of that sin, is to deny the clear teaching of Scripture. The author of Hebrews is clarifying this principle when he refers back to Proverbs 3:11–12, which states, "My son, do not despise the chastening of the LORD, nor detest His correction; for whom the LORD loves He corrects, just as a father the son in whom he delights." In fact, the author of Hebrews goes on to declare further, "If you endure chastening, God deals with you as with sons; for what son is there whom a father does not chasten" (Heb. 12:7)? Not only does this loving discipline prove the love of the Father for the child, but also proves that the child is indeed His beloved son. Going even a step further to pound the point home the next verse proclaims that the son who is without this loving discipline is not part of the family. Here is a New Testament author writing under the inspiration of the Holy Spirit, proclaiming this truth from the Old Testament and confirming its truth in the life of the born-again believer in Christ. It is not true to these Scriptures to claim that when a born-again believer is involved in and cherishing the very sins for which Jesus Christ died on the cross that the Father would have absolutely no chastening response.

> "When you know the truth of chastening from God's Word, you can look beyond the correction and trust in the Father's motive of love."

We are still very much loved, but for our own good we sense a conviction that something isn't right. We, as truly born-again children of God can never lose our relationship, but we most definitely can lose our intimacy and fellowship when we have ongoing, cherished sin in our lives. Let's look further at the security of our relationship in Christ. Dr. Warren Wiersbe shares this truth in his, *Expository Outlines on the New Testament*:

> "Christians do sin; but this does not mean they must be saved all over again! Sin in the life of the believer breaks the fellowship, but not the sonship" (10).

I think this spiritual conviction and uneasiness between Father and son is illustrated (however imperfectly) by an experience with my son many years ago. When my son was in elementary school, I noticed him in our two-story house one day throwing a basketball up the stairs. He would throw the ball up to the top of the stairs hitting the back wall and then let it roll/bounce back down the steps. I could foresee the possible disaster with the ball breaking something upstairs, so I firmly told him he could play outside with the ball. I clearly explained that I didn't ever want to see him throwing the basketball up the stairs again. He promptly said, "Yes sir," and went out to play. I don't recall the exact time frame, but some time later I came home after work and headed up the stairs to the shower. I noticed something that looked out of place as I trudged up the steps. Right at the top of the steps I noticed a bunch of dirty clothes, and I think a clothes hamper stacked in front of the wall. I went over and carefully pulled some of the stuff away from the wall still curious. It was very easy to see why the mysterious stuff was stacked in that spot after I pulled it away. There was a mysterious hole in the wall about the size of a basketball. I of course went straight to him to inquire about the hole. He began to tell a story about how it got there with what he considered the pertinent issues that would put most trial lawyers to shame. As the judge of this trial, I knew that one fact overrode all others. If he had not disobeyed and continued to throw the ball up the steps against the wall, the hole wouldn't be there.

As I started the sentencing phase of this short trial, I was not in a frame of mind to have a wonderful time of fellowship and play together. My love that is beyond words for my son was not in question as my love is eternal. My son had specifically and repeatedly disobeyed my instructions. For his own good and his future growth into a great young man of discipline and character that will enjoy a life of fulfillment (as he has certainly become), until there was confession, repentance, and an apology, our intimacy and close fellowship was on pause. It was a disobedient action which resulted in the consequence of an intimacy breach.

> " The free flowing joy of our usual intimate communication and him jumping up into my arms was hindered. Our relationship as father and son could never be changed. He is my son. He was born into my family."

He cannot be somehow unborn out of my family when disobedient. He will always be my son. Nothing he could do could make him cease to be my son. He is David Hyskell, the son of Mark Hyskell, and the grandson of Joseph Hyskell. He could fall into deep sin which would break my heart, but he would still be my son. He could disgrace me and even live as a criminal, but he would remain my son. When he disobeyed, there was no threat to his family position as my son, only the need for him to ask forgiveness toward the restoration of paternal intimacy and testimony. It was needful and appropriate that he ask forgiveness even though his forgiveness was assured and settled in my loving heart before he even asked. It would not have been appropriate for him to go on like nothing had happened and not ask forgiveness because he knew his forgiveness was assured. That would simply reveal he was taking advantage of my love and forgiveness. There was a good reason that Christ Himself taught His disciples to "ask forgiveness" in the Model Prayer in Matthew

6:12. Again, he could not possibly lose his relationship with me, but he could at times lose sweet fellowship with me.

Rest assured that you are absolutely secure in Christ when you have been truly born-again as we spoke of previously. When you have been spiritually born again you cannot be unborn. You are then forever his child and that relationship and love will never be in question. Whole books have been written on our security in Christ which I will not attempt here (though it is a very joyous and assuring study), but let me share a few words of encouragement with you about your spiritual security in Christ.

Secure in Christ

"Therefore, if anyone is in Christ, *he is a new creation*; old things have passed away; behold, all things have become new" (2 Cor. 5:17, author's italics). Without presenting a lengthy theological dissertation on these few verses which is not my purpose here, I will share some brief thoughts in reference to security. When you surrender your life to Christ and are spiritually born by the power of the Holy Spirit, you are transformed into a new creation. You cannot be un-transformed spiritually any more than you could be unborn physically after that new, eternal transformation has occurred. That radical transformation by the power of God is eternal and cannot be reversed any more than a beautiful butterfly could change back into a cocoon and reverse its metamorphosis back into a colorful caterpillar crawling on the branch.

"My sheep hear My voice, and I know them, and they follow Me. *And I give them eternal life, and they shall never perish*; neither shall anyone snatch them out of My hand" (John 10:27–28, author's italics). Over and over again in the New Testament Jesus spoke about giving eternal life. In this verse He proclaims clearly that they will never perish. The spiritual life that Jesus gives is eternal, everlasting, without end, forever. It is secured by the hand of Almighty God and can never be stolen away or lost because of His unalterable promise.

"In Him you also trusted, after you heard the word of truth, the gospel of your salvation; in whom also, having believed, *you were sealed with the Holy Spirit of promise, who is the guarantee of our inheritance until the redemption of the purchased possession,* to the praise of His glory" (Eph. 1:13–14, author's italics). This may be one of the most intriguing scriptures concerning eternal security in the New Testament. A long chapter could be written on numerous words within these two verses. "Sealed," "Holy Spirit of promise," "guarantee," "inheritance," and "until the redemption" could each be singled out for exhaustive exposition. The word "sealed" is an expressive word in the original language that is used several times. MacArthur describes the original meaning of this word when he explains,

> "The sealing of which Paul speaks here refers to an official mark of identification that was placed on a letter, contract, or other important document. The seal usually was made from hot wax, which was placed on the document and then impressed with a signet ring. The document was thereby officially identified with and under the authority of the person to whom the signet belonged.
>
> That is the idea behind our being sealed in Him [Christ] with the Holy Spirit of promise. The seal of God's Spirit in the believer signifies four primary things: security, authenticity, ownership, and authority" (11).

"We are eternally sealed by the Holy Spirit of God who is the eternal promise and guarantee of our inheritance with/in Christ. We could not be more secure than when we are in Christ."

Flowing out of a perfect love for you, the Father will not allow you to continue down a destructive and painful path of sin without conviction that is intended to pull you back to spiritual health and wholeness and intimacy with Him. As a matter-of-fact, it is greatly encouraging to know that the very fact of this conviction in your life is absolute proof that the Father loves you, and that you are His child. The very fact of God's loving conviction and discipline in our lives not only assures us of His love, but that we belong to Him, and He will not stop drawing us back to health and intimacy.

Dad's Concern

While we are assured that we are absolutely secure in Christ when we have truly been born again, my dad, Dr. Joseph F. Hyskell, who had numerous earned degrees and had preached and taught the Word of God for fifty-six years, had another great concern. The troubling question for him was not whether we are eternally secure when we are truly "in Christ," but whether we are really "in Christ" when there is a habitual and prolonged lifestyle of sin. His great concern was that many who claim to be a Christian have no scriptural evidence in their lives to support that claim. Though he and I would both be quick to acknowledge that only the Lord can truly know the heart of each person, he was nonetheless troubled as a pastor and missionary for his people. So, he spent the last several decades of his ministry trying to give people some truth principles from Scripture that would help them evaluate their own spiritual condition.

Dad's concern never attained any wide exposure here in America so I wanted to give voice to a few of those principles from a little booklet he wrote called, *Who's On Board*. In the introduction Dr. Hyskell gives a foundational statement when he writes,

> "The person who thinks he is saved because of his own assets, achievements and status in the Christian community, is not really saved. The reason he is not saved is because he is not trusting solely in the efficacious shed blood of Christ for atonement of sin" (12).

For brevity's sake I will paraphrase a few of his points that reveal evidence of a spiritual change that is commensurate with being truly born again.

First Peter 2:9 states, "But you are a chosen generation, a royal priesthood, a holy nation, His own special people, that you may proclaim the praises of Him who called you out of darkness into His marvelous light." We are His own special people (one version renders it "peculiar" people) who have been called out of darkness and into His light. Is there something different (spiritually transformed) in your life that reveals you have been set apart (consecrated) by the Lord and live in His light?

First Peter 1:22 says, "Since you have purified your souls in obeying the truth through the Spirit in sincere love of the brethren, love one another fervently with a pure heart." Are your motives, goals, and lifestyle different (spiritually transformed) and do they reveal a purified heart of obedience? Do you have a fervent love for brothers and sisters in Christ with a pure heart?

Second Peter 1:3–4 proclaims, "As His divine power has given to us all things that pertain to life and godliness, through the knowledge of Him who called us by glory and virtue, by which have been given to us exceedingly great and precious promises, that through these you may be partakers of the divine nature, having escaped the corruption that is in the world through lust." Dad focused on the phrase, "partakers of the divine nature." Are you becoming more like Christ and His attributes of love, mercy, and kindness that reveal His divine nature (spiritual transformation) within you? Has there been enough change in your life (like Christ) to clearly reveal the divine nature to others?

First John 3:14 says, "We know that we have passed from death to life, because we love the brethren. He who does not love his brother abides in death." This kind of love is not a superficial label so often used in our country, but a deep, sacrificial love as was evidenced in the life of Christ. How much true, sacrificial, Godly love do you actively show toward your brothers and sisters in Christ? Would there be enough evidence of Christ's love (spiritual transformation) to convict you? Though I have not articulated and developed these principles as Dad was able to, I hope that these evidences of spiritual change from my dad's heart are helpful to you.

The Call to Holiness

A heart of purity is vital for our intimate intercommunication with the Holy Spirit. It is no secret that God expects His children to be holy according to His Word. Again, this is not possible if we are trying to live righteously by the mere strength of our own self will to keep religious duties instead of putting our focus on Christ and living by His empowerment within us. First Peter 1:14–16 says, "as obedient children, not conforming yourselves to the former lusts, as in your ignorance; but as He who called you is holy, you also be holy in all your conduct, because it is written, 'Be holy, for I am holy.'" Paul also passionately speaks of living our lives to honor the Lord in Romans 12:1–2, when he states, "I beseech you therefore, brethren, by the mercies of God, that you present your bodies a living sacrifice, holy, acceptable to God, which is your reasonable service. And do not be conformed to this world, but be transformed by the renewing of your mind, that you may prove what is that good and acceptable and perfect will of God."

One of the key themes of holiness in Scripture is separation. Separation from sin that dishonors God and for which Christ shed His blood. We are called upon to be a separated people (not isolated), not a spiritually polluted people that have been so heavily influenced by the world that the resemblance is striking. Paul speaks to the Corinthian Christians about being spiritually separated from the horrendous evil influences in Corinth which was one of the most pagan environments of the time. It is a classic passage in 2 Corinthians 6 about separation from evil and remaining true to Christ in the midst of that environment.

The Nelson Study Bible note on verses 17–18 states,

"Come out...be separate: Paul was not encouraging isolation from unbelievers (see 1

Cor. 9:5–13) but discouraging compromise with their sinful values and practices. He was urging them (and us) to maintain integrity in the world just as Christ did (see John 15:14–16; Phil. 2:14–16)" (13).

Paul was not talking about isolation from the world but dedication to Christ while in it. He was talking about not adopting their sinful values and practices, so they could see the difference. Sweet brothers and sisters in Christ please hear my heart. If we capitulate to secular culture then we degrade our spiritual saltiness and shine that reveals Christ. The mandate of the Great Commission from Christ Himself was to be His instrument to influence the world, not to be influenced by it. Oswald J. Smith comments on the separated life when he says,

"People seem to have the idea that we must mingle with the world and become like it in order to win souls and influence lives for God. Yet when a man falls into a deep well no one ever dreams of jumping down alongside of him in order to get him out. Instead he stays away up at the top and from there lets down a ladder or rope and thus lifts him up" (14).

A Contemporary Trend

It is unfortunate that some popular twenty-first century churches have little to say concerning a life of holiness through the empowerment of Christ. Holiness is something that is discounted whether intentional or unintentional, and something that is not in spiritual vogue. Among some groups it seems to be considered as some kind of Old Testament, ritualistic practice not in sync with our enlightened spiritual life and freedom in Christ. It is viewed as an outdated and depressing legalism that will stifle the positive movement and emotion of our spiritual lives and our ability to become the best we can be. In some circles, every teaching is constructed to feel good and avoid the subject. This fails to honor the divine context and present the balance that God included in His Word.

For some who have been caught in the trap of capitulating to secular culture, living in sin is also discounted to the point of being presented as almost inconsequential. Some who consider themselves Christians seem to have slipped away from the exhortation of truths like Romans 12:1–2, and live by many or most of the same standards the secular world does. Through a deafening silence on the subject, many who have no solid foundation are made to feel like it is really alright, or at the very most, no big deal as they are covered by grace anyway. Timothy Keller shares Dietrich Bonhoeffer's warning about what he called, "cheap grace." He wrote,

> "Dietrich Bonhoeffer was appalled at how many in the German church capitulated to Hitler in the early 1930s, and in response he wrote his great work *The Cost of Discipleship*. There he warned about the dangers of what he called "cheap grace," the teaching that stresses only that grace is free, so it doesn't really matter how we live. The solution, he said, was not to return to legalism, but to focus on how seriously God takes sin and on how he could only save us from it at infinite cost to himself. Understanding this must and will profoundly reshape our lives" (15).

The amazing grace of God through our Lord Jesus Christ and our forgiveness through His incredible sacrifice is also frequently used as a "pass card," especially in the lives of those who are new in the faith or who have never grown in the faith or their honest study of God's Word.

> "*I*nstead of seeing this amazing grace and forgiveness as a motivation for loving obedience in response to the infinite cost of Christ becoming sin for each of us, many seem to view it through a cultural lens of no restraint which places the flesh in charge."

This sets a dangerous precedent that is not scripturally accurate and leads to more fleshly living. This "anything goes" mentality whether spoken or unspoken is desensitizing, dangerous and scripturally flawed. The flesh is of course drawn to the idea of no restraint and is emboldened by the conception that sin has virtually no deleterious spiritual impact. The result is that those whom the Lord has called to be salt and light to influence the world are becoming more influenced by the world. Many times the salt is losing its saltiness and the light is growing dim. The sad proof of this is in the worldly lifestyles that are prevalent in portions of the church today. When speaking to this issue of continuing in sin because of the incredible truth of super abounding grace, did Paul not say, "What shall we say [to all this]? Are we to remain in sin in order that God's grace (favor and mercy) may multiply and overflow? Certainly not! *How can we who died to sin live in it any longer*" (Rom. 6:1–2, Amp., author's italics)?

Another prevailing practice in some current churches that fails to proclaim the whole counsel of God's Word, seems to be that everything has to be light and bright, warm and fuzzy, comfortable and nice, and positive and fun. The truth is that even as loving human parents, we don't interact that way with our own beloved children when there is a problem or destructive pattern because we know intuitively it is not best for them. Do we not realize that our heavenly Father who loves us perfectly would address destructive patterns in our lives through His Word? You know in your own heart that it is not best to give your kids everything they want and never discuss responsibility and accountability. We all intuitively know and believe the truth of this important principle and have seen the tragic lives of those who have wandered in life with no loving direction and discipline. Spiritual responsibility and accountability is no less important. In reality, along with the unspeakable joy and promises and treasures we have in Christ, we need the not-so-fun loving discipline from our loving Father to keep us grounded in the faith. We need the not-so-fun conviction from our loving Father to get us back on track. We need the not-so-fun uncomfortable reminder from our loving Father to pull us away from the sliding board to spiritual deception and even blindness.

> "We need the not-so-fun words of truth from our beloved pastors in the pulpit that rightly divide the word of truth instead of picking and choosing only our most comfortable passages."

God desires his blood bought children to be obedient, not out of legalistic drudgery but out of loving gratitude for the unspeakable gift of redemption through the greatest gift of all history. The theme of living a holy life that is worthy of Christ in scripture is beyond debate. It is called for clearly and repetitiously: In Ephesians 4:1: "I, therefore, the prisoner of the Lord, beseech you to walk worthy of the calling with which you were called…" In Colossians 1:10: "That you may walk worthy of the Lord, fully pleasing Him, being fruitful in every good work and increasing in the knowledge of God." In 1 Thessalonians 2:12: "That you would walk worthy of God who calls you into His own kingdom and glory." In Titus 2:11–12: "For the grace of God that brings salvation has appeared to all men, teaching us that, denying ungodliness and worldly lusts, we should live soberly, righteously, and godly in the present age…" Jesus Himself made it plain when He said, "If you love Me, keep My commandments" John 14:15, and "He who has My commandments and keeps them, it is he who loves Me" (John 14:21). Add to this list the previously mentioned 1 Peter 1:14–16 and Romans 12:1–2, and you could also add a whole host of other scriptures. He expects His children to live a life that is distinctly different as His Spirit is resident within us and has given us the power and authority to live differently and impact the world. Living like the world doesn't impact the world for Christ. Living like Christ as His love shines through us impacts the world for Him. Obedience should be the normal, loving response for a child of God. It is the desire of the new nature to please the heavenly Father, though the flesh tries to interfere.

We Can Live Holy Lives

The enemy and worldly culture have strategically attempted to make it appear like this is an impossible fairy tale that is only for biblical characters or super saints. The impact of these attempts, especially when coupled with our permissive culture, have heavily influenced thinking even in the church. This influence has led some to believe that living a holy life is good for the preacher's talking points and not much more. The holy life has been successfully framed as a pie-in-the-sky mirage. It looks good and sounds great but it's not real. Perhaps someone you love and respect has become convinced that it is impossible to live a holy life. Maybe you struggle with that peer pressure and the environment of contemporary culture and have been influenced to believe it is just not realistic. Let me explain some ways we have been cleverly conditioned to believe that distortion.

When we hear someone talk or write about living a holy life, many times there is an immediate reluctance to believe it is really possible based upon our experiential understanding of the flesh and its strong pull in our lives. We know all too well our poor track record in dealing with the flesh. We remember behaviors and actions that were anything but holy. Our failures force our minds to accept the supposed reality that we lack the capacity to truly live holy lives, so therefore the only alternative we can envision is to believe it must be impossible. That leads to further confusion when we see these Scriptures that call us to live a holy life and walk in a way that is worthy of Christ. I want to share a couple of thoughts that may help clear some of the confusion. First, we need to consider what living a holy life looks like. Second, we need to regain an accurate scriptural concept of the source of a holy life.

Living a Holy Life

First, let's consider what it would look like for us to live a holy life. Jesus Christ was the only one who ever lived who was perfectly holy in every respect and never once sinned. That is an indisputable fact of Scripture: "For we do not have a high priest [Jesus Christ] who cannot sympathize with our weaknesses, but was in all points tempted as we are, *yet without sin*" (Heb. 4:15, author's italics). All the rest of us have sinned and to one degree or another still struggle with it. Therefore, it is obvious that for us to live a holy life does not mean sinless perfection. That may be the mental picture many have as they think about a holy life which leads them to think it is impossible. It may also be the mental picture imposed by the culture that completely rejects (and despises) the scriptural concept as untenable. However, our heavenly Father who has numbered every hair on our head and knows us better than we know ourselves including our flaws has repetitiously called us to live a holy life. So we know that we can and it becomes a question of how.

We live a holy life only through the indwelling power of the Holy Spirit as we walk in Him, not through any kind of religious devotion or power of self will. Religious devotion based on our power of self will, will always fail. Paul explained, "I say then: Walk in the Spirit, and you shall not fulfill the lust of the flesh" (Gal. 5:16). The word "walk" in this verse is a continuous action word that speaks of our consistent and habitual lifestyle. In a previous book I explained,

> "So what does this really mean to walk in the Spirit? Albert Barnes breaks it down this way, '...This is the true rule about overcoming the propensities of your carnal natures, and of avoiding the evils of strife and contention. Walk... the Christian life is often represented as a journey, and the word walk, in the scripture, is often equivalent to live...if we live under the influences of that Spirit, we need not fear the power of the sensual and corrupt propensities of our nature.'

In reference to the original language here, Dr. Donald Campbell explains, 'the verb peripateite is a present imperative and is literally translated, keep on walking.'

In order to not fulfill the lust of the flesh, we are to live our lives under the influences/control of the Holy Spirit of God Who lives within us. This is an imperative in our lives that is to be an ongoing, consistent lifestyle. We cannot live this way if we are living a life that is controlled by the flesh. We can only live this way as the Holy Spirit of God is directing and controlling us and our hearts are yielded to Him. When we walk in the Spirit by His empowerment within us, we watch Him accomplish His supernatural purposes through our lives" (16).

The Source of a Holy Life

" The truth is we can live holy lives because of what Jesus accomplished on the cross. We can live righteous and holy (not perfect) lives, not because of the power of self will, but because of the empowerment of Christ within us."

No Longer Slaves but Free

One of the exciting truths of Romans 6 is that we are no longer under the authority and bondage of sin. "Knowing this, that our old man was crucified with Him, that the body of sin might be done away with, *that we should no longer be slaves of sin. For he who has died has been freed from sin*" (Rom. 6:6–7, author's italics). Sin has no power over us other than what we give it. In Christ we are freed from the "power" of sin. In this world we of course are not removed from the "presence" of sin and its temptations, but we are most certainly freed from the power and authority of sin's dominion over us through Christ's finished work on the cross. Scripture gives us the great news when it says, "And you, being dead in your trespasses and the uncircumcision of your flesh, He has made alive together with Him, having forgiven you all trespasses, having wiped out the handwriting of requirements that was against us, which was contrary to us. And He has taken it out of the way, having nailed it to the cross. Having disarmed principalities and powers, He made a public spectacle of them, triumphing over them in it" (Col. 2:13–15). Christ won at the cross and through His forgiveness and empowerment, we have been made alive together with Him, and we walk in that victory.

We don't have to be taken captive by those sinful thoughts. We don't have to feel powerless when temptations come. We are dead to the old man and alive to the new man: "I have been crucified with Christ; it is no longer I who live, but Christ lives in me; and the life which I now live in the flesh I live by faith in the Son of God, who loved me and gave Himself for me" (Gal. 2:20).

Reckon: Count It as Fact

Those without Christ and His victorious empowerment are under the authority of sin. Those who by grace alone have Christ's empowerment resident within them are not. So you may be wondering how you actually apply this victory that Christ won at the cross. The Scriptural truth that we must understand and apply is to "reckon" ourselves as dead to sin. This is a word that means we must count what God has declared about us to be fact. Paul explains this truth when he says, "Likewise you also, *reckon yourselves to be dead indeed to sin*, but alive to God in Christ Jesus our Lord" (Rom. 6:11, author's italics).

We must believe God's Word and know it has happened. We must account that it is the truth that it is. We must truly believe God's

Word and then act upon it accordingly as we live out that truth. In this area of the Christian life, what you don't know can hurt you.

Through the years I have seen so many have such a struggle with lust. The truth be told, we all struggle with it to one degree or another, but many seem to be overcome and dominated by it, especially with the exponential growth of the internet. As I have met with them they have tearfully confessed to this domination and ask, "Why can't I overcome this lust of the flesh and live like the Lord wants me to?" They proceed to tell me how this domination of lust is destroying their marriage, their family, and certainly their spiritual lives. I am so grateful that the priceless Word of God gives us an answer. We reckon it to be so and then we walk (removing any of the enemy's insidious tools/weapons against us) in that truth by His power. As we just learned previously, Paul states the answer this way: "I say then: Walk in the Spirit, and you shall not fulfill the lust of the flesh" (Gal. 5:16). There is the answer! The Amplified Bible explains the same verse this way, "But I say, walk and live habitually in the (Holy) Spirit—responsive to and controlled and guided by the Spirit; then you will certainly not gratify the cravings and desires of the flesh—of human nature without God." It is living under the control and guidance of the Holy Spirit through His divine empowerment in you. This underscores even further the vital importance of living in intimacy with Christ.

Realizing that God has given us this unspeakable power and victory to live lives that please Him, it is certainly understandable that God expects us to implement it and live in that victory as we have seen in the preceding scriptures. When we don't apply His victory which is resident in us and live in bondage as if His victory didn't occur, God graciously chastises us because He loves us and wants to guide us back to victory through the empowerment of Christ. God will certainly allow us to endure the pain of learning our lessons because He loves us. Just as there wasn't sweet fellowship and communication with my son when he had specifically disobeyed my instruction, so God will help us learn and grow. Just as any loving parent knows the importance of loving discipline when their child is doing something dangerous that will cause them harm or even long term ruin, so our loving heavenly Father lovingly disciplines us to rescue us from destructive behavior. When there is confession and repentance, there is also restored intimacy and fellowship. We need to keep the lines of communication open by living in the power of the Holy Spirit within us to honor the Lord and keep a pure heart. The characteristic of our lives as those who love Christ should be striving to honor Him through His empowerment though we know we fail at times. Here's the truth. You can live in victory through the power of Christ within you and you can know His will through the inner communication of the Holy Spirit as He speaks to your heart through a peace or unrest. He wants you to hear His direction! Live in His power according to His truth and you will hear His direction.

Final Question to Ponder:
Is my heart open and prepared to hear and obey God's voice or is it too crowded with the desires of the world and self?

Chapter 7

The Confirmation Of God's Word

Our Treasure Book

The greatest source of the mind of God and His will for us is the unspeakably precious Word of God. God has blessed us immeasurably by giving in written form the expressions of His heart for us. The Word of God is a treasure book of unfathomable price. Abraham Lincoln proclaimed his estimate of the value of God's Word when he said,

> "In regard to the great Book I have only to say it is the best gift which God has given to men... They might lay down tons and heaps of their heartless reasonings alongside a few of Christ's sayings and parables, to find that He had said more for the benefit of all our race in one of them than there is in all they have written. They might read His Sermon on the Mount to learn there is more justice, righteousness, and mercy in it than in the minds and books of all the ignorant doubters from the beginning of human knowledge" (1).

In God's Word we find all the promises and principles needed for every situation in life. Unfolded in its pages are the answers to questions the world is desperately asking. The tragedy is that the world is rejecting the true answers to their questions and accepting answers from flawed sources that lead to destruction: "And they will turn their ears away from the truth, and be turned aside to fables" (2 Tim. 4:4). You either believe in absolute truth from the Creator, or you believe in truth as it is defined by the created.

Please understand that truth as it is defined by the created, who are finite and flawed and reject the truth (or even existence) of an infinite God, will inevitably lead to conclusions that are finite and flawed. Therefore, truth as it is defined by the created, though gladly received and believed by the secular culture, is in reality pseudo-truth.

In our hands, we have the expression of the mind of God for our lives. We enjoy in the Scriptures the ultimate in decision-making counsel. The greatest counselor in the universe has carefully spoken to the issues in life. He has written a best-selling manual about how to live the abundant life and make the right decisions. His counsel is counsel that already knows the future. His counsel is counsel that knows us intimately, better than we even know ourselves.

If someone told you they had a treasure map which would lead you to unbelievable riches you would drop everything to get to it. You would lose no time in getting the map and studying it more intently than you had ever studied anything in your life. You would dissect every detail and commit to memory as much as possible. You would keep it in a safe place and treat it like the gold it represents. That piece of paper would be priceless to you. It would be the answer to your dreams. You would follow it without question in order to find the treasure.

It is startling that we have a treasure book of this magnitude that will lead us to riches far beyond what money can buy, and many times we treat it like yesterday's newspaper kept for the bottom of the bird cage. We study it, if it happens to be convenient. We listen to thoughts proclaimed from it with sleepy eyes and minds on Sundays as we look at our watches to see when the service will be over. We ignore it as though we have better things to do. We shed many tears and cry aloud about the need for direction in our lives and we leave the answer book on the coffee table.

> "*We* wonder why God doesn't seem to be specifically directing us when we have laid aside His manual of directions."

The Skeptics

Some would say the Bible is without answers for our lives in the twenty-first century and that it is hopelessly outdated. They would toss it aside as some ancient novel that is without much merit for our enlightened and intelligent minds. They would cast doubt on it as a source for real-life answers. Nothing could be further from the truth! All of those enlightened doubters and intellects have been blinded by the master deceiver in his continuing strategy to pull us away from the true truth.

I can guarantee you the enemy will use our culture and everything in his diabolical arsenal to keep you away from the truth of God's Word. One of the ways he attempts to do that is to have a multitude of voices in the culture casting disparaging and demeaning remarks at God's Word. Some of those voices go even further and make claims that the Bible is not legitimate at all. They claim it is not from God and simply the writings of ancient men who wrote the stories passed down from generation to generation and that they are simply exaggerated fairy tales.

The Truth about the Truth

I want you to be prepared to stand against this onslaught with truth. Peter spoke truthfully and forcefully concerning God's Word in 2 Peter 1:16–21. He said that he and the other followers of Christ did not make up stories about Christ but were actually eyewitnesses to His life and miracles. He said we actually watched Him as He was transfigured before our eyes. "And He was transfigured before them. His face shone like the sun, and His clothes became as white as the light" (Matt. 17:2). He said we watched Him as He spoke to Moses and Elijah: "And behold, Moses and Elijah appeared to them, talking with Him" (Matt. 17:3). He said we actually heard the voice of the Father out of heaven: "While he [Peter] was still speaking, behold, a bright cloud overshadowed them; and suddenly a voice came out of the cloud, saying, this is My beloved Son, in whom I am well pleased. Hear Him" (Matt. 17:5)! He finishes his thought in 2 Peter 1:19–21, when he proclaims, "And so we have the prophetic word confirmed, which you do well to heed as a light that shines in a dark place, until the day dawns and the morning star rises in your hearts; knowing this first, that *no prophecy of Scripture is of any private interpretation, for prophecy never came by the will of man, but holy men of God spoke as they were moved by the Holy Spirit*" (author's italics).

Rest assured that Peter and the other apostles were eyewitnesses of the miracles of Christ, of His death, burial, and supernatural resurrection. This was not some scribe in a cave somewhere creating fantastic tales. This was not a grandfather with diminished mental capacity creatively spinning a story for his grandchildren. These were real men, with real lives, with real minds, and real eyes, and real ears who touched and experienced Christ and His miracles in real historical time. Peter, under the inspiration of the Holy Spirit, states in this passage that we have the miraculous life of Christ confirmed, the prophetic word of the Old Testament confirmed, and then he speaks of the New Testament writings of the Apostle Paul as scripture in 2 Peter 3:15–16, as another confirmation. Paul, also under the inspiration of the Holy Spirit, further confirms both Old Testament and New Testament as inspired Scripture when he states, "All Scripture is given by inspiration of God" in 2 Timothy 3:16. Though it is not my purpose here to present a detailed defense of the inspiration and canonicity of Scripture (which would be greatly enjoyable), if you would enjoy taking this study further and digging into a comprehensive defense of God's Word, I would encourage you to get the excellent book by Josh McDowell titled, *The New Evidence That Demands A Verdict*. This book deals effectively with multitudes of the most pertinent questions concerning God's Word including how the books of the Bible were accepted as part of the canon of Scripture. McDowell was a doubting skeptic. Check out what he found. His testimony in the front of the book is also amazing.

Our Relevant Resource Manual

The Word of God is the most relevant resource manual of the twenty-first century, or any century! It is without peer in addressing the current issues of life that face us. It has been my experience that God speaks through His Word with supernatural accuracy and relevancy. God has used His Word to give me answers for every day decisions in life. God has also given me answers for major decisions I was facing from numerous books in His Word including Hebrews, Job, Romans, and even Chronicles. I am grateful beyond words for the way the Lord has spoken to me and given me guidance and direction through His precious Word.

As we look for God's perfect will in our lives, it is vital that we study, prayerfully meditate, and look for God's answers to us out of His Word. This is the one of our three keys to knowing God's will that is most often overlooked or given a passing glance. This is the element that has been largely forgotten in American Christianity, even many times by those who have a love and high respect for the Word of God. It has been the target of special attack by the forces of hell because they know the treasure it can be to the child of God who begins to get a glimpse of its divine impact. Many Christians have missed some of the greatest blessings of life that Christ has already provided. These blessings are available for implementation and yet they remain unused. Dr. John MacArthur Jr. shares a beautiful illustration of this truth. He writes,

"A poor man had wanted to go on a cruise all his life. As a youngster he had seen an advertisement for a luxury cruise, and ever since, he had dreamed of spending a week on a large ocean liner enjoying fresh sea air and relaxing in a luxurious environment. He saved money for years, carefully counting his pennies, often sacrificing personal needs so he could stretch his resources a little further.

Finally he had enough to purchase a cruise ticket. He went to a travel agent, looked over the cruise brochures, picked out one that was especially attractive, and bought a ticket with the money he had saved for so long. He was hardly able to believe he was about to realize his childhood dream.

Knowing he could not afford the kind of elegant food pictured in the brochure, the man planned to bring his own provisions for the week. Accustomed to moderation after years of frugal living, and with his entire savings going to pay for the cruise ticket, the man decided to bring along a week's supply of bread and peanut butter. That was all he could afford.

The first few days of the cruise were thrilling. The man ate peanut-butter sandwiches alone in his room each morning and spent the rest of his time relaxing in the sunlight and fresh air, delighted to be aboard ship.

By midweek, however, the man was beginning to notice that he was the only person on board who was not eating luxurious meals. It seemed that every time he sat on the deck or rested in the lounge or stepped outside his cabin, a porter would walk by with a huge meal for someone who had ordered room service.

By the fifth day of the cruise the man could take it no longer. The peanut-butter sandwiches seemed stale and tasteless. He was desperately hungry, and even the fresh air and sunshine had lost their appeal. Finally, he stopped a porter and exclaimed, 'Tell me how I might get one of those meals! I'm dying for some decent food, and I'll do anything you say to earn it!'

'Why, sir, don't you have a ticket for this cruise?' the porter asked.

'Certainly,' said the man. 'But I spent everything I had for that ticket. I have nothing left with which to buy food.'

'But sir,' said the porter, 'didn't you realize? Meals are included with your passage. You may eat as much as you like'" (2).

He Cherished God's Word

I have been very blessed and fortunate to have enjoyed some wonderful, godly teachers, and professors through the years. Each of them have taught me invaluable lessons and have had an impact they will never know. As I think about God's Word and my love for it, I think of one of those professors, Dr. Cliff VanNote. He was a large and jolly man full of life and the joy of the Lord. He was an inspiration just to be around. One thing in particular has always remained etched in my mind about Dr. VanNote. He absolutely loved and cherished the Word of God like few people I have ever known. Because of his great love for the Word, he seemed to be on a mission in life to teach others to love it also. His enthusiasm for study of the Word was contagious to us young preacher boys. We marveled at how he took it apart, parsed every word and studied every nuance of a particular verse just as an archaeologist would carefully uncover ancient remains or as a biologist would dissect an interesting species. Sometimes my best friend "Digger" (Danny McCartney) and I would go by his little apartment to find out what new and exciting truth he had learned from God's Word that day.

I will never forget one day that Digger and I went by his apartment to chat a few minutes. As we began to ask what he had been studying in God's Word, his eyes lit up and he jumped up out of his chair to give us a real-life illustration. He insisted that I get up and jump on his back. Now Dr. VanNote had previously had experience as a wrestler and he was the size of man that could probably carry several of us. I hesitated, but at his insistence, I jumped on. He began to take dramatic steps around the room with me on his back, explaining the meaning of certain words that had to do with the idea of bearing burdens. He shared with great excitement and joy as he impressed upon us the real-life meaning of those words. This was one of the true joys of his life and it radiated from his face and his emotional words.

After all these years, I have vivid memories of riding around that room for several minutes on the back of a big hearted man who sincerely loved the Word of God. He taught me some of the truths for life that I still live by today. As I've pondered that sweet memory, I think of the way Jesus has carried me so many times. I think of the way the Word of God has pictured for me the matchless love of Christ.

There are so many things we can learn from the Word of God. There are countless treasures we can find in its priceless pages. In fact, I believe we can study God's Word all our lives for sixty, seventy, eighty years and still be learning new and exciting things as we take that final glorious step into His presence. I must confess I don't remember a lot of our class material that Dr. VanNote taught, but I will never forget the man's love for the Word of God. I found out many years ago now from a mutual friend that Dr. VanNote had gone to be with the Lord. This makes the inscription that he wrote in my Greek New Testament all the more precious to me. Of all the things that he could have written, he wrote a phrase that has had a profound and lasting effect on my life.

"*H*ere is what my beloved teacher and mentor wrote, 'Mark, Love the Lord with all your mind and all your heart—love Him through the Word.'"

Listen to that phrase again. Love Him through the Word. That exhortation will echo through my mind throughout the rest of my life. He taught me to love Him through the Word, and I still have tears in my eyes right now as I write this over thirty years later.

That is my hope and prayer for my Christian family. It is imperative we understand the undiscovered treasures we are missing in leaving the Word of God out of our lives. It is vitally important we return it to the proper place of importance in our lives and confess the tragic error of ignoring the most priceless and unique book of all history. We must energetically and enthusiastically study God's Word for the answers that we desperately need in life. As my friend has said, we must, for our sake, "love Him through the Word."

The Benefit of Study

Contrary to popular practice, we should understand that reading is not all there is to studying. With many pieces of literature, a casual reading would suffice, but with the priceless Word of God, never! As a pastor friend of mine has said, "We can thread words through our eyes and never really comprehend what is being communicated." We can read many times with little or no real attention to meaning and application. Just as some students develop the skill of looking directly at the teacher with an attentive face while being mentally in another world, so we sometimes read with our brain in another world. We've probably all done that at times.

An all-knowing God has shared priceless truths through His written Word. Treasures beyond compare are on its pages. Simple truths and deep truths are found in its storehouse. Life-changing principles are available to lift up the brokenhearted, to bring salvation to the lost, to heal the wounded, to calm the raging storm, to meet life's practical needs, to bring the prodigal son back to the father, to restore broken relationships, to bring conviction and correction and to give direction in the decisions of life. With a book of this magnitude, we will rob ourselves of the life-changing treasures with mere reading.

Studying with Spiritual Discernment

When I was young I had an experience that the Lord used to teach me a lesson about spiritual discernment. I had a friend that had asked me a question about a particular issue with which he was struggling. I loved him and wanted to help, so I sat down to answer his question from God's Word. I was very excited to share this wonderful truth from God's Word that had impacted my life and I knew could set him free.

With joy and passion, I began to explain this wonderful truth. As the Holy Spirit was leading and empowering me, I expounded this nugget of truth and how its application could make an indelible mark on our lives. When I looked at my sweet friend for a response, there was a puzzled look. I immediately assumed I had failed in making it clear, and so I proceeded point by point to simplify and clarify what I had just shared. Again, it was evident my friend was not understanding or comprehending the beauty of this truth and I was again frustrated with myself. He just could not understand or grasp this truth no matter how I explained it.

Please understand this was no disparagement of any kind toward my sweet friend. This was a highly intelligent person, in many ways above my pay grade. The Lord used this as a life lesson for me and made it clear (later as I was praying) that this was not about IQ, intelligence quotient. This was about SSQ, spiritual sight quotient. In a passage that speaks of the Holy Spirit revealing truth to us Paul explains it this way: "But the natural man does not receive the things of the Spirit of God, for they are foolishness to him; nor can he know them, because they are spiritually discerned" (1 Cor. 2:14). Then I understood the real problem. When a person hasn't been spiritually changed by Christ and indwelt with the Holy Spirit, there is a lack of spiritual sight and therefore of spiritual discernment. They may be incredibly intelligent while lacking spiritual sight, wisdom, and discernment. Studying God's Word does not yield up its deep treasures to the natural academic, but to the supernaturally endowed child of God.

This certainly does not mean that when we have the Holy Spirit of God indwelling us and giving us illumination that we immediately understand everything and are the instant repositories of all spiritually discerned truth. What it does mean is that as we prayerfully study with a dependence upon the Holy Spirit to guide us and teach us, we see things through His lens. A. W. Tozer states,

> "The soul has eyes with which to see and ears with which to hear." He went on to say, "As we begin to focus upon God, the things of the spirit will take shape before our inner eyes. Obedience to the word of Christ will bring an inward revelation of the Godhead" (John 14:21–23) (3).

When we study the precious Word of God, it should always be with a conscious dependence upon the Holy Spirit for discernment to see exactly what God wants us to see. We can then joyfully begin to mine the spiritual nuggets of truth that transform us by the renewing of our minds. Paul put it this way: "And do not be conformed to this world, but be transformed by the renewing of your mind, that you may prove what is that good and acceptable and perfect will of God" (Rom. 12:2).

The Benefit of Repetitious Study

As a boy on the farm, one of my jobs was to milk and take care of the cow. It was fascinating to me how the cow seemed to be able to chew all day. Even when the cow hadn't eaten any more grass, she could stand there and chew for hours. I discovered the reason behind this bovine mystery. After the cow has chewed her food, she then swallows it. That would be the end of the chewing with a human, but not with a cow. As I would watch the cow closely, a little later her body would jerk upward like she was hiccupping. Then to my amazement, she would start chewing again. She hadn't taken a bite of new food. It is referred to as a cow "chewing her cud." I learned that the cow regurgitates the swallowed food and chews it some more.

That might sound a bit gross, but I guarantee you that cow will never have a stomach ache from rushing through her food like so many of us do. It is chewed thoroughly. It has been used and reused and enjoyed to its fullest extent.

If we desire to know God's will and God's way, we will have a desire to study repetitiously. We should go over and over a passage of spiritual food asking the Holy Spirit to reveal exactly what He knows we need to see. We should examine it again and again. We should meditate on it and then digest it, and then chew it some more as we search for all the life-giving nourishment God intends for us. We should dive into the Word of God over and over with all the energy and excitement of a gold miner who hit the mother lode. It is known that some of our great preachers would read a passage fifty times while preparing to preach from it.

With repetitious study of God's Word we will also gain more ability and wisdom. There is another interesting item I need to share about my cow experiences. After I had milked for a few years, I began to experiment with my expertise in milk control. I began to knock flies down off the wall with a single shot of milk from my expert hand turning up that udder while milking. The powerful stream of milk from the udder was amazingly accurate in the hand of one who had practiced hundreds and thousands of times. I would enjoy watching for cats coming in the barn door and plaster them right in the face with a stream of milk. When I was late milking in the evening, the cow was very full of milk. I would see how much pressure was available and try to see how far I could shoot a stream of milk. It was udderly incredible (Sorry, I had to do one milk joke). I estimate that I could shoot about ten to fifteen feet outside the barn door from my stool. That would be a total shot of around twenty-five feet.

Because of the repetition of my task, my hands became very strong and I became efficient and able to do more than the average milker.

When we spend a good deal of prayerful time in God's Word, we will, with the teaching and illumination of the Holy Spirit be able to see more than the average reader. We will draw closer to God. We will be more aware of God's ways. We will become more accurate and able in our use of the Scripture as we study to show ourselves approved. We will begin to understand the deeper things of God's heart as we dig deeper. We will be capable of rightly dividing the Word of Truth.

> "*We* will be more in tune with the heart of God, and therefore, able to discern His will for our lives more accurately."

To use my milking illustration, watching a professional milker explain milking once a week won't build the tremendous hand strength and milking ability that comes from your own regular time in the barn, milking. Also, hearing a message on Sunday or reading the Bible occasionally will not develop the strength of spiritual insight, character, and intimacy with the Father that comes from quality time on a consistent basis. I can't explain all the benefits, many of which I believe we aren't even aware. I do know that it is transforming in more ways than we even see. A while back I met a new friend who after a few weeks shared some kind words about my life and testimony. I am deeply aware that what she saw was not some kind of religious devotion, but the light of Christ in me. Jesus is the source of true light and He said, "Let your light so shine before men, that they may see your good works and glorify your Father in heaven" (Matt. 5:16). Even though they may not understand that light, they will see it and it will leave an indelible mark.

The Benefit of Systematic Study

One of the journeys of exciting discovery for me has been to systematically study my way through each book of the Bible from Genesis to Revelation. At times during this study I take longer on a passage as the Holy Spirit peaks my interest and sometimes not as long on others. At times I will get thrilled with the stunning illumination on a topic or even a word and will dig into it for weeks. Therefore, sometimes I study from Genesis to Revelation in a couple years and sometimes in eight to nine years. In my personal time of study (which is separate from my preparation study for teaching and preaching), I find it has the most impact as I ask the Holy Spirit to show me all He wants me to see and then follow His guidance as to the amount. If I find I am studying just to complete a certain amount for my check off list, it seems too rigid even though there is nothing wrong with a certain goal each day when done in the right spirit. If studying a certain amount each day such as a one-year study Bible works well for you, then by all means go for it.

It is very wise and an incredible journey of spiritual growth to develop a habit of systematic study. To have a system of studying the whole Bible every year or two, or longer if you are diving deeper into specific themes, will uncover treasure that will not only feed you, but give you answers to life's questions. The time will differ from person to person with various schedules, but the consistency and determination to study through the entire sixty-six books of the Bible will enrich and change a person's life radically.

There are numerous reasons why a system of study that will take you through the whole Bible is so valuable. First, when we study a piece here and a piece there, we tend to have a fragmented understanding with no overview of the whole. It will be difficult to truly understand a fragmented piece outside the divine context that surrounds it. It has been said that a text without its context is a pretext. Second, the hit and miss approach, also called the open and point method, leaves us open to some serious problems with misapplications of our understanding of God's will. Third, in not systematically studying the whole of Scripture, we miss out on many astounding promises and treasures God has so lovingly given. Lastly, it is incredible to me how the Lord has used a systematic study all the way through the Bible to give me answers in my life. I may be three or four years into my journey through the Bible and on a specific day in a specific circumstance or great struggle God will use the exact verse(s) where I am to speak to my heart and bring me to tears with the divine answer I needed. Our loving Father knows where we will be and what we will be struggling with and will honor our systematic search and provide divine answers. Amazing!

The Benefit of a Controlling Overview

The contexts of a passage, a chapter, a book, a testament, and of the whole Bible are very important. Without this proper understanding of the unit, we run the dangerous risk of misusing God's precious Word. A pastor friend of mine would methodically share with the church family the first three rules of interpretation. These were not the official rules of biblical interpretation that we learn in seminary, but the point was very clear and it stressed proper importance on this subject. He would say, "The first three rules of biblical interpretation are, context, context, context." Be very careful to read the whole passage, the whole chapter, the whole book, the whole testament, and eventually the whole Bible before building whole theologies on a small portion. Hendricks and Hendricks speak of the importance of context when they write,

> "So whenever you study a verse, a paragraph,
> a section, even an entire book—always consult
> the neighbors of that verse, that paragraph, that
> section, that book. Whenever you get lost, climb
> a 'contextual tree' and gain some perspective" (4).

I love their suggestion, "climb a contextual tree." They go on to detail five different kinds of context in this "must read" book for those who love to study the Word of God and want to discover more tools.

A bizarre experience I had may help illustrate this point about the danger of removing a verse from its context.

I Was Accused of Murder

The stunned look on her face spoke volumes. My secretary had come hastily into my office and nervously told me I needed to come out and talk with the guys in the lobby of the church. I could tell by her facial expression it was going to be an interesting encounter to say the least. As I followed her into the hall lobby, I was introduced to two very uniquely dressed men. They wore gunny sack robes down to their feet, they were barefooted (not sure what they do in the winter time), they wore white headbands, and they carried small satchels on their shoulders. I introduced myself and invited them to my office. As we sat down they informed me they were called, "Christ Brothers." They began to share various concepts they believed the Bible taught.

They began to share some bizarre thoughts. They told me that Jesus had returned and that they knew where He was. I shared with them that I found that very interesting, but that it had no scriptural backing. I then shared with them a passage on the return of Christ and what it will be like when He truly does come back to earth again. This angered them, and though I don't remember the exact sequence of this conversation thirty-five years later, I believe they continued for a while trying to share some of their other strange beliefs.

The really bizarre one, which clearly illustrates the danger of a doctrine with no context, is when they informed me that anyone eating meat was a murderer. This one was a shocker. This of course made me one of the worst serial murderers in history, so I inquired about their spiritual basis for this belief. They directed me to an incomplete portion of Isaiah 66:3, which says, "He who kills a bull is as if he slays a man." That phrase was the complete basis for their doctrinal position which made me a murderer. They built a lifestyle of vegetarianism around that verse (actually a small part of that verse) and at the same time called most of us in America murderers. Can you believe it?!

That verse has absolutely nothing to do with their claim. Further, it was God Himself who told them to kill the animals and offer the sacrifices! God is speaking of the abominable sacrifices of the Israelites and the fact that their hearts were turned away from Him. They had turned to their own ways and had blasphemed God. Their sacrifices had become a stench and a sin before Him. These false prophets had failed to even read the rest of the verse that they misused. This vividly reveals the danger of building beliefs on a portion of Scripture, without its proper context.

There's one further interesting note on the colorful "Christ Brothers" I'd like to share. As we were discussing these issues in my office, I noticed one of them reaching for his satchel. As I kept watch out of the corner of my eye, I saw him grab some odd paraphernalia out of the little brown bag. He had some little white papers and a little bag of stuff that looked strangely like weed. Having grown-up in the sixties and seventies, it was apparent to me that the guy was beginning to roll something to smoke and it wasn't tobacco. I was stunned! Here were two guys who claimed to be on the road for Jesus. I blurted out, "What in the world are you doing?" With a slurred sixties kind of hippie voice, his classic response was, "These are just God's green herbs man!" With that enlightened comment, I rest my case!

I also used another illustration to highlight the critical importance of context when I explained in a previous book,

> "One of the most glaring examples of removing a scripture from its context is currently being used by the secular world almost as a fad. It is, 'You shall know the truth, and the truth shall set you free.' I have called it a 'hijacked truth.' It is a wonderful truth of scripture that, with its proper context, takes the student to a God-ordained, accurate destination of understanding.

Without its God-ordained context, the truth is hijacked and ultimately leads the student to whatever premise is being espoused by the user.

This wonderful truth from Jesus viewed with its God-ordained context adds the accurate overview for a genuine understanding. The Bible says, "Then Jesus said to those Jews who believed Him, 'If you abide in My word, you are My disciples indeed. And you shall know the truth, and the truth shall make you free'" (John 8:31–32).

This true meaning is radically different from the way most people are using it. Within its God-ordained context, there is a conditional statement. Jesus said, 'IF you abide in My Word, you shall know the truth, and the truth shall make you free' (John 8:31–32, paraphrased). Needless to say, most people using this phrase know nothing of abiding in His Word. They are simply using a phrase that sounds good but is completely divorced from its full meaning, completely superficial, and hijacked from its original intent" (5).

The Danger of the Open-and-Point Method

The open-and-point method can also be a dangerous way to study. Again, we don't have the protection of the context of thought from the Holy Spirit. This method could well have touched the lives of many Christians with an encouraging word from God, especially in the beautiful Psalms, and I am in no sense discounting your encouraging message from God, but it could also mislead people seeking real answers, especially someone who had committed themselves, before opening the Bible to follow whatever instructions they would find. This could be someone who is at the end of their proverbial rope and is desperate to follow any solution.

The danger of this method is illustrated by the humorous story the old preacher shared with his people on Sunday. He exhorted them to beware of the open and point method and shared the outcome of one poor soul. The preacher explained that this desperate person had blown the dust off his Bible and was tearfully asking God for answers. He was desperate and had determined he would follow whatever exhortation he discovered. He randomly opened his Bible with eyes shut and put his finger on the verse. He then opened his eyes excited to see God's answer under his finger. The verse he read was, "And he went out and hanged himself." He recoiled in horror and decided he must need to try it again to receive his answer from God. Again, he randomly opened his Bible with his eyes shut and placed his finger on another verse. He opened his eyes and desperately looked under his finger to read, "Go thou and do likewise."

The open and point method not only fails to use the important context of a particular passage, but it can sometimes be dangerously misleading. Just as any of us despise being misquoted or having our words taken out of context (which is so often done in the media), so does God and His words are the most important of all time with eternal weight. Although it is fun to use this open and point method sometimes, it is to be understood for what it is. It may be good for an encouraging promise out of the Psalms, but it is not careful and accurate study of God's Word and His will for our lives under the direction and context given by the Holy Spirit.

The Danger of Missing the Treasure

One of the strongest reasons for a systematic study through the whole Bible is what we miss without it. When we fail to study any major portion of God's Word, we miss the unfathomable treasure contained therein. God doesn't waste His words. He didn't bring His Word to fruition just to be filling space. He isn't guilty of useless verbiage. Every part of God's Word is precious and needful. The Holy Spirit of God inspired the following words through the apostle Paul to Timothy his son in ministry. "All Scripture is given by inspiration of God, and is profitable for doctrine, for reproof, for correction, for instruction in righteousness, that the man of God may be complete, thoroughly equipped for every good work" (2 Tim. 3:16–17). The NIV translation renders it, "All scripture is God breathed." All of it is God-breathed, which is the meaning of the original word "inspiration" here and it is very profitable for our lives, especially when we are trying to find and follow God's will. What a tragedy to miss a treasure so valuable!

Some would agree but with certain reservations. They would claim they enjoy and gain spiritual food from most of the Bible, but not all of it. Through the years people have shared with me that they have become bored or uninterested in certain portions of the Old Testament, such as Chronicles and Numbers. They seem to be able to gain the spiritual nourishment they are looking for in some books but not in others. I understand those sentiments.

Here was my approach as I began to study many years ago. You can call it old school or meticulous or whatever you desire. Knowing that all scripture is God breathed and is profitable for my spiritual growth and all of it contains a divine reason for its inclusion, I determined to read every word believing God and searching for how He might use it in my life. Though I understand and sympathize with their struggle with certain parts of scripture and that's okay, it was intriguing to me that I began to see answers from God even in Chronicles. Recently, as I was reading through the Old Testament again, I was desperately needing an answer from God in my own life. I needed the touch and confirmation of God's Word in my heart as I studied. God knew my need and He gave me His answer about deliverance, which was the desire for which I was praying. It was one of those times when the scripture jumps off the page and into your heart. I was filled with joy and knew that God had again used His Word in my life. All of God's Word is a treasure.

The Benefit of Applying the Treasure

One of the disheartening realities of American Christianity is that we study and yet many times we don't apply what we learn. We know much of what the Bible teaches, but we don't apply much of what it teaches. Many of us have a good knowledge of the doctrines of the church and the commandment of the Great Commission, but we don't put much of it into practice. We have been preached to more than any country maybe in history, and yet we seem to do less application. We seem to have become in many regards a country of hearers and not doers. Even within the ranks of ministry there are too many who play the double life.

The great preacher of yester-year, Charles H. Spurgeon said of them,

> "May we never be priests of God at the altar, and sons of Belial outside the tabernacle door; but on the contrary, may we, as Nazianzen says of Basil, 'thunder in our doctrine, and lighten in our conversation.' We do not trust those persons who have two faces, nor will men believe in those whose verbal and practical testimonies are contradictory. As actions, according to the proverb, speak louder than words, so an ill-life will effectually drown the voice of the most eloquent ministry" (6).

We must be obedient doers of the Word and not shallow hearers only if we expect God to give us supernatural leading concerning His will for our lives. No matter how much we learn while studying, the service for which God called us will never get done until we are obedient. God fully expects us to be obedient to His Word, not just to know it, but to do it. James 1: 22–25 says with great clarity, "But be doers of the word, and not hearers only, deceiving yourselves. For if anyone is a hearer of the word and not a doer, he is like a man observing his natural face in a mirror; for he observes himself, goes away, and immediately forgets what kind of man he was. But he who looks into the perfect law of liberty and continues in it, and is not a forgetful hearer but a doer of the work, this one will be blessed in what he does." The obedient doers (not perfect ones) are the ones upon which God is seeking to pour a double portion of His blessing. They are loving, obedient children that God will use in supernatural ways for His honor and glory through the empowerment of His Spirit.

> "*W*hen we fail to apply what God has shown us in His Word, we stunt our spiritual growth. We do ourselves a great disservice by much learning and very little living."

We lose out on multitudes of blessings. We leave ourselves in the category of neglectful children that miss God's best. We should be honest with ourselves and admit that we aren't really as serious about finding and following God's will as we might claim if we really have no desire for application. Let's be honest with ourselves and move forward into the fullness of His blessing. Application of Scripture to our daily lives through the power of the Holy Spirit is the great builder of spiritual growth. As we apply Scripture to our lives we are following the guidance of the Holy Spirit and we are refusing to be conformed to the world, so that we will be transformed by the renewing of our minds. Then our lives will prove what is that good, acceptable, and perfect will of God.

The Benefit of Seeking God's Will in His Word

When studying the precious Word of God it is important that we are being spiritually attentive as we look for God's will. Go to God's Word with prayerful dependence on the Holy Spirit and with the intention and anticipation of finding God's will. Again, we don't want to pull something out of its divine context to suit our desired purposes, but we do want to have an eager heart that is seeking the will of God through His Word. The precious Holy Spirit speaks to our hearts in many ways. Allow me to share a few which have direct bearing on our subject. The Holy Spirit speaks conviction, comfort, and contentment to our hearts through His Word as we are genuinely seeking to find and follow God's will.

The Holy Spirit Speaks Conviction

When God is lovingly trying to lead us away from something that is not in line with His will, He will speak through His Word with conviction. It is wonderful while at the same time painful that God loves us enough to actually communicate with us in this way. Each time we approach the Word of God, it should be with the prayer that God will reveal to us anything that would hinder our hearing Him clearly and being in the center of His will.

> "We should seek to be convicted of barriers we have erected knowingly or unknowingly, of wrong turns, of clever deception that has taken us captive and of simply taking God for granted at times and not expressing our love for Him as He deserves."

We should seek God's daily direction from His Word with our spiritual ears listening. Anything less than an open heart to the Holy Spirit's conviction, is less than God's will for us, and leaves us vulnerable to the one who comes only to steal, kill, and destroy.

One detrimental aspect within our Christian community is that very few approach God's Word in this way, with an open heart to His loving conviction. Our immediate reaction is to run. Remember the poem "Conviction Grace" in chapter 3? See conviction through the lens of grace and love, instead of through the lens of anger and resentment as you grow in your love relationship with Christ. Even more tragic, very few approach God's Word at all. It is left on the proverbial and literal shelf. God will convict our hearts if we are spiritually lethargic and neglectful of the greatest book on the planet that He has given for the purpose of directing us. That conviction is His love speaking because the Bible is God's authoritative will for us, and His desire is for us to know that will. Heed these wise words from the Psalmist and be blessed: "How can a young man cleanse his way? By taking heed according to Your word... Direct my steps by Your word, and let no iniquity have dominion over me" (Psalm 119:9 and 133).

The Holy Spirit Speaks Comfort

When we are in need, God knows. When we hurt, He sympathizes with those hurts. When we feel like giving up, He will carry us. Speaking of Christ as our great high priest, Scripture proclaims, "For we do not have a high priest who is unable to sympathize with our weaknesses, but One who has been tested in every way as we are, yet without sin. Therefore let us approach the throne of grace with boldness, so that we may receive mercy and find grace to help us at the proper time" (Heb. 4:15–16, HCSB). When we realize not one sparrow falls without the Father's notice, we know He cares deeply for us. The Holy Spirit will speak comfort through His Word if we are seeking. He will comfort us when we are hurt and totally frustrated if we will look into His glorious book of promises and hear Him speaking to our hearts.

Through the traumas of life, God's Word is a tower of strength and a place of great refuge for me. Sometimes while waiting on the timing of God's will, we need God's comfort. Look to the Psalms, which have ministered incredible comfort to so many. We need the assurance of God's forgiveness when we have fallen. We can look at the life of the great Psalmist, David, who knew what it was to fall and be in need of forgiveness and restoration of joy. We can be lifted up and encouraged by the tender love of God in our lives. We can see our painful cut washed off, the medicine lovingly applied, and the tears wiped away by the greatest love of the universe. When we look into God's Word, we seek comfort: "Blessed be the God and Father of our Lord Jesus Christ, the Father of mercies and God of all comfort, who comforts us in all our tribulation, that we may be able to comfort those who are in any trouble, with the comfort with which we ourselves are comforted by God" (2 Cor. 1:3–4).

The Holy Spirit Speaks Contentment

One of the most beautiful ways the Holy Spirit speaks to our heart through His Word is with contentment. This is one of the main features of knowing God's will through His Word. When we are gripped by the Holy Spirit with a portion of His Word, it is priceless. When the Holy Spirit communicates through a verse or passage that immediately speaks the answer for which we have been searching, it is a heavenly experience. You are immediately aware God has spoken to you. You are filled with excitement as you contemplate being spoken to personally by Almighty God. The load of wondering and searching is lifted from your back by an unseen hand. You know the contentment that God has intended for you in your search for His perfect will. Your question is answered, your dilemma is settled, your direction is sure, and your heart is content. What a marvelous touch from the Master. The confirmation of God's Word in your decision-making is exciting and fulfilling. There is nothing in this world like it! "I will never forget Your precepts, for by them You have given me life" (Psalm 119:93).

Conclusion

The Word of God is many things to our lives. It is understanding: "Through Your precepts I get understanding; therefore I hate every false way" (Psalm 119:104). God's Word lights our way: "Your word is a lamp to my feet and a light to my path" (Psalm 119:105). God's Word is our treasure: "Therefore I love your commandments more than gold, yes, than fine gold" (Psalm 119:127)! God's Word gives us peace: "Great peace have those who love Your law, and nothing causes them to stumble" (Psalm 119:165). God's Word is enduring: "Heaven and earth will pass away, but My words will by no means pass away" (Matt. 24:35). God's Word is spirit and life: "It is the Spirit who gives life; the flesh profits nothing. The words that I speak to you are spirit, and they are life" (John 6:63). God's Word looks all the way into the deepest recesses of your soul: "For the word of God is living and powerful, and sharper than any two edged sword, piercing even to the division of soul and spirit, and of joints and marrow, and is a discerner of the thoughts and intents of the heart" (Hebrews 4:12).

If a person is really serious about finding and following the will of God, they will also have a serious desire to study the Word of God. The Word will teach us, lead us in God's direction, and answer the questions of our searching heart if we will seek it with a holy passion and energy empowered by the indwelling Holy Spirit and not our own strength. Though the world rejects God's Word and prefers to create their own pseudo truth according to their own limited knowledge and desires, here is the ultimate truth from the unlimited God of the universe: "The entirety of Your word is truth, and every one of Your righteous judgments endures forever" (Psalm 119:160). Whatever you do, don't leave God's Word out of your life. Seek the treasure. Find the treasure. USE the treasure!

Final Question to Ponder:
Am I consistently seeking God's truth principles and answers for my life in His Word, or am I neglecting it?

Chapter 8

Putting The Three Keys Together

Real-Life Illustration

*M*ost of us receive great benefit from a real life illustration. When we see a truth fleshed out in terms of everyday life, our learning many times moves from an intellectual concept to assimilated understanding. Many times Jesus used illustrations right out of people's everyday lives to convey truth they could comprehend and apply. My dad also told me many times while preparing messages that illustrations are the windows of the house that allow people to see inside. With that in mind I feel it would be most helpful to you to hopefully move these three keys from intellectual concepts to assimilated understanding with an illustration from my life.

Our church family in Florida was a wonderful place to be. It was a growing church with some of the sweetest, most loving people in the world. I was a thirty-two-year-old associate pastor/youth minister who was enjoying my country home and my church with my wonderful wife, daughter, and son. Our church had constructed a beautiful Family Life Center that was a cutting edge facility. God had blessed us greatly, and I believe it was evident to the whole county.

A Peace and Unrest in My Heart

After serving at the church for several years, I began to have questions in my heart about my role as a youth minister. Somewhere in that period of time my pastor and friend, Bro. Lynn also shared with me about some of the things he was sensing about the Lord's direction for the future. I began to pray about whether the Lord was leading me toward a new chapter in my ministry, and I was beginning to have doubts that I should continue in that ministry family. I was also questioning whether God desired to lead me in a whole new direction. It was a difficult time of ministry in my heart as I know it was for Bro. Lynn also, but God was growing me.

After struggling with the nagging doubts for quite a few months, and a few heartfelt discussions with Bro. Lynn, I began to feel I was supposed to seek God's leadership and direction for my life and ministry elsewhere. I began to sense I was out of place, though I cannot definitively explain that feeling to anyone who hasn't experienced it. I now realize this was a prime example of the unrest in one's heart I spoke of in chapter 6. There was an uneasiness in my spirit that wouldn't go away. It was not the kind of thing obvious to everyone. In fact, it might have only been obvious to my family and our staff who knew me well. I did not feel that peace and contentment that God gives when we are exactly where He wants us to be. I'm speaking of that inner peace that is in our hearts even when we would prefer to be elsewhere. With this leading in my heart, I was beginning to look for the doors through which God might lead.

The Opened and Closed Doors

I began to feel God was definitely closing the doors in Florida. He began to lay further education on my heart at that time. I had enjoyed completing a BA and an MA degree, but had always felt that someday God wanted me to further my education. As I looked into the various seminaries that God might lead me to, He touched my heart in a special way with The Criswell College in Dallas, Texas.

I took some vacation time and drove the long trip to Dallas. I had many hours in the car to share my heart with God and to sense His love and tender direction. I listened to wonderful Christian music and filled myself with praises to Christ. I shed many tears that trip as I thought about leaving the loving Christian family with whom we had grown so close.

I had begun to sense the Lord opening doors in Dallas. Dr. Paige Patterson was especially used by the Lord to encourage me in that direction. When I arrived, I went to talk with Dr. Patterson (The President of Criswell College) in his office and seek his counsel. He was a great encouragement and instrument of compassion that God used to further confirm my steps toward Dallas and The Criswell College. I was now sensing the Lord was opening doors to the Dallas area and was closing them in Florida. I was also sensing a peace in my heart about the move, while continuing to experience unrest about staying in my current assignment. Now, I knew the last piece of the pie with these three keys was the confirmation of God's Word. I knew that with a major move in my family's life that God would give absolute assurance of His perfect will if it was in fact His will. That's what I was seeking. That was what my heart still needed for an immovable spiritual confidence.

The Confirmation of God's Word

It was a great "defining moment" the day God answered my prayer for the confirmation of His Word in this move. I had gone to chapel at the Criswell College on the week I had come to visit. I enjoyed the hearty singing of the students as I joined my voice to theirs and the atmosphere of Christ's love that seemed to literally engulf me that morning. I listened to the beloved president, Dr. Patterson, as he made some announcements and proceeded to make several comments that revealed a master prankster with a quick wit. The students and the faculty enjoyed every syllable of his comments, and there was a love pointed back toward him that was akin to children looking up to their beloved Dad. It was just what God had intended for me and I was totally at peace. I was ready to hear from God.

Dr. Patterson introduced Dr. Charles McLaughlin as the speaker in chapel that morning. I had never seen him before in my life, but he was respected by Dr. Patterson and that was good enough for me. Dr. McLaughlin seemed to be dripping with love that day as he came to the pulpit. It was obvious he was a sweet man who had spent many years walking with Christ. He spoke that morning from Hebrews 11 on the life of faith.

It was intriguing that he would be speaking about the life of faith on the only day I had traveled across the country to be there. It was a great step of faith I was staring at, to move my family from loved ones in Florida to a city in Texas where we didn't know anybody. Dr. Patterson was the only person that I knew in Dallas, other than Dr. Burns, another Criswell professor whom I knew from another seminary. Faith was definitely the issue. I didn't really know anybody; I didn't have a job, or a place to live. I didn't have a church ministry to come to and I didn't even know which part of the city we would choose to search for our home. I truly did not know where we would be going. There were no details, only God's direction.

What I did have, were doors that seemed to be closing in Florida and opening in Texas, and an unrest about remaining in Florida while feeling a complete peace and excitement about moving to Texas. I had two of the three elements I had learned to look for to be sure I was following God's will rather than my own. Though I didn't know it when I walked into chapel that morning, the third element would come from God's Word through the message of Dr. Mac. As he was preaching from Hebrews 11, I felt the great peace of God in my heart. He finally came to verse eight, which says, "By faith Abraham obeyed when he was called to go out to the place which he would receive as an inheritance. And he went out, not knowing where he was going." Boom! The spiritual explosion hit me. The tears started streaming down my face and a lump jumped up in my throat. I was in that moment gripped and assured as the Holy Spirit spoke His answer by way of application to my waiting heart. It was one of those unexplainable experiences when the Scripture actually jumps

176

from the pages of the Bible and into your heart. It was a supernatural answer. It was God speaking to me in such a loud and clear way that it was overwhelming. I knew in that wonderful moment that God had confirmed my direction from His precious Word.

It was perfect. Abraham was told to go and he obeyed the voice of God even though he had no details on where he was going. He just knew God had spoken to him to step out in faith and trust God's direction. If you look in my old study Bible today, you will see the words, "Coming to Texas" written out to the side of Hebrews 11:8. God had said to go. Even though I had no details on where or how, we were going. God's direction had been given and confirmed and it was time for one thing, obedience.

My Personal Answer

One of the beauties of God's Word is that He can speak to you personally concerning your own life. I don't imagine that anyone else in chapel that day got the exact same answer I did, though it is possible. Most likely, there was no one else there that day who got hit with the power of the bomb that exploded in my heart. Certainly God was using His Word to speak to everyone there in many different ways, but I'm speaking about that special communication of the Holy Spirit as He answers a major decision/direction prayer in a personal and powerful way. Those are the times when the Scripture jumps out at you and you are overwhelmed at the personal communiqué from Almighty God. Those are priceless times when you can't fully explain what happened, but you know what happened.

I want to be clear on this issue. There is one actual historical interpretation of this verse proclaiming Abraham's faith/obedience to God's directive. However, there are many applications of this "truth principle" of stepping out in faith to trust God's direction. This was not a scripture taken out of context with a forced application to fit the desired circumstances. It was simply the Scriptural "truth principle" speaking of a man whom God called upon to step out in faith. As the Holy Spirit forcefully applied that truth to my heart that morning, it then became a matter concerning my actions of stepping out in faith and trusting my God. It was about me going forward in God's direction, even though I didn't know the details of where, and the confirmation in my heart that I was being called to take that step of faith.

There have been many times in which God has given me His answers through the truth principles in His Word. I have shared this one personal experience to illustrate and illuminate the working of the three elements mentioned in chapters five, six, and seven, and how they worked in my own life. I pray this brief testimony is an encouragement to you that you can do the same. If you know Christ, you have the same indwelling Spirit within you. There are, of course, those clear directives in God's Word such as the Great Commandment in Matthew 22:37–38, and the Great Commission in Matthew 28:19–20 for which we already have our marching orders. There are also many times when certain quick decisions have to be made from the peace or unrest in your heart and the knowledge of what will be in line with God's Word from your accumulated prayer and study. However, most of the important decisions in life can be made with the spiritual confirmation of putting the three elements together; at least, that has been the case in my life. It is a wonderful assurance to have the absolute confidence we are moving in God's direction. That is what so many are desperately searching for today.

My Prayer for You

My prayer for you, my sweet friend, is that you will find and follow God's perfect will for your life. Do not listen to the lies of the enemy that it cannot happen. It is very obvious that God has a will and plan for us. It is also very obvious that He wants us to know it, because His heart's desire is for us to fulfill it. Stop living in the past and jump in now! "Forgetting those things which are behind and reaching forward to those things which are ahead..." (Phil. 3:13). You can do it!

" *The* way won't always be an easy one, but, it will always be the right one and in the end the most fulfilling one."

The unspeakable rewards will far outweigh the difficulties along the way. As Paul says in Romans 8:18, "For I consider that the sufferings of this present time are not worthy to be compared with the glory which shall be revealed in us." I passed a car the other day that had this very inspiring message written on the back window in large letters, "The pain that you've been feeling can't compare to the joy that is coming" (Rom. 8:18). You can be a champion for Christ. Even if it seems you have failed at everything else (I think many of us struggle with that feeling), you can be a real winner and a person who will leave an impact on this world if you will surrender everything into His hands and determine that nothing will stop you from finding and following God's will. May the Lord supernaturally empower you and bless you as you go. In Christ you can!

Final Question to Ponder:
Am I being attentive to the confirmations that God is giving me?

III

Progressions Toward Knowing God's Will

1. Discouragement: The Great Defeater
2. Prayer: The Great Ingredient
3. Lordship: The Great Issue
4. You: The Great Champion

Chapter 9

Discouragement: The Great Defeater

Dealing With Discouragement and Depression

*O*f all the roadblocks thrown in the way of the Christian seeking to find and follow the will of God, discouragement can be one of the most deadly. Though it doesn't appear like a serious problem at first glance, its force has toppled more than a few great warriors. Its painful grip has been felt by all, and its deadly grip has been experienced by too many.

Discouragement and depression are favorite arrows in the devil's quiver. He shoots them as an expert because of his vast experience. If I am being honest and transparent, I am being hit by a few even as I write this book. He knows the perfect places and times to shoot them into the heart of his victim. He knows these arrows can cause deadly infections if left embedded without medical treatment by the Great Physician. He realizes that a small wound can become a very serious problem with the proper amount of time and neglect.

If you are now hurting and discouraged and wondering if there is any real hope, or if in the past you have been, this chapter is shared out of love and compassion for you. The good news is that God is more powerful than anything you may be facing, including discouragement and depression. If you are in a dark place right now, my prayer is that you will cry out to the Lord, listen to His voice as

He prompts your heart, and continue to read asking Him to restore your hope.

God Is Able

Sweet friend, God is all-powerful. He is still on the throne! Though sometimes your circumstances may scream He is not, that is a lie meant to keep you trapped down in your dark hole of depression. The enemy also incessantly whispers the same thing, but it is a lie. Your problem hasn't dethroned Him or pulled Him from His place of ultimate authority. He reigns and He loves you more than anyone else ever could. He wants the best for you more than you want it for yourself. He wants to use your life in a supernatural way to impact lives for Christ. His desires toward you are love, strength, and restoration to fulfill His purpose, not discouragement and depression to fulfill the enemy's purpose. Jesus said, "The thief does not come except to steal, and to kill, and to destroy. I have come that they may have life, and that they may have it more abundantly" (John 10:10). He loves you so much that He paid the ultimate price for loving you. He died that you may have life and have it more abundantly.

God is the one who spoke the world into existence. He created it out of nothing. A. W. Tozer spoke of the awesome power of God when he wrote,

> "The Word of God is quick and powerful. In the beginning He spoke to nothing, and it became something. Chaos heard it and became order; darkness heard it and became light. 'And God said...and it was so' (Gen. 1:9). These twin phrases, as cause and effect, occur throughout the Genesis story of creation. The said accounts for the so. The so is the said put into the continuous present" (1).

To put it simply, He is absolutely, positively, without question, able and willing to speak hope into your life and bring restoration. He spoke and there was light. He spoke and there was an atmosphere. He spoke and there were seas, land, and vegetation. He spoke and the stars responded. He spoke all creatures into existence. He created man, then woman. He commanded the waters to flood the earth. He commanded them to recede. He parted the mighty waters of the Red Sea. He made water come out of a rock and food fall from heaven. He made the lame walk, the blind see, the dead walk out of the grave, and the sun stand still. He caused the barren to give birth, the poor to find plenty, and the enemy to drop dead. He made the rod turn into a snake, the donkey speak, the mountains shake, the water into wine, the winds be still, and countless other actions that manifest His omnipotence. There is absolutely no doubt that inconceivable power sits on the throne of heaven. Because He did all that, you know in your heart of hearts that He is more than able to intervene in your life and with one word of Almighty authority command hope to return. From David's broken heart he cried out, "Restore to me the joy of Your salvation, and uphold me by Your generous Spirit" (Psalm 51:12).

God Is Wise

When God allows us to go through the fiery furnace, as in the case of Shadrach, Meshach, and Abed-Nego, it is to burn off the bands of bondage and make us stronger through His empowerment to fulfill His purpose and bring Him glory. Just as the Hebrew children were thrown into the furnace, sometimes we wonder why God allows the circumstances He does. Though they courageously proclaimed their absolute loyalty and devotion to the Lord regardless of the outcome, sometimes we cry out and even show our anger. We come to the end of our rope. We prepare ourselves to give up. We look for a way out. We get desperate. We even scream and weep and tremble. Sometimes we do give up and cry out, "I quit!"

A Startling Lesson

I will never forget him screaming in my face. He was a huge, mean man that seemed bent on hurting me. His name was Senior Drill Sergeant Perry. He informed me, like a Doberman with teeth barred informs the mailman that he was going to be my mother, my father, my brother, and my sister for the next two months. I had just been yelled off the bus for my basic training in the United States Army at Fort Leonardwood, Missouri. It was a rude, very rude awakening!

Through two grueling months this mean, hateful man and his staff of hateful DI's (Drill Instructors) made my life miserable. Though his insane staff did most of the dirty work, I always knew he was behind it all. He made a point of pushing me farther than I could go. He and his henchmen intentionally made me mad and got me up in the middle of the night for the sheer joy of harassment. He made me continue to clean my weapon when it didn't need cleaning. He humiliated me in front of my whole company of fellow soldiers. He made me crawl under a barbed wire fence until I was bleeding. He dropped me for pushups until complete exhaustion had taken over for the sheer delight of it. He dropped me out of a chopper in the middle of a forest in the middle of the night and told me to avoid capture by the enemy (veteran experienced soldiers) while they were swarming and searching for me to drag me back to a POW camp (staffed by other drill sergeants that weren't happy to be there). He screamed in my face in such a way that I wondered when he was going to take a bite. He was a genuine nightmare in combat boots. I just couldn't understand this man and his ways, and anger was welling up in me.

At one point, I had had all I could take. One day as we were standing in formation and looking directly into the bright sunlight, I was squinting my eyes because of the glare. He called me out in front of everyone and accused me of sleeping while he was talking. I immediately responded with, "No I wasn't!" After my response he immediately punished my whole platoon making sure they all knew it was because of me that they were suffering through extra pain and hardship. Also, that weekend, which was supposed to be my first days off, he dropped me off at a five-acre field of tall grass with a push mower and two large cans of gas and told me he would see me later as they drove away. Needless to say I thought of him all weekend as anger boiled inside of me.

Touching My Heart Forever

After all those terrible weeks of wondering what I had gotten myself into, I saw something that changed my thoughts, and to some degree my whole life perspective. We had finally made it through basic training and were preparing to graduate. The weeks had gone by slowly and the drill instructors had gotten worse as time went on. I was looking forward to getting as far away as possible from these terrorists called, "Drill Sergeants." We had gone to great pains to get ready for graduation. We had starched uniforms, polished brass, spit shined shoes, and everything was immaculately in place. We looked like the soldiers you see on TV marching in formation and looking sharp. Just as we took our positions in the formation to march to the graduation ceremonies, Senior Drill Sergeant Perry had a few words to say. They were words that would end up touching my heart forever.

He began to share his heart. He told us that everything he had tried to do over the past eight weeks was done for the sole purpose of keeping us alive if we found ourselves stepping off a plane in Vietnam. He said we were good men and that he cared about us. I was stunned. He shared with us that he didn't always enjoy doing some of the things he did, but he knew for our sakes, he had to be as hard as possible. He had to prepare us for the hellish scene we might have to face in the near future. The final picture lodged in my heart is of this huge man, barely able to get his words out, a man that I believe had killed men in combat, that had seen the worst of a bloody, brutal war, yet he was barely able to speak because of emotion. I have tears in my eyes now as I think about him all these forty-six years later.

I learned a valuable lesson that day. Although I couldn't understand at the time, this man cared for me. He had my best interests at heart, though it seemed that the opposite was true.

"*M*any times what appears to be love in this world is not love and many times what appears to not be love is the epitome of it."

All the pain, the trials, the struggle, the emotion, and all that time was for my benefit. I certainly wanted to crawl out of it many times, but that day I was glad I didn't. I love Senior Drill Sergeant Perry and the other DIs. I doubt that I will ever have the privilege of seeing him again, but if I do, or if he ever sees this book, I want to thank him for teaching an eighteen-year-old kid one of the most important lessons in life. That lesson is the critical importance of basic training and of one who cares enough to push you and prepare you for battle.

Though I am in no way comparing Senior Drill Sergeant Perry to our great Heavenly Father, I am using the "truth principle" that I learned to understand an important feature of my life. I know that even though I don't understand my circumstances, though I may get weary, frustrated, tired, and angry, even though I may see no light at the end of the tunnel, and even though I may be ready to give up, my precious Father in heaven loves me, intimately. He is preparing me for further service. He is perfecting the skills needed for the future conflict. He has my best interests at heart. He knows exactly what I need. I know that although He would fight any foe for me, He must do what He knows is best. I can sense the compassionate tears in His voice as He shares His love for me. Though there are many times I would like to crawl out of the situations I am in, after He has taken me through them, I'm glad that I didn't. I can cling to the wonderful assurance that God loves me sacrificially and unconditionally which was proven on a hill just outside Jerusalem.

"*I* might not understand the circumstance, but I understand the love of the One behind it."

I will be very honest with you. I didn't understand these things when I was younger, but I take great joy in looking back at His love and faithfulness as I understand them better now. The apostle Paul said, "For this reason I also suffer these things; nevertheless I am not ashamed, for I know whom I have believed and am persuaded that He is able to keep what I have committed to Him until that Day" (2 Tim. 1:12). He also explains his assurance in Christ when he states, "Who shall separate us from the love of Christ? Shall tribulation, or distress, or persecution, or famine, or nakedness, or peril, or sword? As it is written: 'for Your sake we are killed all day long; we are accounted as sheep for the slaughter.' Yet in all these things we are more than conquerors through Him who loved us. For I am persuaded that neither death nor life, nor angels nor principalities nor powers, nor things present nor things to come, nor height nor depth, *nor any other created thing, shall be able to separate us from the love of God which is in Christ Jesus our Lord"* (Rom. 8:35–39, author's italics). Hallelujah! Nothing can separate me from Him, not even death! That is your greatest assurance to hold on to. Hold On!

Caution with the Causes

The causes for discouragement are as varied as the people that experience them. Thousands of things seem to be able to set off the great defeater in our lives. Sometimes small things do the trick for the adversary and at others it is major trauma. Whatever the cause is, it is always wise to seek God's guidance and develop prudent caution. When you see certain trigger points occurring as they have before, you can discern a setup. We can be better prepared to deal with the same set of thoughts or circumstances by being watchful and vigilant. First Peter 5:8 gives us this warning when it says, "Be sober, be vigilant; because your adversary the devil walks about like a roaring lion, seeking whom he may devour." The Amplified Bible adds more descriptive language when it states, "Be well-balanced—temperate, sober-minded; be vigilant and cautious at all times, for that enemy of yours, the devil, roams around like a lion roaring [in fierce hunger], seeking someone to seize upon and devour." We can, with Godly wisdom, be ready and prepared for the battle by being alert and by putting on the whole armor of God detailed in Ephesians 6. Though all our experiences differ and I am sure you can insert your own experience at this point, let me share one of the causes of discouragement within the life of a minister that will also have application to your life.

The Monster of Failure

Of all the numerous challenges which the minister faces, few can have the devastating effect of the perception of failure (something all of us from every walk of life deal with), especially when you feel like you are failing God in what He has called you and equipped you to do. I want you to notice that I wrote, the perception of failure. Many times, it is nothing more than the nagging perception of failure which we allow to simmer that causes the most extensive damage. Some of the greatest preachers of recent history have experienced this monster. Dr. Warren Wiersbe, in his informative book, *Walking With The Giants*, shares of many great preachers of yesteryear who faced severe discouragement. He speaks of F. W. Robertson:

> "The young man died at the age of thirty-seven after only thirteen years of ministry; and when he died, he considered himself a failure" (2).

Of the great scholar Alexander Maclaren he writes:

> "Surprisingly, Maclaren was haunted all his life by a sense of failure... He sometimes spoke of each Sunday's demands as, 'a woe', and he was certain that his sermon was not good enough and that the meeting would be a failure" (3).

Of R. W. Dale, he writes:

> "A dark thread of depression ran through Dale's life, and often he spoke of 'the strange, morbid gloominess' that he had to battle, sometimes for weeks at a time" (4).

Of Joseph Parker, he says:

> "Yet, beneath Parker's rough exterior and dramatic pose was a feeling of inferiority that tortured him" (5).

In reference to a book written on the life of J. Hudson Taylor, Wiersbe writes:

> "But the real bombshell in the Pollock book is his claim that in 1869, during the darkest hours of the mission, Hudson Taylor was so discouraged that he was tempted to end his own life" (6)!

After his death, W. E. Sangster's son found a handwritten note which his father had written that stated:

> "'I am a minister of God and yet my private life is a failure in these ways...' Then he listed eight areas of defeat. He concluded: 'I have lost peace... I have lost joy... I have lost taste for my work... I feel a failure...' He ultimately found victory, although at times his depression was so acute that he considered resigning from the ministry" (7).

It is known that Spurgeon haggled with severe depression. George W. Truett was ready to quit the ministry because he was so discouraged with self-guilt after a hunting accident in which he accidentally shot a friend. I personally heard Billy Graham in a TV interview say that he felt he had failed in many things in his life, though on a personal note my own father surrendered his life to Christ and was saved at one of his crusades. Another young minister wrote the following in his personal journal at a difficult time in his life while he was waiting and wondering if God was ever going to use him. He wrote,

> "I am now in the bottom of a hole that I never thought I would be in. I'm tired of trying. I'm ready to give up working part-time and going to school. I can't take care of my family decently. I can't pay my bills and have to call my parents to send money. I can't find a church that wants me after being in the ministry full time for nine years. I've been looking for a ministry for the whole one year and 30 days that I have been here, without one positive response. I feel like my ministry and gifts are being wasted. I find anger in my heart which I never dreamed would be there. I call it frustration to others, but there is also anger. I am beginning to wonder if God has called me to preach. Between singing and preaching, I've always wondered. I am emotionally tired of beating my head against a brick wall. I am hurt and I am hurting and I don't understand. Oh God, if You really want to use me in Your ministry, I've got to know. I've got to know or my heart will give up even if my body continues to go through the motions. Oh God, if You've called me to preach then give me a church or I am going to give up. If You haven't really called me to preach, I can't go on. Oh God, give me a church to pastor, or I quit" (8)!

This young minister was not saying he would quit in a spoiled kind of way. He was saying it with a humble, pleading, and broken heart. He was going through a breaking process. God was breaking him much the same way a cowboy has to break a wild horse in order to make it mature, productive, and reliable. If you would have asked this young minister before this period in his life if he had ever seriously considered giving up, he would have said, "Of course not!"

> " *I* know this young minister quite well, you see, he is me."

To be honest, I didn't want to share this part of my life. Though it is always painful to share weaknesses, God has answered specific prayer to let me know that He wanted me to share this moment with you. I never thought that I could feel and say those things, but I did. Again I say I would never have shared this experience of my own accord, but my Lord said to include it. I must conclude that He will use it as an encouragement to another heart that is struggling. You see, God did answer my humble prayer. He put me exactly where He wanted me to be in His perfect time. He has blessed me graciously and abundantly. He is using me to His honor and glory.

Focus on His "After"

Let me share a special encouragement from God's Word in the midst of difficulty. First Peter 5:6–10 shares many vital truths with us, but there is one phrase in particular that I want you to focus on. That phrase is, "after you have suffered a while" in verse 10: "Therefore humble yourselves under the mighty hand of God, that He may exalt you in due time, casting all your care upon Him, for He cares for you. Be sober, be vigilant; because your adversary the devil walks about like a roaring lion, seeking whom he may devour. Resist him, steadfast in the faith, knowing that the same sufferings are experienced by your brotherhood in the world. But may the God of all grace, who called us to His eternal glory by Christ Jesus, *after you have suffered a while*, perfect, establish, strengthen, and settle you" (author's italics). That was one of those touching moments when the Holy Spirit used those words from Scripture to grip my heart and encourage my soul. What an encouragement to my heart those few words were. He was assuring me that though I was moving through a difficult time, the end result would be that He would instill maturity, a strong footing, strength, and a settled trust and confidence. From that day many years ago, until now as an older pastor, that phrase has continued to be an incredible encouragement to my heart.

> "*I*f you are walking the path of suffering, put your focus on His 'after.'"

The Trap of Believing the Label

Zig Ziglar, the well-known Bible teacher and motivational speaker from Dallas said in his Sunday school class one morning at First Baptist Church of Dallas as I was there listening, "Failure is an event, not a person." As I thought about that statement, I realized even more that many people think of failure as their identity. Their whole life is pervaded by the awful hiss of the word that sounds strangely like the hiss of a serpent in a garden. They have ceased to think of themselves as who they really are in Christ and have submitted to believing they have metamorphosed into a failure and will always be a failure. They have fully accepted that definition as their life truth though they may never admit that to anyone else.

To be honest, I believe there have been times in my own life when I actually have believed that is who I am. Yes, as someone who has studied God's Word all his adult life, I know the Scriptures that speak of my identity in Christ and being more than a conqueror through Him. I have memorized numerous scriptures that speak of my position in Christ, the unlimited power of the Holy Spirit within me, and my inheritance as a child of God. I have even seen the power of Christ manifested in defeating dark spiritual forces. However, I am just being real and honest about the internal dialogue in my mind at times after particularly crushing failures and spiritual attacks. My mind would whisper, "You are one, big, hunk of failure. You will never amount to much. You ruined your life years ago. You can't function like others can…no wonder you are going nowhere fast" and the list of self-inflicted wounds (with a hissing voice in the background) could go on and on.

Sometimes a pastor has really poured his heart and soul into study and prayer through the week, he has done spiritual warfare, he feels God's hand on him, and he has prepared in every way possible to be able to explode with the power of the Holy Spirit of God in the pulpit. Then the anticipated Sunday morning comes. He preaches with unusual freedom and clarity. He senses the power of the Holy Spirit flowing through him like water through a fireman's hose. The invitation time comes and the plea is made. The pastor takes his traditional place in front of the pulpit to wait on those who will respond. The first verse is sung and nobody makes a move. He speaks reassuringly to himself, "Nobody usually moves on the first verse anyway." The second verse is sung and still nobody comes. This time the accusing thoughts begin to roll like water over the falls. Self-accusation begins to spew out like a Roman candle at a July 4th celebration. "I could have done more this week," he says to himself. "I could have encouraged more people to go out on visitation. I could have shared the gospel with more people. I could have spent more time in prayer. I could have sent out more cards and letters. I could have made better preparations for my message. I could have communicated with more love. I could have, I could have, I could have…" and as all these thoughts roll through the slide projector of the mind, one preeminent theme superimposes itself over them all: "I AM A FAILURE!"

At times we ministers unfortunately judge our whole worth and success by certain numbers. You can insert your own false standard of success for your life here. We would probably claim that we don't, but it is always there in our minds and it is weaponized by some who judge "everything" by numbers. We meticulously watch the attendance in Sunday school for any downturn which would signal our failure. We carefully keep track of the number of baptisms for the current year as opposed to the previous year. If we don't surpass last year's number, we believe we have failed miserably and sometimes begin to think about leaving the church. If the membership of the church doesn't grow at a faster rate than the previous year, we are enveloped in a depression and discouragement that threatens our spiritual health and in many cases our physical health as well. If the offerings aren't what they should be, and they almost never are, frustration gnaws at us. We know it is our responsibility for not sharing enough stewardship emphasis. We perceive we have failed to have the right numbers, the prosperous numbers, the impressive numbers, the expected numbers, and the supernatural numbers as do some of the "other" churches.

> "Though we masterfully put on a good face, deep down, many times we feel like failures."

Though I certainly am not speaking on behalf of vocational ministers and I am sure many of them don't struggle with these issues, especially after they have matured through the years; I have certainly had many pastor brothers through my journey that have, and this is meant as an encouragement to them.

Sometimes ministers have problems within the family. We have an argument and are no longer the unstained, pristine examples we expect ourselves to be. Perhaps we've made a bad financial decision and have been caught up in the credit card mania which should only be for carnal people. We have a problem with our teenagers and feel the sting of hypocrisy when sharing about godly parents. We have failed to spend the appropriate time in God's Word. We have slipped away from the habit of a daily quiet time of prayer because we have poured ourselves so thoroughly into our preparation and study. We wonder sometimes to ourselves, "How can I possibly stand and preach the Word of God when I have failed God so badly this week?"

Again, though we are skilled at putting on a good face, we still feel the sting of failure. We then sometimes become blanketed with a suffocating cocoon of discouragement. All my pastor brothers who read this will be able to relate to some degree as I hope all of you will in your own journey of dealing with being constantly self-critical. While in this cocoon some years ago, I wrote the following prayer poem to the Lord which I have never made public before:

"Desperately Trusting"

The numbers are dwindling, each one takes a toll
The pews are so empty, it tortures my soul
I cry out to God, this cannot go on
I'm dying inside, though a smile I put on
They're dying and sick and moving away
Oh Lord please, don't take another today
I feel like a failure, like I've failed You Lord
A good church should grow, be fulfilled and restored
I cannot go on, without Your embrace
The future looks dim, please fill me with grace
Though I cannot see, just around the bend
My hope, and faith, on You still depend
I'm believing this Red Sea will part by Your hand
That Jericho's walls before You can't stand
I'm desperately trusting that chariots of fire
Will conquer and burn up my enemy's desire
I cry out in pain from the depths of my soul
GOD MOVE!
GOD SPEAK!
AND SHOW YOUR CONTROL (9)!

Whatever your position in life or however these principles apply in your journey, the monster of failure has more than likely come after you. When we don't feel we've made the grade, we feel like failures. When we don't measure up to our peer group's standard of success, we feel like failures. When we don't accomplish what our good friend does, we feel like failures. When the jaws of this beast really get a hold of you, it becomes very difficult to kill and sometimes you just try to keep it in the cage. We struggle to ignore it and claim it isn't there. We try to say we will not allow it to continue to have a hold on us. Usually we will not even let anyone else know we feel that way. It is a lonely place because a pastor doesn't feel it is appropriate to share these struggles with the very ones he is trying to help past their struggles, and feels he should protect his beloved wife and family from them. We fast and pray to seek God's wisdom and strength. We fill our days so full we don't have any time to think about it. We try to deal it a death blow in our own strength or according to our own plan. We plod on and on like real troopers, but seem to have little effect on the beast still very alive in the cage.

My Sweet Friend Didn't Make It

To take this issue to another level and illustrate the depth and bondage of prolonged depression without finding freedom through the power of Christ, please listen to the following. With some hesitance I feel compelled to share a few words about a sweet friend of mine who struggled greatly with depression. Knowing him, I believe he would want me to share if it could help minister some insight and encouragement to someone else. I wrote the following thoughts shortly after I found out that Tom had tragically ended his life after a lifelong struggle with the chains of depression and its twin brother hopelessness. It has been less than a year as I write this, and it is still difficult. With permission from his sweet wife who we love, I share these words to honor his life and help someone else.

Tom was a good friend in my small group Bible study for four years, with a beautiful family, and I grew to love him and enjoy him greatly. I have rarely laughed so hard as I did when Tom was telling stories or giving his input in our study and discussion times. Games and trips were always more fun with him around. He was one of those rare individuals that was not only a beloved character, but was just naturally funny without trying. He could just look at me and I would laugh. We would joke with each other on an ongoing basis and sometimes say just one special word that would make us both laugh out loud. He was a beloved and special part of our family and it is hard to believe that he is gone. It is safe to say that he will be missed deeply from all of us who experienced his quick wit, his giving heart, his warm hugs, and his magnetic personality.

Appearance, especially a very humorous facade can be very deceiving, as it was with Tom. I know that underneath that unique wit and funny persona was deep hurt. He shared a few things in our small group concerning some of his struggles, but I certainly didn't know the depth of it until later, though I'm sure his family did. It is intriguing to me that some of the funniest people in our world seem to be at the same time some of the most tortured inside. My thoughts run back to Chris Farley, a very famous comedian in America that I thought was one of the funniest people of all time. If I spoke of a classic skit he did about living in a van down by the river, many of you would have an immediate memory. I rarely laughed so hard as when I saw him perform and yet he died sad, lonely, and addicted.

A Humor Mask?

We all ask ourselves questions when we face this kind of loss and heartache. Is the humor an escape mechanism? Do they use humor to mask the underlying pain for a while? Is the greatest humor evidence of the greatest internal pain? Is great humor created from great pain? Does the humor give them a short reprieve from facing difficult reality and dealing with those things that are destroying them like whatever addictions are present? Do they essentially hide behind it? Do they finally live through humor so much that it becomes their only coping mechanism? Do they finally realize that no amount of humor can mask the overwhelming needs of their tortured soul, lose hope, and make a decision that they cannot live another day? After trying to overcome the bondage of various addictions in their lives for many years, what finally clicks that pushes them to actually carry out that final decision? Do they end up pushing everyone away that tries to intervene? Should we try to have a heart-to-heart talk with someone we love that seems to live through humor while giving us some signals about the depth of their struggle and pain? How can I possibly understand this better to rescue someone before it's too late? And the list goes on.

For some who I have loved like Tom, it became overwhelming. Though I know his sweet family did everything they could think of to help rescue him, he had been pulled into such a dark place by the enemy of our soul that he saw no way out and no hope. On top of that I believe that the enemy had filled Tom's mind with the lie that he was beyond hope and help and that he was nothing but a burden to his family and everyone else. I believe in his last days he thought it was too late for him and that his constant string of failures would only lead to more and worse failures. I believe he had truly come to believe that his identity was failure. If that has been the dialogue in your mind, then I pray that your heart will hear these true words. That was not true for him, and it is not true for you!

What I feel sure of is that this loving man would not want you to follow his path. He would want you to see the signs and do whatever is necessary to get off the road before you get to where he was. I believe he would want you to avoid any addiction in your life because it exponentially adds to the darkness and gives the enemy a stronger foothold. If you already struggle with the grips of addiction, I believe he would want you to join groups like Celebrate Recovery that will surround you with spiritual support and resources. I believe he would get in your face and say, "Do whatever is necessary to get help now and not travel as far as I did down that road!" I believe he would say, "Look at your beautiful wife, your beautiful kids, and your beautiful grandkids that need you." I believe he would say, "You can do it, you must do it, get off the road now!"

I have sat through funerals like Tom's with many questions cycling through my mind and tears rolling down my face. For me the questions continue. Some of them will most likely never be answered this side of heaven. Having been in pastoral ministry for over 40 years and trying to help many sweet, loving people through some dark times, it is still difficult though I have a much clearer perspective now. There are a couple things that I think are very important to remember. First, we cannot judge the depth of these struggles by the externals as those who are depressed become quite skillful at camouflage. Second, this problem is very serious like a cancer of the soul and if not overcome through the power and authority of Christ and the love and support of the body of Christ, it can be deadly. Do not take it lightly and try to overcome it in your own strength. Don't hesitate to reach out to trusted spiritual leaders and friends in your life who can help refer you to all kinds of great Christian counseling and resources, and to some loving prayer support you need.

I have shared briefly of Tom's story for a few reasons. One is that I want to be Tom's voice in giving you a wake-up call if you are in a dark place. Listen to his voice. Another reason is to let you know that you are not alone. Others are struggling also, even though they put on a beautiful mask. Most importantly I want you to know that you are not beyond hope and help.

"There are no chains on you that Christ can't break!"

That is the absolute truth! Hear this truth from Jesus Himself when He said, "All authority has been given to Me in heaven and on earth" (Matt. 28:18). He has all authority! There is nothing in your life that He does not have authority over. When you surrender everything to Christ and place your trust completely in Him, He will speak in His ultimate authority and speak hope into your heart. I have shared about Tom's struggle as a provocative wake-up call but want you to hear these following words as your hope. I have known hundreds of people Christ has delivered from the chains of darkness. I have seen many that were convinced there was no hope and certainly no freedom because of their bondage and addictions, including one young man who told me his story years ago. He was in such a dark place of depression that he was sitting in a room by himself with a .357 Magnum in his mouth. Ready to pull the trigger he desperately cried out to the Lord one last time as his last hope. Though he had no strength or hope of his own, Christ heard him and spoke hope back into his life. He is now a loving servant of Christ, living in freedom and serving Him with joy. His story can be your testimony. Yes it can! Christ is waiting. Surrender it all and cry out!

Understanding My Sense of Failure

I will finish my story. In my personal journey the depression had to do with a terrible sense of failure in ministry; however, I believe that the principles and perspectives from my life that follow will be helpful for you to apply to your own life regardless of your position or situation. Many times we miss the reason behind our discouragement and depression. The real cause is secluded behind the veil of emotions. We fight to deal with a problem, sometimes without having any understanding of what brought it on. We tend not to look back and analyze (relive) the circumstances that brought us to this painful point. We try to assess the problem without looking at the core issue. Therefore, our strategy fails.

I Feel Like a Failure

As I looked at my ministry and began to try to understand this terrible sense of failure and the unshakable discouragement, I began to realize I had been judging myself and my ministry from the wrong set of success guidelines. I began to look at the reasoning behind the sense of failure, and I saw that to a great degree, it was simply my own definition of success (and the definition of many churches) that was the problem. It was my standard of measurement that caused much of my problem. Please think through this faulty reasoning with me and apply it to your own life and situation to see it through a new lens.

A Flawed Standard of Spiritual Success

I was judging myself and my ministry on the basis of worldly success. It was a sanctified and religious version, but the way I was approaching it was worldly nonetheless. It was what I had seen so many others do. It seemed it was the accepted standard that many followed. I was judging my success or failure according to several sets of numbers in the life of the church. Without fully realizing it at the time, they had become my spiritual barometer. If certain goal numbers were not reached, I felt like a failure. When certain giving initiatives fell short, I chalked it up as my failure. When other numbers were not what I expected them to be, I felt like a failure. This feeling of failure was compounded when certain people would use numbers as weapons to assert pressure and additional pain which just compounded the sense of failure.

The plethora of numbers can take on a life of their own and become stifling as you get caught up in a numbers game. I didn't realize it at the time as a young minister, but that was my thought process. I was striving to faithfully share the gospel and preach the Word of God, but many times the responses were disappointing which once again would add to a sense of failure. As I contemplated this dilemma I thought, "What can be said of the great missionaries that gave their whole lives preaching to see a handful of souls saved in a foreign land or jungle somewhere? What can be said of missionaries like Jim Elliott and his young missionary buddies in Ecuador who were speared to death on a river bank before even reaching the tribe for Christ? Were they completely unsuccessful? Was their work without spiritual merit? Were they pathetic failures because of certain numbers?" I knew in my heart they were absolutely not failures in God's eyes.

God's Standard of Spiritual Success

Let me be quick to state that numbers are good and useful and were created by our perfect God. Some of those precious numbers are of infinite worth in that they represent precious people for whom

Christ died. Some of those numbers help us to be good stewards of the gracious resources God has provided. Other numbers give us the ability to meet pressing needs and minister the love of Christ in foreign places. Numbers were not the problem. My misuse of numbers was the problem. Measuring my ministry success by my own imposed set of numbers, instead of by my priority of love for God and faithfulness to His call in my life was the problem. I came to realize the true measure of success in God's eyes. That true measure is clearly seen in Christ's response to a young lawyer. When a young lawyer asked, "Teacher, which is the great commandment in the Law?" Jesus surprised him by saying, "You shall love the LORD your God with all your heart, with all your soul, and with all your mind. This is the first and great commandment. And the second is like it: you shall love your neighbor as yourself. On these two commandments hang all the Law and the Prophets" (Matt. 22:36–40). Wow! There you have it from the lips of the Master Himself. He clearly defined the top priority of all priorities. Concerning this unexpected but powerfully penetrating answer from Jesus, Dr. Francis Schaeffer states,

> "Here is what really matters—to love the Lord our God, to love his Son, and to know Him personally as our Savior. And if we love Him, to do the things that please Him; simultaneously to show forth His character of holiness and love in our lives; to be faithful to His truth; to walk day by day with the living Christ; to live a life of prayer" (10).

After all the hours and all the papers in Bible College and seminary, I realized that my number one priority is to love God with all my heart, soul, and mind. I am to love God with every fiber of my being. I am to be governed by my love and faithfulness to Him. I am to be faithful to love the Lord personally and the outflow of that intimate love priority will be success in His eyes.

It hit me like a light coming on in a dark room. Yes, I had heard it before, but now it took on real meaning as it became the fabric of my heart. If I'm loving God with all my being and faithfully sharing the gospel and preaching the Word of God as He has called me to do, I am successful. Can you hear me, my sweet pastor brothers out there in the small churches (the vast majority of churches), or my beloved compassionate missionaries out there in the jungle somewhere, or my beloved pastors and leaders in earthquake/drought-ravaged Haiti, or my beloved pastors in the jungles of the Philippines that walk hours and swim through a river to minister to a handful of people. That is success! That is, I realized I am successful according to the most important standard. Will I make mistakes? Most definitely! Will I be less than perfect and have problems like everyone else? You bet! The wonderful assurance is that even though I make mistakes, God loves me and is proud of me as I strive and stumble to be all He wants me to be through that priority love relationship. His hand is on me and His eye is trained on my heart.

Asking Myself Questions

I asked myself questions and answered them. It's all right to do that, you know? Can I be a success in God's eyes and pastor a small church? Yes! Can I be a success in God's eyes and not have all the impressive numbers that are always moving up on the graph? Certainly! Can I be a success in God's eyes without enjoying the exposure of the well-known ministries? Absolutely! Can I be a success in God's eyes when I don't see people coming down the aisle every time I preach? Judging from testimonies of some preachers in Scripture and many faithful missionaries, most definitely! I don't want you to misunderstand what I am saying. It's important to explain that if we are faithfully proclaiming the good news of the Gospel, and going out to share, consistently, that God will bless with souls being saved, and the time and the numbers will be completely in His sovereign hands. Sharing the gospel of Christ is simply part of our spiritual DNA. This is in no way a defense of ministers who don't share the gospel and preach the Word of God, but it is an effort to say to my hurting ministry comrades and church families that are faithfully ministering in smaller churches throughout the world, you can throw off the cloud of guilt and discouragement, knowing that you are successful in God's eyes when your loving priority is the priority commandment of Christ Himself.

God expects faithfulness and empowers us to be faithful. When we are lovingly faithful to Him and to the ministry to which He has called us, we are successful. We are responsible for loving faithfulness, not results. Each time we share the gospel, whether the person receives Christ or rejects the good news, we are successful. Each time we faithfully preach the Word of God in the power of the Holy Spirit, without compromise, we have been successful whether or not someone walks the aisle. When we are faithfully growing deeper in our daily love relationship with Jesus Christ, and we are faithfully striving to preach God's precious Word and lovingly shepherd the flock, God looks at us and sees success.

Discouragement makes us feel like giving up on finding and following God's will. Maybe you've given up on finding God's will. Tired of the endless grind? You have vowed to quit? You have decided it's easier to go your own way and survive. You will fade into the background and live as others seem to do. You will give up on unrealistic ideas of walking in the center of God's perfect will. It's too hard. You've gone too far. There's too much pressure! Please stick with me a little longer.

Decisions by Discouragement

I still remember the shock of what he said to me in the truck that day. Don (not his real name) was a young father that had completed his seminary training several years ago. He was still driving a courier truck in Dallas while waiting on God to open a door of ministry. He was an experienced courier who was teaching me the ropes as I rode along in his truck and carefully watched him that day. He shared with me that he had talked to at least one hundred churches over the last several years looking for a ministry. The discouragement was evident in his voice as he recalled several of the experiences he had encountered. Not one of those ministry interviews had worked out for him and his young family. He had seen each door close through this painful period in his life. His waiting had progressed from uncomfortable to painful discouragement. With a tinge of anger and rebellion in his voice, he proceeded to tell me of a new job. He accepted this job due to his inability to secure a ministerial position. He was now ready to strike out on his own and take whatever came along that would meet the financial needs of his family. Then the shock came.

Though I tried not to show any response on the outside, when he told me where he was going to work, my heart sank like a cannonball. Not only had he given up on finding a ministry position, he had moved completely out of the realm of jobs appropriate for a young minister whenever God did finally open up a position in His timing. His words stunned me. He said, "I'm going to work for Coor's Brewing Company." Though I fully understand that to our contemporary secular culture that would be just fine, for someone who had been called by God to preach the gospel and spend the rest of his life serving the Lord, it was a move in the wrong direction. As I struggled to figure out what to say, all kinds of things were running through my mind. He had graduated from one of the most prestigious seminaries in the country. He had some wonderful skills. He was young and had a lot going for him.

> "*I* kept shoving the question at myself. Would I ever give up like that? Would the time come that I would just give up trying and give my life to a secular job of that variety?"

I finally asked him what I had been pondering. I said, "Why in the world would you do something like that?" His response was that Coor's was the only one who had offered him enough money for his family to live on. Though I felt compassion for his plight, the inner part of my being bristled at his rationalization. I tried my best to put myself in his position. I remembered very difficult and bleak times for my family when I had started school and was desperately seeking a position in ministry. There were many times we literally had to pray for God to provide food. There were times that God had to miraculously provide to pay small bills. Money came from totally unexpected sources time and again. There was an especially low time when I was at home one day without even a quarter to go across the toll bridge and look for a job, but I never conceived of the idea of getting a job that would require me to compromise my Scriptural convictions and call from God. God had always met our needs even though it was sometimes at the last minute and always uncomfortable.

I will never forget that training day in the courier truck with Don. The tragedy of a Christian young man with great potential, deciding to move away from his calling, will always be etched in my heart. It will always be a caution light flashing in my heart when I catch myself getting caught up in the "wanting to quit syndrome." His story is unfortunately all too common. The end result of this choice is very obvious. His is a road to disappointment, and not enjoying the blessing and fulfillment of God's unique ministry purpose for his life. It is the wrong road the devil disguises to look like the right road. It is the compromise that leads to real failure. It is the tearful testimony of great regret that I shared about previously of my older friend in seminary who didn't listen to and follow God's voice in his heart. I never had any more contact with Don after that, but I hope and pray that he returned to God's direction for his life and used his wonderful gifts to glorify Him. Please don't make your decisions on the basis of discouragement, anger, and depression as it will only lead to regret.

Am I Losing My Mind?

I will open one more dark closet of my life. I will share one last experience that only my family and closest friends even know about. It is difficult for me to share, but I pray that the Lord will use it as some kind of help in your life.

Some years ago, after pastoring for many years I had an experience that took me further down a dark hole of depression than I had ever been before. For well over twenty-five years at that time, I had always just plowed through every hurt, discouragement, personal attack, and failure as they came my way. I had watched my dad just power through all kinds of horrendous hurt in his life and keep on going so that's what I tried to emulate. As with most of us, my heart had been absolutely crushed numerous times from people (and the enemy behind them) who had lashed out in bitterness, anger, and hatred, and of course great betrayal. It was one thing for the attacks to be poured out on me, but when they affected and hurt my wife and kids, it was almost more than I could endure. I had at several times truly wanted to quit and felt I couldn't go on, and if I'm being honest had pretty much packed my bags to move to the mountains in some remote place and never have to deal with people again. However, after much prayer and comfort from my loving Father, I would continue out of love for Him and knowing His design and purpose for my life.

After numerous times of being truly heartbroken and crushed through many years, I found myself once again the recipient of pointed bitterness and anger and rejection. I tried to deal with it once again as I always had by praying and plowing through and disregarding the extreme hurt and now depression in my heart. I didn't realize at that time that these hurts had been accumulating over the years and had never really been fully dealt with or healed. I had stuffed all that hurt and rejection down and just kept adding to it and turning the crank as with a Jack-in-the-Box. Please hear my loving caution if you are at that point. Don't just keep powering through it in the stubbornness and power of your own will, as even that can come from a place of self-pride.

My Breaking Point

Finally, no more could be stuffed in and my heart and mind rebelled at the decades long accumulation and abuse. I was physically sick and emotionally in great pain, as I had been many times before.

But now, there was one more overloaded part of me that pushed me over the edge. My mind! On top of the physical sickness and the emotional crushing, my mind started to spin out of control. That may not make any sense, but that is the only way I know to describe it. My thoughts started to spin like the spin cycle on a washing machine and I couldn't stop them. I became fearful that I was about to lose touch with reality and fall off of a mental cliff. It progressed to the point where I was telling my wife which Christian psychiatric hospital to take me to if she had to take me somewhere.

When I was a young minister, I am sad and embarrassed to say that I looked at some of my friends who had gone through break-downs (emotional stress) as weak and negligent in not standing strong on the promises of Scripture and the authority and position we have in Christ. In my young and immature self-confidence, I began to spout my dismissive answers with scriptures added though I had never walked in their shoes. Now I was standing in their shoes and all the immature bravado was gone, along with all my quick answers. I had always taken care of it before (or so I thought), but now my strength was helpless. The only thing I could manage to do in the midst of my spinning thoughts was to cry out to my Father. Please help me Lord and do what only You can do!

> "Here's what I really want you to hear. He answered! He is faithful! He loves me and He heard me and I know that He loves you and will hear you."

The Lord stopped the spinning in my mind which I had no control over and during the next few days gave me a new direction and a sense of peace. Over the following months, He used some incredibly loving brothers and sisters in Christ to pray for me and my family, to love us unconditionally, to stand with us and meet our needs and to start a wonderful healing process. For those of you who were part of that beloved family you know who you are and each of you will always have a very special place in my heart. Please hear me.

Your spiritual healing will not come from your strength and prideful self-will to power through; it will come as you humbly acknowledge your complete dependence on the Lord and His strength. When you have no strength left, as you surrender everything to Him and cry out for help, He will begin to fill you with His strength.

Two Roads to Depression Avenue

I have been fascinated through the years to watch numerous documentaries on the Iditarod Trail Sled Dog Race. This grueling race which is over 1,100 miles and takes nine to fifteen days (or more) to complete takes place in Alaska over some of the most rugged and dangerous terrain anywhere. Temperatures plunge way below zero with blizzards that produce whiteouts and zero visibility. It is an incredible test of endurance of a man and his beloved dogs. Though everything about the race fascinates me, as a dog lover I am particularly interested in them.

There are various breeds of dogs used to pull the sleds from Alaskan breeds to Siberian breeds and many more that we don't usually hear much about. In fact, many of the dogs I have seen look very different from what I have pictured, but they are all elite athletes with the same heart for pulling the sled. What these dogs endure during this race is in my estimation, heroic. The temperatures alone along with the winds and snow seem torturous. I've seen pictures of a snow swept landscape and to my amazement a dog's head begins to break through the surface of the snow as he stands up and shakes himself after a time of rest. The risks are real. They may get hurt during the race and endure great pain. They may struggle through storms like the rest of us have never seen. They may even fall into an unseen crevasse and be severely injured or even lose their lives, but they were born for this and they love to pull.

As I've listened to the mushers speak about their dogs and interact with them, it is quite obvious they have a deep respect and love for them. Their connection is quite remarkable. What is also remarkable is what they explain about these dogs and this grueling race. They say that these dogs absolutely love to pull the sled. It is what they live for to pull the sled. They derive their greatest joy in life from pulling the sled. They are born and bred to pull the sled. It's in their DNA. They explode with excitement and yelps when they are being hooked up to the sled. They can't wait to strain against that harness with their team and pull the sled. They are living out their innermost desire and purpose when they are pulling the sled. This is truly what they were designed to do by their Creator and is their joyous purpose in life. They are sled pullers.

Please allow me to make a couple of applications to our lives that I think will make sense. God has designed each one of our lives with gifts to fulfill His purpose. Even before birth the Psalmist explains, "Your eyes saw my substance, being yet unformed. And in Your book they all were written, the days fashioned for me, when as yet there were none of them" (Psalm 139:16). I could add more scriptures that also confirm this truth, but I think this one describes the point well.

> "God has fashioned all your days and designed you with a divine purpose."

Can you think with me for a moment about those eager, athletic sled dogs? Can you imagine what it would be like if after they were born they were permanently attached to a six-foot chain (what does 6 feet remind you of?) by their doghouse "never" to pull a sled? They would eat their food with the rest of the team and then watch as their parents and siblings and friends were all hooked up to the sled with tails wagging and yelps of delight getting ready to pull the sled with all of their hearts. They would hear the musher give that exciting command to pull and they would take off into the pristine snow to fulfill their purpose and mission. They would watch them disappear into the distance as the happy yelps grow faint. Day after day, week after week, month after month and year after year always on the chain. Always watching. Always hoping for the next training run. Six feet and no further. No running. No pulling. No wind in their face. No challenge. No barking with delight and finally no hope. A heart that was made to pull but now only pulls on a six-foot chain. That would be tragic right? Cruel and depressing right? They would still be alive (depending on your definition of alive) but not full of joy, fulfilling their designed purpose in life.

Here are two roads in life that will lead to depression. One of those is to be divinely designed with a purpose and never living out that purpose. The other is to take that divinely designed purpose and use it only for yourself. Some are continuing to travel this first road out of fear implanted by the enemy. They are unwilling to step out in faith and live out their purpose. The thought of storms and the crevasses keep them on the chain. Some have also traveled this second road by taking the gifts God has given them and using them only for their own benefit whether for money and fame or some other reason. Both of these roads will lead to depression sooner or later. It is not a matter of if; it is a matter of when. Regardless of the time frame the end result of not living out the purpose for which you were designed in the freedom and power of Christ is sad and depressing. You are alive, but are you really living?

Guarding Your Mind

There is a constant assault on your mind especially in our contemporary American culture. It is a nonstop barrage of worldly input designed to dominate your thoughts and therefore strongly influence the way you live and what you believe. The enemy's intention is of course to pull you away from life-giving truth and freedom in God's Word and into a clever counterfeit that "looks" like truth and freedom. If we are not aware that this stealthy assault is going on, we become dangerously vulnerable to accepting thoughts and behaviors that dishonor the Lord and lead us away from real truth and also from the real power of the Holy Spirit. Whole books have been written concerning the battlefield of the mind and I am grateful for them. However, my intention here is to share a few brief principles that I hope will help you guard your mind against the worldly infiltration as you seek to find and follow God's will for your life.

The Meditating Mind

One great way to guard your mind against the constant barrage of worldly input is meditation on God's Word. As the Psalmist is speaking about the life of a blessed man who rejects the input of ungodliness and who is fruitful and prospering he proclaims, "But his delight is in the law of the LORD, and in His law he meditates day and night" (Psalm 1:2). I find it intriguing that this verse speaks of a connection between the desire of his heart and the contemplations of his mind. As we grow in the intimacy of our loving relationship with Christ, our love for the life-giving truth of His Word will also increase.

> "*O*ur study of God's Word will change from a checklist devotional duty to a delightful anticipation of spiritual impact. What was previously a religious exercise will transform into a search for spiritual gold."

That delight and excitement will result in a lifestyle of meditation on the unsearchable riches of God's Word which will dominate and shape the thought life instead of all the destructive input shaping it.

As a brief note of practical help, it has been my habit of life for many years to study a smaller portion of Scripture in the morning asking the Holy Spirit to illuminate some truth to meditate on through the day. It can be as small as one word or sometimes the truth principle from a whole paragraph that can be summarized in a few words. Many times I will highlight the word or words, underline it and write a note to myself in the margin. For me this reinforces the truth in my mind and provides a visual note. Webster's defines *meditate* as,

"To focus one's thoughts on: reflect on or ponder over" (11).

So through the day I reflect on and ponder over this truth, what it means, and how it applies to my life. As I'm going to bed at night, I rewind my visual notes and recall what I have learned.

The Dwelling Mind

Another way to combat the constant barrage of ungodly material that is so pervasive in our American culture is what I will call the "dwelling mind." Though there is admittedly a significant overlap between the dwelling mind and the meditating mind, my hope is that a different facet of this truth will be helpful to you. Paul speaks clearly about this issue when he writes, "Finally brothers, whatever is true, whatever is honorable, whatever is just, whatever is pure, whatever is lovely, whatever is commendable—if there is any moral excellence and if there is any praise—dwell on these things" (Phil. 4:8, HCSB). I love the word "dwell" here that is also used in the New American Standard Bible and speaks of a strong, intentional focus. He says let your mind make its home here. Let your thoughts spend focused time enveloped in these godly characteristics. Let your spiritual focus kickback in the recliner and spend some time. This intentional focus coupled with a whole list of Godly characteristics speaks to me of the bigger picture of a whole thought life that is wholesome; whereas, I think of meditation as more directed to a particular truth.

Think of the bigger picture of your thought life like the whole pie instead of just one piece that you are savoring. Dr. Lightner explains,

> "Six items are mentioned as objects of a wholesome thought life, and each one is introduced with whatever. In the Greek 'whatever' is plural, which suggests that several things could be included under each heading" (12).

As you move through your day, intentionally dwell on those things that are Godly as you reject those things that are not. After the previous verse (7) speaks of the supernatural peace of God guarding our hearts and minds, H. C. G. Moule states,

> "He begs them to give to their minds, thus 'safeguarded' by the peace of God, all possible pure and healthful material to work upon, of course with a view to practice" (13).

Make it an intentional practice to dwell on, keep in view, and retain in one's thoughts, those things that are Godly and that honor the Lord. This guards the spiritual integrity of your mind.

The Renewing Mind

It is important for you to be fully aware that there is an unrelenting attempt to conform you and your mind to this world system that is opposed to God. It is ongoing and pervasive. The enemy who is behind the world system is prowling around like a cat stalking its prey. Your mind is the prime target and the goal is to conform or mold your thoughts into those of that world system.

One of the most beloved teachers at Dallas Theological Seminary, Dr. Howard Hendricks and his son Bill wrote one of the most outstanding books of our time on Bible study methods titled, *Living By The Book*. In the very beginning of the book Dr. Hendricks states,

> "Shortly after I became a Christian, someone wrote in the flyleaf of my Bible these words: 'This book will keep you from sin, or sin will keep you from this book'. That was true then, and it's still true today. Dusty Bibles always lead to dirty lives. In fact, you are either in the Word and the Word is conforming you to the image of Jesus Christ, or you are in the world and the world is squeezing you into its mold" (14).

This molding is done strategically over a period of time in an incremental way in an attempt to keep you unaware of the molding process. This is the prime reason we need to remain vigilant. If left unchecked this process will not only lead to assimilation with the beliefs and values of the world system, but will be a foothold for the enemy to cause confusion, barriers in your spiritual walk, discouragement, and depression.

Fortunately, we have the answer to avoid this strategic attack. It is imperative that there is an ongoing renewing of our minds. Paul exhorted the Roman Christians, "And do not be conformed to this world, but be transformed by the renewing of your mind, that you may prove what is that good and acceptable and perfect will of God" (Rom. 12:2). Notice he is speaking to Christians. In the previous verse, he is exhorting them to present their bodies as a living sacrifice and in this verse, he is following that up with his exhortation concerning the renewing of their minds. This word "transformed" in the original language is the word from which we derive our word "metamorphosis." This transformation takes place through the renewing of the mind by the God-breathed truth of His Word through the indwelling power and illumination of the Holy Spirit. This ongoing renewing of our minds through the truths of God's Word will be transforming and give you the corresponding discernment to avoid the enemy's attempts at molding us.

Conclusion

Sweet friend, don't get caught up in the trap of giving up on God's plan for your life through discouragement and depression. Regardless of your position or station in life, the only real joy, peace, and fulfillment in this life comes from finding and following God's perfect will. Though many try to make you believe they are doing fine after walking away from the Lord, they are either lying or completely deceived by the manipulations of the devil. The time "will" come when you will see how wrong they were. True life comes from the author of life. True purpose in life comes from following the true

Master of life, Jesus Christ. Fulfillment comes from the fulfiller of life. Though discouraged and ready to quit, realize that the Lord is with you. He loves you deeply. He knows your hurt and is aware of the depth of your need. He can fill you with hope and desire again. He can lead you out of the hole. He can wrap His arms around you and show you His power. He has promised to meet your needs if you trust Him completely as He renews your mind. He is the most wonderful, precious support in life. He will never leave you or forsake you. If someone has moved, it has been my experience that it is not Him. He is waiting. You can really trust the Lord!

"My Anchor"

When darkened clouds surround my soul,
When hurt and pain around me roll,
Whatever come my lot may be
His loving hand still anchors me.
When words have cut me like a knife,
When hatred causes bitter strife,
Whatever come my lot may be
His loving hand still anchors me.
When sickness tears my loved ones down,
When death's cold stare has come around,
Whatever come my lot may be
His loving hand still anchors me.
When purpose fades and questions rise,
And burning tears have filled my eyes,
Whatever come my lot may be
His loving hand still anchors me.
When those we love have gone astray,
Have broken our hearts and saddened our day,
Whatever come my lot may be
His loving hand still anchors me.
Whatever the storms, whatever the gales,
Whatever pain blows against my sails,

Though battered and torn my boat may be,
HIS LOVING HAND STILL ANCHORS ME (15).

Final Question to Ponder:
Am I keeping my focus on Christ and His indwelling power
in my life and saturating my mind with the transforming
truths and promises of God's Word which prove I am more
than a conqueror, or am I dwelling on the failures and
fears and worldly viruses that are tearing me down?

Chapter 10

Prayer: The Great Ingredient

The Importance of Prayer

*W*hen it comes to finding and following the will of God, prayer is an indispensable ingredient. Leonard Ravenhill speaks of the critical importance of our prayer life when he says,

> "No man is greater than his prayer life. The pastor who is not praying is playing; the people who are not praying are straying… Poverty-stricken as the Church is today in many things, she is most stricken here, in the place of prayer. We have many organizers, but few agonizers; many players and payers, few pray-ers; many singers, few clingers; lots of pastors, few wrestlers; many fears, few tears; much fashion, little passion; many interferers, few intercessors; many writers, but few fighters. Failing here, we fail everywhere" (1).

This is a stinging rebuke of prayerlessness and may be uncomfortable, but it may ultimately also be helpful to provoke us to see the truth and to see what we are missing. Prayer is the wonderful privilege of communicating with Almighty God. We share our hearts with our Heavenly Father and sense His love. We cast our cares upon Him knowing that He truly cares for us. We intercede for others and lift them to the throne of grace. It is truly one of the most important ministries of the Christian's life.

As with the study of God's Word, prayer is one of the most neglected privileges of contemporary Christianity. It is the great throwaway in the mad dash of typical life in our country. Abraham Lincoln's heartfelt proclamation reads like today's newspaper and should convict our hearts as he shares,

> "We have been the recipients of the choicest bounties of Heaven. We have been preserved these many years in peace and prosperity. We have grown in numbers, wealth and power as no other nation has ever grown.
>
> But we have forgotten God. We have forgotten the gracious Hand which preserved us in peace, and multiplied and enriched and strengthened us; and we have vainly imagined, in the deceitfulness of our hearts, that all these blessings were produced by some superior wisdom and virtue of our own.
>
> Intoxicated with unbroken success, we have become too self-sufficient to feel the necessity of redeeming and preserving grace, too proud to pray to the God that made us! It behooves us then to humble ourselves before the offended Power, to confess our national sins and to pray for clemency and forgiveness" (2).

I fear that many of us have been fooled by the enemy into relegating prayer to a low priority. Some of us have developed the habit of saying grace over the food and feeling good about our diligence. We fall into the trap of giving God a few brief moments of our valuable time each day and tell everyone how we pray daily. We have digressed to the point that many don't even know what a true prayer life really is and the different elements of prayer.

How can we stand in the battle and do spiritual warfare without prayer? How can we ask for our needs to be met without prayer? How can we get comfort in our time of need without prayer? How can we ask God to open and close doors without prayer? How can we ask the Lord for a peace or an unrest in our hearts without prayer? How can we ask God to give us confirmation from His Word without prayer? How can we find and follow God's will for our lives without prayer?

How can we be obedient to God's Word without prayer? The answer is painful and simple. We cannot! This is not some routine religious duty we fulfill to complete our spiritual checklist. This is the highest privilege of communication with our loving heavenly Father Who sits on the throne.

Through many years of studying God's precious Word, practicing a lifestyle of prayer, and reading many books by the wonderful Christian leaders of our day, God has blessed me. He has given me a small glimpse of the importance of prayer. He has grown me in the elements of prayer. He has given me an earnest desire to develop an intimate and balanced prayer life in order to stay close to Him and know His will. He has touched my heart in unspeakable ways through the sweetness of His voice. It hasn't been an audible voice in my life. As Dr. Adrian Rogers so aptly said for many years, "It wasn't an audible voice; it was much louder than that." I concur with this great role model of preachers everywhere. God's sweet voice in my heart is wonderfully powerful, touching, and clear.

"*I*t is the greatest privilege of my life to enjoy loving communication with my heavenly Father."

The Elements of a Balanced Prayer Life

The following elements of prayer which have become my daily habit are most definitely not original. They have come from the teachings of God's Word and have been skillfully clarified and explained by many of the great Christian pastors and leaders of our day. I am very grateful and indebted to them for their impact on my prayer life. With this humble recognition, I would like to briefly describe for you the five elements of a balanced prayer life that have been part of my daily habit. I acknowledge that some great prayer warriors and authors have used different titles to describe these elements and use them in various orders. I appreciate all of them and their contributions to this vital spiritual lifestyle. I am not sharing some inflexible formula or rigid dogma concerning the elements of prayer as that leads us away from the intimacy of communication with our Lord and into a legalistic structure. I am sharing brief descriptions of some elements of prayer that I hope will help you deepen your intimacy and facilitate your growth in communicating with the Lord.

Also, I would like to encourage you in your prayer life by showing you the way to be assured that your prayers will be answered. I pray that we in America come to the realization that a life of true prayer is a life of true power. Too many have developed spiritual muscular dystrophy in their prayer life.

> "To live victoriously in Christ, we must live victoriously through intimate, empowering communication."

Confession

I have chosen this as the first element in my prayer time because of the need for spiritual cleansing, which facilitates my intimacy with the Lord. Though I usually begin my prayer time by briefly thanking God for His love and expressing my love and praise to Him, it seems in my heart the appropriate order to then begin with confession. Starting with the element of confession is important because of the vital need to deal with anything not pleasing to God in our lives that might hinder our spiritual intimacy and communication as we have discussed previously in chapter 3, "Knowing Cleansing." It would be impossible to enjoy wonderful fellowship and communication with the Lord when there is cherished sin and rebellion in our hearts and His loving conviction ringing in our spiritual ears. I have illustrated this relational hindrance previously in sharing about my experience with my son and the hole in the wall in the section, "A Heart of Purity" in chapter 6.

One of the verses engraved on my mind since I was a very young man is Psalms 66:18, in which the Psalmist says, "If I regard iniquity in my heart, the Lord will not hear." I have also addressed this principle in more detail previously in the section, "A Heart of Purity" in chapter 6. This scriptural principle of a pure heart before God and the loss of intimacy when we insist on cherishing or holding on to things that dishonor Him is one key that has prompted me to begin my prayer time with confession.

> "Rather than running away from conviction and correction, I want to make sure I open my heart to the all-seeing searchlight of the Holy Spirit and run toward His loving correction. I desire to ask Him to reveal anything I need to confess."

I want to humble myself before God and denounce anything with which He isn't pleased out of love and gratitude. I want to stay clean before God so that my sweet fellowship with Him will be unhindered. I want to live my life in such a way that there is no barrier of disobedience or rebellion to the full and powerful working of the Holy Spirit in my life. I want to be sure not to go on praying through a regimented routine and fooling myself about God's hearing and answering, when He is in reality chastising me to draw me back into true intimacy. I want to strive to live my daily life in such a way that any sin would be accompanied by a quick and sincere confession. I want to make sure to have nothing between my soul and the Savior.

Whatever else I may mess up (and I have messed up plenty), I will strive to listen to the Holy Spirit's conviction and never let anything stay between my precious Savior and me. Many people tend to reject conviction and I understand the reason. At this point in my life I tend toward receiving it in order to deal with it even though it is still difficult. Whatever other relationships I may have difficulty with and whatever other fellowship I may miss out on, I want to never, ever, miss out on His. Certain things can be forgotten for a time without causing unspeakable loss, but not the practice of confession with its accompanying cleansing and forgiveness applied. The things the Father chooses to do through my life are only possible by the power of the indwelling Holy Spirit which flows out of my loving intimacy with Christ. If I really cherish His intimacy, I will also choose to lovingly submit to His conviction.

Can you grieve God as a born again Christian? According to scripture you can. Paul instructs the Ephesian Christians, "And *do not grieve the Holy Spirit of God*, by whom you were sealed for the day of redemption" (Eph. 4:30, author's italics). This whole section of scripture is a clarion call to put off the old man with the sinful behaviors and put on the new man in Christ. Paul exhorts them, "that you put off, concerning your former conduct, the old man which grows corrupt according to the deceitful lusts, and be renewed in the spirit of your mind, and that you put on the new man which was created according to God, in true righteousness and holiness" (Eph. 4:22–24). MacArthur addresses this issue of grieving the Holy Spirit when he states,

> "All sin is painful to God, but sin in His children breaks His heart. When His children refuse to change the ways of the old life for the ways of the new, God grieves." He goes on to say,

"Grieving can lead to quenching (1 Thess. 5:19)
and to a forfeiture of power and blessing" (3).

Yes, you can grieve God by living in sin and continuing the corrupt and lustful lifestyle of the old man. Yes, you do need to confess this sin and ask forgiveness for grieving the Father even though you are absolutely, eternally secure and "sealed for the day of redemption." Father I confess this sin to You and ask You to forgive me for dishonoring the unspeakable sacrifice of my Lord Jesus on the cross that already paid for it.

Even the wisdom literature of the Old Testament addresses this concept of confession with a divine truth principle when it states, "He who covers his sins will not prosper, but whoever confesses and forsakes them will have mercy" (Prov. 28:13). To attempt to hide, cover up, or camouflage sin with excuses, labels, spins or denials has always been a destructive path. It is like trying to hide or cover up cancer. At some point the evidence will become obvious. It is also wise to remember how ludicrous it is to even think we can hide something from our God who sees everything. We see this truth vividly proclaimed as the Psalmist says, "O LORD, You have searched me and known me. You know my sitting down and my rising up; *You understand my thought afar off.* You comprehend my path and my lying down, and are *acquainted with all my ways. For there is not a word on my tongue, but behold, O LORD, You know it all together*" (Psalm 139:1–4, author's italics). You cannot hide your words or even your thoughts from the Lord.

The Master's Model Prayer

If you want the ultimate confirmation of our need for confessing and asking forgiveness for our sins, we have it from the lips of the Master Himself. Not only is it from the Master, but it was specifically given as a model prayer for His disciples to follow. Having seen Jesus pray many times and realizing the importance and power and intimacy of prayer in His life, His disciples desired that blessing also and asked that He would teach them to pray. So He teaches them what is many times referred to as the "Lord's Prayer," which is really a model prayer. It was not intended to be some kind of religious liturgy only to be recited, though that recitation from a pure heart is a wonderful expression. He intended it to be a model outline of major elements in their prayers. Long discourses have been written on the major elements within this prayer which is not my purpose here. Rather, I want to spotlight the portion of His model prayer which states, "And forgive us our sins, for we also forgive everyone who is indebted to us" (Luke 11:4). The NIV renders this verse, "Forgive us our sins, for we also forgive everyone who sins against us." We ask forgiveness as we also manifest the forgiving heart of Christ within us.

Finally, there are certain scriptures that should make their way into our memory for use on a daily basis. First John 1:9 is one of them. It states, "If we confess our sins, He is faithful and just to forgive us our sins and to cleanse us from all unrighteousness." This is a gem to be used and employed on a daily, hourly, and even moment to moment basis as needed. It is a wonderful promise. We know God is faithful and just to fulfill His promises. It is also conditional. The verse begins with an "if" clause. If we follow God's direction with a genuine heart, then He will produce the promised results. It is an everyday miracle with which God has blessed us. Use it!

Thanksgiving

Thanksgiving is a sorely neglected element in the prayer life of many Christians. You would think it would be prevalent after all the unspeakable blessings a loving God has showered upon us, but many times it isn't. Many have an unbalanced prayer life because of the total exclusion of everything other than that for which they ask or beg. Many spend countless time in prayer practicing the element of petition, or asking God to give them something or protect them from something. The other small percentage of their prayer time is a passing thanks to salve their conscience about a lack of intimacy, ungratefulness, and the conviction of neglect.

If we would consider the enormous blessings we enjoy in Christ, we would shout thanksgiving to the throne. If we could truly grasp the scope of God's promise, "My grace is sufficient for you," we would swell with gratitude and excitement. Dr. John MacArthur Jr. shares the story of this truth bursting into the thoughts of C. H. Spurgeon as he writes,

> "The story is told of Charles Haddon Spurgeon, who was riding home one evening after a heavy day's work, feeling weary and depressed, when the verse came to mind, 'My grace is sufficient for you.'
>
> In his mind he immediately compared himself to a little fish in the Thames River, apprehensive lest drinking so many pints of water in the river each day he might drink the Thames dry. Then Father Thames says to him, 'Drink away, little fish. My stream is sufficient for you.'
>
> Next he thought of a little mouse in the granaries of Egypt, afraid lest its daily nibbles exhaust the supplies and cause it to starve to death. Then Joseph comes along and says, 'Cheer up, little mouse. My granaries are sufficient for you.'
>
> Then he thought of a man climbing some high mountain to reach its lofty summit and dreading lest his breathing there might exhaust all the oxygen in the atmosphere. The Creator booms His voice out of heaven, saying, 'Breathe away, oh man, and fill your lungs. My atmosphere is sufficient for you'" (4)!

Thanksgiving should come from a deep well within us and be a well-used element of prayer in the life of every Christian. To humbly thank God for all the things He has done, is to show true love and gratefulness. To use thankfulness little or not at all, is to show our lack of spiritual maturity as we use God for our own purposes.

I heard an intriguing comment on thankfulness one day. I was talking to Dr. Homer Lindsay, the great pastor of First Baptist Church of Jacksonville, Florida who is with the Lord now. As a youth pastor at the time, I tried to learn as much as I could from this man (from my few, brief interactions and reading his books) whom I admired and used as a role model. One day I asked him a question. I said, "Dr. Lindsay, if there was one thing we could build into our Christian young people of today, what would you say it should be?" I guess I was expecting various comments I had considered beforehand, but his answer was brief and to the point. He said, "Mark, I think it would be thankfulness." I have shared that comment many times through the years since that day and I continue to meditate on it.

Truly, if Christians, young and old alike, were sincerely and deeply thankful for the unfathomable blessings of God, most everything else would fall into place. We would strive to be lovingly obedient in every aspect of life as we live out of thankfulness and gratefulness for the unspeakable gift of Christ's sacrifice on the cross. Remembering all God has done for us, the life of obedience would take on a new brilliance and splendor. Our love would grow moment to moment. We would readily give Him our all. After all, Jesus paid it all. What a wonderful miracle of the matchless love of God. A heart that is truly thankful will be a heart that spends time thanking.

I remember some years ago as I was interacting with some of our pastors in the Philippines about their prayer lives, and one of them stated in genuine honesty that after he prays for a few minutes he feels like he runs out of things to pray. I certainly understood what he was talking about with reference to the kind of traditional prayer that one might offer in a church service. However, when I began to share about these different elements of prayer and especially Thanksgiving, the Lord opened up a new understanding of intimacy through our prayer life for all of them. A spiritual light dawned on them and smiles began to spread across their faces.

As I began to talk about numerous things in my own life for which I was thankful it became immediately apparent to all of them that we could spend unlimited time just on this one element. With that new perspective the real problem was not running out of things to pray, but running out of time to pray.

Praise

With the element of Thanksgiving, we thank God for what He has done. With the element of praise, we worship and adore Him for who He is. Though there is some overlap between the two, there is a difference. We seem to have largely forgotten that we are exhorted to, "Enter into His gates with thanksgiving, and into His courts with praise. Be thankful to Him, and bless His name" (Psalm 100:4). It is revealing that too many of God's people enter His presence with nothing more than requests and demands.

A time of praise to God is part of a balanced prayer life. My time of praise has become an intensely sweet time of beautiful communion with the Lord. I bow before Him and wonder at His awesome power. I stand with my mouth shut and my heart open before the Creator of the universe. I lift my sacrifice of praise to the Lord of lords and the King of Kings. I worship the indescribable One on the throne who loves little me. Listen to the apostle John's incredible description of the risen Christ as he said, "His head and hair were white like wool, as white as snow, and His eyes like a flame of fire; His feet were like fine brass, as if refined in a furnace, and His voice as the sound of many waters...and His countenance was like the sun shining in its strength" (Rev. 1:14–16). I see myself as hopelessly without adequate words as John was before the shining One who is the Word. I cry in praise to my precious Heavenly Father who would even allow me to step inside the rent veil, torn apart from top to bottom when Jesus cried, "It is finished!" I burst out into songs from my heart.

The reason several of these balancing elements have been largely overlooked is very obvious. In a society like ours, we've gotten so busy with our fast-paced living that we have to some degree forgotten the Giver of life. We have become so overloaded with many good things that we have left out the best things. We usually pack so many things into each day, that there is only one thing left by the end. Exhaustion! God deserves our personal praise. In a few moments, days, months, or years we will stand face to face with the One whose eyes are like a flame of fire and realize our busy lives weren't as important as we thought.

> "As a minister I've been by the bedside of many sweet ones who were in their final hours. There has not been a single time in all these years I have heard one of them say, 'I sure wish I had spent more time at work!'"

We will stand (or fall prostrate) before awesome omnipotence and be amazed that we could have gotten our priorities so far out of proper order. We will stand in that gleam of the fire of God and wonder at our lack of proper praise.

Many times as I begin to sing a song of praise to God, I imagine the greatest symphony ever assembled to accompany me. Countless musicians playing with supernatural abilities human words cannot describe. I hear heavenly strings as they play with unearthly beauty, and the monstrous brass section as they erupt on the refrain. Awed by the huge percussion section as it brings the crescendo to a level that can only be borne by immortals, I lift my voice to a level that can be heard Heaven-wide as I sing out with all my might of His incredible greatness and glory. What a heavenly experience available to us all. Whether you think you can sing or not, lift your voice with all the praise you can imagine to God who is worthy to be praised. He will love it!

Intercession

Intercession is the element of prayer whereby we intercede for others. We pray to God on their behalf. We pray for God's intervention on behalf of our family, our friends, our country, our church, our mission work, and our world.

This is a vital ministry of the church in the twenty-first century, perhaps even more vital now than at any point in history. Our country has driven down the road of immorality and sin at such a prolific speed that we are now on the verge of running off the cliff. We are running at breakneck speed toward the cliff of spiritual destruction as there is a growing rejection and even overt hatred toward the only One who can prevent the plunge. You may remember certain cartoon characters that would be running like a freight train toward a cliff. They wouldn't see the danger ahead until they had run off the edge of the cliff and found themselves in midair. In that moment they would look back with surprise and terror and then plunge to the bottom of the gorge. There would be a small puff of smoke as they hit the ground at the bottom. The character would then get up and continue on his way. The tragedy is that the cartoon character can get up again, but real people after leaving this life without Christ cannot.

I believe the ministry of intercession has its champions who never get praise (and don't want any). Some of these champions of prayer are those elderly ladies and men who sacrificially give of their time to approach the throne of grace for others. They shed tears of compassion and wield a power that is unknown to many pastors. They pray earnestly that God would intervene in the life of the prodigal sons. They lift their hurting pastors to God's throne for encouragement and help. They pray for the families that are tearing apart at the seams. They ask God's healing in the life of the ill. They bombard the throne with the needs of those lost neighbors. They plead for the needs of their church and country. Let me share a personal illustration from my own life of one of those prayer warriors.

Bernice the Intercessor

"Her name was Bernice. She was smiling when I met her one day in her nursing home room. I was pastoring a church and had gone to the nursing home to visit some other friends. A deacon from church had mentioned her and told me what a blessing she had been to him as he ministered there.

As I walked into her room, the light of Christ on her face and in her life was evident. I sat down and began to talk with Bernice, thinking I would try to be an encouragement to her. Though her spirit was bright and full of life, her body was not. With numerous health issues that came from many years on this earth, she now rarely even made it out of her room. She was in one little room at the end of one of several halls. This secluded little spot unknown to all but some family and a few friends was where she would live out the rest of her limited days.

As we began to talk, I realized this was different than most of my visits to the nursing home. This was not a sweet soul just waiting to die. She still had a purpose in life, though most would wonder what that could possibly be in a little secluded room at the end of the hall in a nursing home. She began to tell me about her ministry for the Lord. She had previously been a member of our church years before but had moved to another church family afterward. She sat in her little chair by the end table with a light and her Bible, and she explained her daily ministry. After her time in the Word each morning, she would enter into a time of intercessory prayer. She would take her pastor's picture out of her Bible, lay it on top of her Bible, and lay her hand on top of his picture. She would then begin to intercede for her pastor and call on the Lord for blessing, healing, strength, wisdom, and favor on his life. I was humbled in her presence as I saw a prayer warrior that would not give up. I was also convicted, as I had wanted to give up recently.

She then told me something that has impacted me to this day. She said that when she heard from our mutual friend that I had come to pastor her old church, she began to call out my name to the Lord each day and intercede for me also. I was stunned by the compassion and ministry of this little old lady. Her spiritual strength and heart for ministry put me to shame. She told me that she needed my picture so that she could put her hand on it each day and call out to the Lord the same way she did for her own pastor. There were tears in my eyes then as there are now many years later as I write. I took her a picture a few days later.

I can't tell you what it meant to a struggling pastor to know that a sweet prayer warrior in a little room at the end of a long hall was putting her frail hand on my picture each day and calling out to the Lord for me. That is a hero of the faith! I can say in all honesty that I believe her spiritual ministry known only to God and a few others had as much or more impact in the kingdom as anything I was doing. When most of the sweet people I visited there had given up and were settled into the waiting and enduring mode, she was using her spiritual gift to make an eternal impact.

I don't know what other gifts Bernice may have had, but I believe she definitely had the gift of helps. She had become a burden bearer with me as I struggled through some difficult times. I didn't get to see her a lot, but it was always a desire of mine when I was out visiting to go to that little room at the end of the long hall and see the sweet prayer warrior who was daily lifting me up to the throne in prayer. There are a few of those moments in life when you know you have had the privilege of being in the presence of someone with which God gave you a divine appointment. She was one of them for me.

Maybe you feel like you are at the end of a long hall in a little room and have very little to give. You know Christ personally and walk with Him but feel like you have little worth in kingdom work. Let me assure you that just as God used Bernice to impact my life and many others, He has gifted you to make an eternal difference. Whether your spiritual gift is more evident to others or known to almost no one, it is known by our Almighty God on the throne. He is not done with you yet! You can make a difference, and when we get to glory I believe that many, like Bernice and maybe you also, will have more rewards than pastors like me. You can lay up treasures in heaven and impact kingdom work no matter what your situation may be. Lord, I pray that whoever reads this book will have your blessing, healing, strength, wisdom, and favor on his or her life as they love and serve you! Amen" (5)!

When we are practitioners of intercession, we show the compassionate love of Jesus in our hearts. We show a selfless form of love, which is in short supply today. We show God we are truly concerned about others and not just ourselves. Our hearts grow warm and tender with the concerns of others, and we are truly following the scriptural admonition to, "Bear one another's burdens, and so fulfill the law of Christ" (Gal. 6:2). I pray that we will be more willing to undertake this vital ministry, even though there is no worldly recognition.

I will close this section on intercession with a personal illustration that is one of the most amazing acts of interceding that I have ever witnessed. It is from one of my heroes of the faith that has been one of the greatest prayer warriors in my life and the one whom I have loved and admired like no one else.

"*S*ometimes communicating the most powerful message requires no words."

Dixie Hyskell: Prayer Warrior-Intercessor

Few times in my life have I been more impacted by the loving act of one human being to another than when I was sitting by my Dad's bed in the final hours of his life. In one act without saying anything to me, my mother preached a message to me that truly summarized her whole life. This is even more miraculous when you take into account that she was five to six years into the progression of Dementia/Alzheimer's at that time and didn't even know who Dad or any of us were any more.

It was amazing for me to see the transformation in Mom at certain periods of time from mentally broken to the beautiful picture of Christ's love that I had always known. While I was sitting at Dad's bedside and praying for him, Mom came in. We didn't say anything to each other, but we both knew we were simply trying to compassionately help Dad in any way possible in these final hours of his life. Mom would walk around the bed trying to fix his sheets and blankets and make him more comfortable. I assumed she would try to fix a few things in the room and then go wandering around in the house as she so often did.

Then in the midst of all this pain Mom did something that made me cry. I watched her get down on her knees at the foot of the bed, take the blanket and sheet off of his feet, lovingly put her hands on his feet and then put her face against his feet like you would caress the face of a baby. She began to weep and pray (coherent, compassionate prayer) for Dad and continued for almost an hour and a half. I didn't say anything... I couldn't. I just watched with tears rolling down my face. This was my Mom who was the greatest prayer warrior I have ever known who literally prayed all night long for me when I was in trouble. In all honesty, without saying a word to me she had preached to me one of the most Christ-like messages I have ever heard. How an eighty-four-year-old could have stayed on her knees for an hour and a half is amazing to me, but I have concluded that after the way she had lived her life, her knees were very accustomed to that position.

Petition

This is the element of prayer usually employed to the exclusion of all the others. Many times we never feel a real need for prayer, until we feel pain. Some come to God only when in a desperate situation. Consider this all too familiar scenario. A person gets caught driving while drunk. The officers give the standard sobriety test on the road and determine the person to be legally drunk. They proceed to arrest the individual and take them to jail for booking. While riding to jail the person begins to desperately pray. "Oh God, please don't let my husband/ wife leave me. Please don't let my boss fire me. Please don't let this cost too much at the bondsman's and lawyer's offices. Please don't let anyone at church find out. Please don't let this be published in the paper. Please forgive me. I promise You on my mother's grave, I will never do this again! I've been stupid. I knew better. I'll follow Your will for the rest of my life. I'll never miss church again. I'll never touch another drop of alcohol if You will just please, get me out of this mess one last time."

Many times I have found myself speaking to someone through glass at a jail making promises to God about how faithful they are going to be in serving the Lord and coming to church as soon as they are released. I am sad to say that I am struggling to remember one time when their promises were kept. Pleading prayers of petition offered solely for self-centered purposes that have nothing to do with genuine heart change and submission to the Lord are doomed to failure.

Although petition is one of the elements of a balanced prayer life, it isn't the only one. Though some use petition in an abusive manner to the complete exclusion of all other prayer, it is a wonderful assurance to know that God's loving grace hears our personal cries for personal needs. I am not implying we shouldn't pray to God when we are in trouble. This is one of the most important times to pray. What I am implying is that some people seem to have no use for God, aside from what they can get out of Him when in a bind. God is to some people a genie to be used; a get out of jail free card; a butler who responds at the slightest wish of his employer; A Santa Claus who will bring whatever you wish; a bondservant. This kind of distorted spiritual behavior and fatally flawed conception of God reveals a self-centered heart problem that must first be addressed.

Far removed from this picture is the perspective of the humble Christian. Realizing he/she deserves judgment and that it is only through the grace of God and Christ's sacrifice that he is freed from it, he responds in true humility. He asks an awesome, praiseworthy God to have mercy and help in his time of need. He recognizes the unmerited blessings of God upon his life and his own inadequacies without the indwelling power of His Spirit. He asks that his needs be met within the realm of the all-knowing wisdom of God. He requests God's intervention with the sincere desire to follow God's direction more closely as he continues to develop his intimacy and love relationship with the Lord.

Petition is a vital ingredient in finding and following God's will. It is my habit to pray for God to reveal His opened and closed doors, to give me His peace about the direction He would have me go, and to confirm these first two through His Word. I then communicate with God each day as I meditate on the things that have happened, seeking His direction in my heart. I synthesize the doors, the peace, and the Word, as I wait on God's perfect timetable. Many times God will be leading in a direction and we will have one or two of these three keys, but God will only give the confirmation of the third when He knows the timing is perfect and it is best for us.

> "The key is to wait on and obey that direction of God within the timing of God. Many times we ask, but do not want to wait on God's answer."

It is scriptural to ask God for our own needs and direction, but it is also vital that we fully intend to obediently follow His direction when given. As Jesus was sharing the parable of the two foundations, contrasting those who are wise and those who are foolish, He said, "But why do you call Me Lord, Lord, and not do the things which I say" (Luke 6:46)?

Knowing Your Prayers Will Be Answered

One of the major questions I struggled with for many years was how to know my prayers would be answered. It is a joy and thrill to let you know that the main answer came from our treasure book, the Word of God. As I was seeking God's answer on this subject, I was studying the book of 1 John. It was one of those gold mine experiences when you know you've found a great nugget and the answer you've been seeking jumps out and grabs you and you shout a "Hallelujah!" that cannot be contained. First John 5:14–15 says, "Now this is the confidence that we have in Him, that *if we ask anything according to His will*, He hears us. And if *we know that He hears us, whatever we ask, we know that we have the petitions that we have asked of Him.*" What an exciting truth. I especially like the word "know." We can know our prayers will be answered if we ask according to His will. This leads us on to the next great question. How can we know we are asking according to His will?

What we know for sure is that God's will is contained in God's Word. That's the key! Praying in accordance with God's revealed will in His Word is praying in accordance with His will. Again, we see the unspeakable treasure we possess in the Scriptures. In God's precious Word He has clearly communicated to us His will that we might be able to pray with confidence. I began to understand, I must pray in accordance with the promises of God's Word in order to know that my prayers would be answered. In essence, I would need to pray the truths of God's Word. I am not talking about an insincere, manipulative mind pulling a word or verse out of context to fulfill the lusts of the flesh or feed our proclivity to use God for our own purposes instead of being surrendered to Him and His will. I have already illustrated in the previous pages the dangers of pulling verses out of their divine context and using them for our own purposes.

I am talking about praying in accordance with God's promises and principles in their divinely given context in a way that ultimately brings glory and honor to our heavenly Father and furthers His Kingdom work. I would pray God's promises to me and know that God would keep them. How can I know for sure that my prayers for forgiveness and cleansing are answered? The answer is, through the Word. It is my daily habit to pray 1 John 1:9. I pray, "Dear Lord, I confess (this word means to [agree together] with God that it is sin) the sin of anger or hatred toward (name), and I claim Your promise to me that if I confess my sins with a genuine heart, You are faithful and just to forgive me of my sins, and to cleanse me from all unrighteousness." I can then know beyond any shadow of doubt that I have received God's forgiveness and cleansing because I have prayed in accordance with His will. It is obvious that the Christian knows this through faith in God's immutable truth. We are not only saved by faith, but we live the victorious Christian life through faith as we reckon it to be as God has decreed it.

As I realized this great principle, a whole new world of prayer opened to me. Now, I didn't have to pray with the shotgun approach, firing off a lot of shot and hoping that something hits. Now I could pray with confidence. Although the Bible does not directly speak to every issue with a definitive negative such as, "thou shalt not" or a definitive positive such as, "thou shalt," it has been my experience that it speaks to every issue in "truth principle." The Lord created us and knows the human psyche and experience better than anyone, so He gave us His inspired Word to give us His direction in this life.

"*M*y Bible study took on a new meaning as I searched for God's will and His glorious promises/ truth-principles to claim. Now the Scripture was speaking personally to my daily needs."

Blessed Assurance

Now I could be assured God would lead me and direct my paths. How? You know the answer, God's precious Word. I found God's revealed will in God's inspired Word. The wisdom book of Proverbs is one of my favorites. It yielded gold on this issue. Proverbs 3:5–6 explains, "Trust in the LORD with all your heart, and lean not on your own understanding; in all your ways acknowledge Him, and He shall direct your paths." Hallelujah! There it is! I trust in the Lord fully, and I don't trust my own understanding. I acknowledge and honor God in all my ways and I will know He is directing my paths. Now you know what to do. Pray the promises.

Let me share a treasure that will astound you. I found the way to get the desires of my heart. Hard to believe? It's true! Psalm 37:4–5 yields up its treasure by exhorting us to, "Delight yourself also in the LORD, *and He shall give you the desires of your heart.* Commit your way to the LORD, trust also in Him, and He shall bring it to pass" (author's italics). Do you see the wonderful "truth principle" here? When I delight myself in the Lord through my love relationship with Him, my heart is filled with His heart. The desires of my heart are wrapped up in Him. Dig in and see the treasures for yourself. We will be like a kid turned loose in a candy store as we search the Scriptures for God's will. There is the inconceivable peace of God in Philippians 4:6–7. There is the unfailing provision of God in Matthew 6:25–33 (key on verse 33). There is the unprecedented power of God in Ephesians 1:18–20. The list will be inexhaustible and exciting as you continue to dig.

Begin to pray within the Spirit inspired context and parameters of God's Word and you will be assured you are praying within the confines of God's will. Then, according to God's Word you can pray with absolute confidence that your prayer will be heard and answered. You will take on an authority in prayer you haven't experienced before, not because of faith in your ability to work up faith, but because of your faith in the trustworthiness of God's Word and your understanding and confidence in this truth. Enjoy!

Final Question to Ponder:
Am I growing in my love relationship with Christ through
a balanced, intimate prayer life, or am I allowing all
the busyness of life to make me miss His voice?

Chapter 11

Lordship: The Great Issue

Following Christ's Call

*W*hen we examine the issue of finding and following God's will and what He designed us to do, we would be wise to look at the foundation or principle of life He has stated repeatedly which supports and encourages it. If we do not seek to understand and internalize that core principle which brings success, then we will not reach our goal. Finding and following God's will and loving Him as our top priority which is clearly stated in Matthew 22:37–38, is an issue of Lordship. Living a lifestyle of Lordship in the power of the Holy Spirit is where the rubber meets the road. It is a question of, "Is He the top priority in my life?"

> " *I*s Christ the central focus of my life or just a player among many others I allow into the mix?"

Following Jesus Christ as Lord is the principle idea, the crux of the thesis, and the priority of the list. To not follow Jesus Christ as Lord not only shows a lack of surrender, but also reveals a misunderstanding of His direction and the clear exhortation of God's Word.

Contemporary Compromise

Contemporary Christianity is besieged with well-meaning people who either don't understand this teaching of Scripture, ignore it, or simply refuse to acknowledge the call of Christ that Scripture clearly defines. That is not surprising in a culture that tends to serve self as the priority. A heart of hedonism cannot be a heart of Lordship. I fully understand that this truth cuts against the grain of contemporary acceptance, but I want to help you move beyond that acceptance and into the power and fulfillment of truly living for Christ.

Many in our country seem to believe they have become the masters of their own fate (essentially they are in control and make all the decisions). I understand that is not what many of them would say in the language of "Christianese" as they speak to others. I have spoken that convenient language myself at times. However, I am referring to deeper internalized beliefs based on lifestyle. In many instances God has become an afterthought or something that is tacked on to what "they" do. Their lifestyle many times contends they have pulled themselves up by their own bootstraps and have made their own way. They have worked hard and set the course of their own direction. Or perhaps, could it be they have just grown cold to the leading and provision of God in their lives from neglect.

> "*Maybe* they have been straying for so long and have become so conditioned by the culture they have grown spiritually dull and blinded to the truth of God's direction, grace, and blessings."

Still others would rather just live their own lives according to their own self-imposed parameters, not having to deal with the real truth and genuine call of Christ. Their spiritual senses have become gradually numbed into comfortableness. After being hurt in one way or another, the tendency is to just go along to get along. I get it! We have all been hurt! I assure you I am in no way discounting the pain you have felt. I just want to help you deal with the hurt in a way that leads to light and freedom and not darkness and bondage.

Whatever the reasons for spiritual compromise, the truth of Scripture is that Lordship is the lifestyle Christ proclaimed numerous times. If we are going to deal honestly with Scripture, we need to step through the fear in faith to acknowledge Christ's words. It is the way to find and follow God's will and fulfill His purpose and plan for each of us. It is the response of the person who is in an intimate relationship with Christ and truly sincere about living within the sphere of God's perfect will. It is the only road that leads to true victory, peace, fulfillment, rest, strength, and contentment. If the influence of the culture has caused you to question this principle, please look carefully at the following scriptures asking the Holy Spirit to speak to your heart about what they proclaim.

What Is Lordship?

Let's begin with a definition of Lord from an English dictionary. Webster explains that a Lord is,

> "One having power and authority over others...a ruler by hereditary right or preeminence to whom service and obedience are due" (1).

Understood within the ultimate context of Lordship as we see in Scripture, the application is easily defined. Jesus Christ is Lord. We speak those words but do we grasp the depth and personal application of their reality? He has ultimate power and authority over others and in fact everything: "And Jesus came and spoke to them, saying, *All authority has been given to Me in heaven and on earth*" (Matt. 28:18, author's italics). Does that sound like He has all authority and that He is Lord? Without question! He is the ruler by preeminence to whom loving service and obedience are due. Scripture proclaims, "And He is before all things, and in Him all things consist. And He is the head of the body, the church, who is the beginning, the firstborn from the dead, *that in all things He may have the preeminence*" (Col. 1:17–18, author's italics). Does that sound like He has the preeminence in all things and He is Lord? Absolutely!

As Lord He is in authority and He is preeminent. To be honest, understanding the concept of Lordship isn't usually the problem; it is the application of the truth that is more often the stumbling block. When one gets a glimpse of the amazing love and grace on display at the cross, the response of loving obedience and Lordship is the desire of the heart, not some legalistic drudgery. That kind of loving obedience bubbles up in one's life like an artesian spring and is never perceived as some religious duty we have to constantly maintain.

On a personal level, Lordship is the complete, loving submission of my life to Jesus Christ as the One who has loved me, saved me, paid my debt, given me abundant life here and eternal life hereafter. He is the one who is my ruler by preeminence and payment, and to Him my wholehearted service and loving obedience are due. It is understanding and accepting that He is my ruler, my controller, my director, my Savior, my King, my Master, and the one in control who loves me more than anyone else. It is also realizing and accepting that I can no longer be my own ruler, controller, director, Savior, King, Master, and the one in control. It is submission to follow His path rather than my own. It is sacrificing what I think I want for what He knows I need. It is trusting and following His direction. Self must be dethroned. Leonard Ravenhill explains that,

> "Much of the barrier to believers' translating the promises of God into fact before the eyes of men is that wretched thing called self. But Paul remembered when his old King Self was dethroned and—what is more—crossed out on a cross (Gal. 2:20). Then Christ was enthroned. And before we can be clean and ready for Him to control, self-seeking, self-glory, self-interest, self-pity, self-righteousness, self-importance, self-promotion, self-satisfaction—and whatsoever else there be of self—must die" (2).

Blackaby, Blackaby, and King speak about the control issue in our lives when they write,

> "While the essence of sin is a shift from a God-centered to a self-centered life, the essence of salvation is a denial of self and a return to a God-centered outlook. We must come to a place where we renounce our self-focused approach to life and turn the attention and control over to God" (3).

Is Lordship a Must?

This is the question many are asking with the cultural bias (and self) shouting the answer is no. The truth is, if the desire of your heart is to find and follow God's will which is contained in God's Word, the answer is a resounding yes! Let's look at a few examples that give us the definitive answer to this question.

Matthew 7:21–27

When considering the issue of obeying and doing the will of God as opposed to just hearing and giving lip service to it, or doing it your own way, we need to evaluate the words of Jesus. Matthew 7:21–27 says, "Not everyone who says to Me, 'Lord, Lord,' shall enter the kingdom of heaven, but he who does the will of My Father in heaven. Many will say to Me in that day, 'Lord, Lord, have we not prophesied in Your name, cast out demons in Your name, and done many wonders in Your name?' And then I will declare to them, 'I never knew you; depart from Me, you who practice lawlessness!' Therefore whoever hears these sayings of Mine, and does them, I will liken him to a wise man who built his house on the rock: and the rain descended, the floods came, and the winds blew and beat on that house; and it did not fall, for it was founded on the rock. But everyone who hears these sayings of Mine, and does not do them, will be like a foolish man who built his house on the sand: and the rain descended, the floods came, and the winds blew and beat on that house; and it fell. And great was its fall."

It is intriguing and tragic to me, after all the good "religious" things these people insisted they had accomplished, that they didn't even know Jesus personally. They didn't follow God's direction in knowing Jesus as Savior and Lord.

> "*L*ike many today they may have insisted they believed (mentally, intellectually, and historically) in Jesus but they continued to do things their own way which simply amounts to religious works regardless of the appearance or label."

They would miss heaven because they hadn't submitted to and followed God's will to personally be born again through the power of the Holy Spirit as they surrendered to Christ (to "know" Him, the Rock). They would be labeled as foolish because of their refusal to apply the Word of God to their lives and actually live out what Jesus had said according to His way through His power. They would find themselves living in a house built on a dissolving foundation of sand, simply because they had heard the Word of God, but had not internalized it and put it into practice. Understanding the spiritual foundations Christ spoke of here are crucial. There was the solid foundation of the rock and the crumbling foundation of sand. Dr. Barbieri explains,

> "The rock foundation represented the Lord Himself and the truths He had been presenting, especially the truth concerning inner transformation. The sand spoke of Pharisaic righteousness which the people knew and on which many were basing their hopes" (4).

Both of them heard His words. Both of them gathered materials. Both of them built a house. Both of them had confidence in their house. Both of the houses probably looked good. Both of them functioned fine in good weather. Both of them had a foundation. Both of them had the rain descend, the floods come, and the winds blow. According to Christ one of them stood strong and one of them had a devastating collapse. Is your life truly built on the foundation of the "Rock?"

Matthew 10:37–39

Lordship also demands priority love according to the Master Himself. Jesus left little doubt as to the quality of love and devotion expected of His followers. He said, "He who loves father or mother *more than Me is not worthy of Me.* And he who loves son or daughter *more than Me is not worthy of Me.* And he who *does not take his cross and follow after Me is not worthy of Me.* He who finds his life will lose it, and he who *loses his life for My sake will find it*" (author's italics). Does that sound like Jesus is calling His followers to make Him the top priority love in their lives? Undeniably!

Love for Jesus is to be the surpassing love of the disciple, or you find yourself essentially telling Jesus Christ Himself that He is wrong and has no right to make such a demand. It is clearly what He said in these verses though culture attempts to spin it, redefine it, deny its relevance and validity in contemporary society or deny it altogether. Many of us in vocational ministry greatly admire C. H. Spurgeon as one of the greatest preachers of yesteryear. After a lifetime of faithful service and what most of us would label as great success, as he was drawing near the end of his life he wrote his commentary on Matthew. Listen to the words of the old warrior as he said,

> "Christ must be first. He herein claims the highest place in every human breast... We must earnestly beware of making idols of our dearest ones, by loving them more than Jesus. We must

never set them near the throne of our King. We are not worthy to dwell with Christ above, nor even to be associated with Him here, if any earthly object is judged by us to be worthy to rival the Lord Jesus" (5).

The one who follows Him as Lord will make Him the top priority and will be willing to take his cross (death to self's control and full submission to Christ's control) and follow wherever Jesus leads. He will be "willing" to lose his life for the sake of Christ (as did most of His original inner circle) that he might truly find and live out real life. How could these sayings of Jesus be interpreted in any other way than Lordship? The truth is, any other interpretive gymnastics of which there are many (due in part to the cultural bias), are rejecting the contextual reality of Christ's words and without scriptural legitimacy.

Matthew 22:36–38

Love and the focal emphasis that Jesus placed on it tell the story of where He thought the highest love should be directed. A young lawyer questioned Jesus and was testing Him when he asked, "Teacher, which is the great commandment in the law? Jesus said to him, *'You shall love the LORD your God with all your heart, with all your soul, and with all your mind.* This is the first and great commandment'" (author's italics).

Though the young lawyer thought he had outsmarted Jesus and backed Him into a corner (which was always an infinitely ludicrous thought), he got an answer that not only answered his clever question, but also answered a much bigger question of life priorities. Jesus proclaimed without any hesitance that this was the first and great commandment. All of the religious rules and regulations which they took such great pride in were actually keeping them in spiritual chains. Jesus proclaimed priority love for God as the answer. In their great book, *Experiencing God*, Blackaby, Blackaby and King explain,

> "Everything in your Christian life, every-
> thing about knowing God and experiencing Him,
> everything about knowing His will depends on
> the quality of your love relationship with God. If
> this relationship is not right, nothing in your life
> will be in order" (6).

Christ's answer to this young lawyer was actually from the Jewish "Shema" (Hebrew for "hear") in Deuteronomy 6:4–5. It was actually the Jewish confession of faith. It was such an important truth for them to remember that they kept it on their lips and in their heart daily. That would be a great practice for us also. Jesus clearly confirms this supreme love as the priority love. One has to be abusive to the text to get anything less than Lordship here. The highest priority of the follower of Christ is to love God with every fiber of his/her being. To focus on following and pleasing the Lord of our lives, we must love God supremely which in reality enables us to truly love our family and others with the highest, most divine love as the full empowerment of His love flows through us to them. When we love Him supremely, then the storehouse of Christ's love flows freely through us.

Romans 12:1–2

God has used the apostle Paul to show us many truths. Among these are his pleading exhortation about how we should use our lives. Paul says, "I beseech you therefore, brethren, by the mercies of God, *that you present your bodies a living sacrifice,* holy, acceptable to God, which is your reasonable service. And do not be conformed to this world, but be transformed by the renewing of your mind, that you may prove what is that good and acceptable and perfect will of God" (author's italics). Dr. Richard Lee explains,

> "The term living sacrifice is a paradox.
> Living means that which is alive, whereas a sac-

rifice was something that had been put to death. However, as contradictory as it may sound, the idea of a living sacrifice perfectly explains the relationship we must have to God if we are to know His will for our lives" (7).

To present one's body as a living sacrifice can only be accurately understood as Lordship. Presenting our bodies to God for His use is the clear picture of loving submission to His Lordship, though some in our culture have moved light years away from it or tried to redefine it. In this Lordship submission we are to refuse to let the world mold us into the cultural bias and to be transformed by the renewing of our minds through His truth. We are to do this so we can prove what is that good and acceptable and perfect will of God. We are His and this is our reasonable (proper, true) service. It has always penetrated my innermost heart to see the verse saying this is merely our reasonable service (though a few other words are used in various translations). Though the flesh bristles and pushes against that concept, it isn't unreasonable at all as our flesh and others would have us think. As a matter of fact when you look honestly at what was done for us, it is completely reasonable.

"*I*t is reasonable that we lovingly submit to and follow the One who went to Calvary and died the worst death of all time (yes, others were crucified, but none carried our sins and the sins of the world) to become a curse for us."

He took my place on the cross. He paid my debt. He set me free. He paid it all. I am redeemed and the price of my judgment is paid. My chains have been removed. I have been taken off the road to destruction and have been permanently placed on the road of eternal life. It is only reasonable that I owe my redeemed life to my Redeemer.

One aspect of Lordship is refusing to bow to the enemy's advances. We are to refuse to be conformed or shaped into the mold of the world. We are to be transformed. The word for "transformed" in the Greek language is the word from which our English word "metamorphosis" comes. We are to be transformed or metamorphosed into what our Lord designed us to be. Our lives will then prove the perfect will of God. We will be the obedient servants of our Lord. A refusal to be conformed to the world is a decision that is in short supply today. Many who call themselves Christians are being conformed to the world's ways and are being told that it's okay. I want to lovingly share the truth with you. According to God, it's not okay and the truth is it's destructive to you. Your path to real life and fulfillment is to be a transformer and not a conformer.

1 Corinthians 6:19–20

Lordship is the only appropriate response from one who belongs to a Lord. Paul writes, "Or do you not know that your body is the temple of the Holy Spirit who is in you, whom you have from God, and you are not your own? For you were bought at a price; therefore glorify God in your body and in your spirit, which are God's." Dr. Paige Patterson comments,

> "Not only did he affirm that our very bodies constitute the Holy of Holies (naos), contrasted once again with the larger temple complex (hieron), but also he declared that the body became the temple by virtue of the fact that God, in the person of the Holy Spirit, indwelt the body.
>
> This is one of the most remarkable features of the new covenant. In the old dispensation, the Spirit of God was active and came upon some, but in the new dispensation every individual believer is personally indwelt by the Holy Spirit, rendering him the temple of God. This, of course, adds

another dimension to the whole aspect of bodily chastity; namely, the believer no longer belongs to himself" (8).

It is one of the great misconceptions of our day that we are free to follow our own fleshly desires. The fact that some actually believe that concept is proof of the predominant influence of culture over scriptural truth. We can of course follow them (with terrible consequences), but according to Scripture we are called to love Christ as our highest priority and to fulfill His purpose and plan for our lives. Actually, we are responsible to the One who has paid the price for our redemption. We are His. He is Master and Ruler, and our response should be one of loving and serving Him and bringing glory to God. Anything less, whether overt or subtle is not fulfilling the clear instruction of God's Word, which shows us God's will. Paul admonished the Corinthian Christians to glorify God with both their body and their spirit because they belong to Him. That's Lordship!

Philippians 3:7–8

"But what things were gain to me, these I have counted loss for Christ. Yet indeed I also *count all things loss for the excellence of the knowledge of Christ Jesus my Lord*, for whom I have suffered the loss of all things, *and count them as rubbish, that I may gain Christ...*" (author's italics). There can be no doubt these verses proclaim that Paul was one who believed in and practiced Lordship. It is little wonder he was used of God to write much of the New Testament. Those who strive to practice Lordship (though failing at times) from a grateful, loving heart are those whom God blesses and uses in supernatural ways. All other things became as meaningless to Paul. I find this continuing progression in my life also. His ultimate prize was Jesus Christ. He gave up everything others would have counted as valuable by this world's standards in order to serve Jesus Christ his Lord. The life of this astonishing man can only be viewed as a testimony to the call and blessings of Lordship through the power of the

Holy Spirit. Lordship wasn't just the key issue of his life; it was his life. Jesus became more than a religious belief or a person of history; He became the joy, the life and breath that Paul experienced. Jesus had authority over Paul's life, and Paul truly made it the vocation of his life to render the proper grateful, loving obedience and service which was due.

The Key Question

Many more scriptures could be brought to bear upon this issue of Lordship, but the case is very clear. The Word of God calls for Lordship from the blood bought children of God. With this fact of Scripture established, the key question is, "Does the consistent characteristic of my lifestyle proclaim Jesus Christ as my Lord?"

"*We* aren't discussing ideas of absolute perfection which the enemy will use; we are investigating the scriptural call of habitual lifestyle flowing out of the love and power of Christ."

Are you living your life with Jesus as the controller or are you usurping the role yourself? Have you been ignoring the truth of this issue hoping you wouldn't be called upon to actually confront it? Sweet friend, this brief Scriptural survey makes it very clear what the Word of God has recorded about Lordship. If you are listening to people who are down playing, discounting, or denying these truths, they are spinning Scripture to appease the current culture or possibly their own hesitance. You need the truth to avoid the culture traps and live in the freedom of Christ.

It would seem that many times we are playing games with God to expect Him to give us His perfect will and direction in our lives when we have shown ourselves to be untrustworthy with the basic principles He has already made clear. His love for us is not in question. Our growth toward maturity through the power of the Holy Spirit is the issue. Are you truly serious about finding and following God's will for your life? Are you really ready to follow what you find? Are you ready to quit playing culture games and get down to real business with your Lord? Are you really tired of the superficiality of your spiritual life, or maybe more disturbing, have you grown comfortable with it? Are you tired of being your own Lord and messing things up?

There's good news! God is just watching and waiting for people who are really serious about finding and following His will. He is not fooled by those who talk a good talk but don't walk a good walk. Remember, God can look all the way into the deepest recesses of the heart. He desires to shower His blessings and power on those who will truly take up the banner and go forward into battle. He wants to make champions of those who will follow Him as Lord, whether that is in a little room in a nursing home praying, or in a leadership position directing. He is looking for a few good men, women, and young people who will refuse to play things according to the world's rules and will step out in faith going forward for their Lord. If you want to be one of those individuals that God uses to touch the world and impact lives with His love in a powerful way, the decision is up to you, but Lordship is the issue.

One of my favorite memories from seminary days was singing old hymns of the faith with all the other preacher boys. We would get together in chapel and belt out our praise to the Lord with everything that was in us. It was like a little piece of heaven to hear a couple hundred students singing and proclaiming the power and majesty of our mighty Lord Jesus Christ! What a joy!

Final Question to Ponder:
Am I loving Christ and following Him
as the top priority in my life?

Chapter 12

You: The Great Champion

Yes, You Can!

*Y*es, you can be a great champion for Christ even if you are in a small room at the end of a hall in a nursing home like Bernice the intercessor in chapter 10. You can make a lasting impact on the world. You can be a somebody in the kingdom. You can leave a legacy. You can be someone others look up to. You can find your niche (God's unique purpose) in life and fulfill it. You can accomplish amazing things. Sweet friend, the great news we have to shout about is, we can do any of the God-sized things that He has planned for us. As the Scripture proclaims in Philippians 4:13, "I can do all things through Christ who strengthens me." Paul shared the good news that regardless of the challenges he faced, whether abased or abounding, full or hungry, having abundance or suffering need, he could do all things through the indwelling power of Christ.

No matter who you are or what you've done, you can be a champion for Christ. It will likely take time as you begin to function within the power of the Holy Spirit and become a strong testimony of His grace, but the fact is you can. That wonderful verse relates the scope of our possibilities and the source of our possibilities. Your life is an exciting possibility in Christ. A life focused on Jesus Christ is the key. Chuck Swindoll says,

"What is the sum and substance of all this? The secret of living is the same as the secret of joy: Both revolve around the centrality of Jesus Christ. In other words, the pursuit of happiness is the cultivation of a Christ centered, Christ controlled life" (1).

The Scope of Our Possibilities

What do you think the scope of, "I can do all things" is? How big is it? Within the will of God for your life, the scope is unlimited. "All things" means that God has a special ministry for you to impact this world and nothing can stop you from fulfilling it. I can do all things means that in Christ you are equipped with the potential for unlimited impact on the world regardless of the circumstances. Dr. Unger says of Paul's statement,

"In Christ he has unlimited potential" (2).

I can do all things means you can do more than you have ever dreamed you could because His power supersedes any and all circumstances no matter how challenging or impossible they may seem. This great verse (truth principle) does not refer to some shallow "carte blance" to indulge self-centered pursuits. It is infinitely greater than that and refers to the indwelling power of Christ to fulfill His amazing design and plan for my life in spite of any circumstances.

God wants us to be the very best in the power of His might wherever He has placed us. You can have a tremendous impact as a committed Christian wherever He has placed you, whether that is in a daily job, in school, in the military, as a full-time Mom, in a nursing home, in full-time ministry or wherever it may be. I believe you can find that particular niche with which God has gifted you and become outstanding, as you exercise it in the power of the Holy Spirit to the glory of God. I believe you can do something no one else can possibly do exactly as you would. I believe you are uniquely gifted and created to be a champion in some area. If God has called you into vocational ministry, realize that there is an unlimited scope of possibilities for your life to turn the world upside down. If God hasn't called you into vocational ministry, He "has" called you into ministry and you can start to dream about the scope of, "I can do all things." The need is great for sold out, vocational Christian ministers, but the need is just as great, if not more so, for sold out Christians in all areas who are ready to walk in His power and impact lives.

One of the most exciting parts of living the Christian life is that nothing can stop us from becoming all God can make us to be. Well, there is one thing that can stop you from becoming that world-changing instrument of God. You can stop you! Outside of your own fear, flesh controlled lifestyle, or lack of faith to trust God fully; there is no limit to what God can accomplish through you. Your life outside of His empowerment and will is the only hold up. God is ready and waiting!

Dreaming His Dreams

When you think about unlimited possibilities, you have to think about dreaming. I think it is critical that we dream big dreams as we pray and search for God's design. I believed that in my twenties, and I still believe that in my sixties. It is very important we develop the dream for our lives based on God's movement as He reveals His will and where He is at work to direct us along the way. As we cautioned before, it is not about us coming up with our own dream and asking God to bless it, but it is about finding and following His uniquely designed dream for us that has His full blessing and resources behind it. It is also essential to becoming all that God wants us to be, for us to refuse to let people or circumstances steal those dreams. It is a tragedy of unspeakable proportions for men or women to let people, feelings, circumstances, or past failures steal the dreams God has planted in their hearts. As a matter of fact, we all have past failures and God can use even those as a witness and testimony of His power and restoration. Moses had great failures with anger, murder, and disobedience, and went on to fulfill God's unique purpose for his life. David had spectacular failures with lust, power, and a terrible family dysfunction that we still learn from to this day, and he went on to win great victories and write many Psalms. Peter had heartbreaking failures with dangerous impulses, and even denial of our Lord, but God used him in supernatural ways to impact thousands of lives for Christ. Christ's inner circle all deserted Him in His darkest hour, yet He used them all. Though they all dealt with consequences in their lives as we do, the Lord empowered them through it all and used them in supernatural ways. The list of failures and restorations flows through the centuries and even the family lines from which Jesus came.

Some of the saddest people I know are those who have given up on their dreams and have submitted to simply existing. Sweet friend, if your dreams have been stolen from you, retrieve them, and if they haven't been, set your mind as a flint that they will never be as you love and serve the Lord to completely fulfill His great purpose for your life in His time. Listen to these inspiring truths that remind your heart that with our Almighty God anything is possible. As an angel spoke to a young virgin girl named Mary about something that had never happened before in human history he said, "For with God nothing will be impossible" (Luke 1:37). Jesus spoke to the blind and they could see. He raised up the lame to walk. He turned the water into wine. He fed thousands with a few pieces of food. He walked on the water and commanded the winds to shut up. He turned the most violent hater of the church into the strongest defender of it. He transformed prostitutes and thieves and murderers! He even called a dead man out of the tomb. He conquered death and rose again! He has not lost His power! He is on the throne! It is no struggle for Him to accomplish His will through your life when you are surrendered to Him.

God is the wonderful Father who plants and nourishes His dreams within us. Satan and his workers are the ones who deceive you into thinking dreams are unrealistic and that God would never use you in a supernatural way. God has big dreams for big dreamers. Even if you don't see the possibilities right now, God has something big for you in His time that is uniquely suited to you. Whatever that mission is, big or small, now or later, you are equipped to complete it. Remain faithful and continue to seek God's leadership and purpose for you in the dreams of your heart.

The Source of Our Possibilities

The reason we have an unlimited scope of possibilities is because of our source. That verse says I can do all things, "through Christ." I not only have an unlimited scope of possibilities for my life, but I have an unlimited source as well. There is no greater source of power in the universe than mine. I can dream big dreams because I have big power through the indwelling Holy Spirit. Jesus said, "All authority has been given to Me in heaven and on earth" (Matt. 28:18). He is the all-powerful sovereign. His power and place are indisputable as we see in Colossians 2:8–10, 15, which says, "Beware lest anyone cheat you through philosophy and empty deceit, according to the tradition of men, according to the basic principles of the world, and not according to Christ. For *in Him* dwells all the fullness of the Godhead bodily; *and you are complete in Him, who is the head of all principality and power*...having disarmed principalities and powers, He made a public spectacle of them, triumphing over them in it" (author's italics).

You are complete in Him! With Jesus as our source we can dream about the possibilities. We can seek God's dream for our lives because we know that nothing is too big for Him to accomplish. The Red Sea wasn't too big for Him to part. Goliath wasn't too big to defeat. The walls of Jericho were not too big to smash. The multitudes were not too big to feed and the stone covering the tomb was not too big to move. Those who would tell you to quit dreaming are those who have lost the vision of God's great plan and purpose for their lives. They are the ones who have lost their own dream of service or never had one. They have been duped into believing God will no longer do great things in our day. They have accepted the dead belief that God has become impotent and that He isn't the same God. Sweet friend,

God is the same yesterday, today, and forever. He has not lost His power nor has He lost the desire to use it through His people. Jesus is our unlimited source. Through His power and according to His special purpose I can truly do all things. Yes, you can!

Conclusion

You can be a great champion for Christ. I know that is true without even knowing you personally because the Word of God opens the door for all who would seriously be transformed by Christ and take the challenge. Do you really want to be somebody special? Are you tired of the temporary and superficial teasing of the world? Are you tired of the void in your life that you can't seem to fill? Are you tired of the treadmill you keep walking on and yet staying in the exact same place? Are you really ready to go all the way for the Lord and make an impact? Are you ready to do what nobody else can do? Are you ready to pray that God will use you to be the greatest man or woman He has ever used in some area?

If you are, you are ready to seriously seek, find, and follow God's will. If that is the case, let me reiterate the principles of this book in a nutshell.

"Knowing Him": You must "know" Christ personally. You must know that you are saved/born again and that you have completely committed your life to Jesus Christ and have claimed Him as your personal Savior.

"Knowing Obedience": Walking with Him you will desire to live in loving obedience to those things you know to be righteous and holy as you are empowered by the Holy Spirit. Your life must be focused on your loving and intimate relationship with Christ which will lead to following the principles God has revealed to you so that He can lead you on to more maturity and obedience.

"Knowing Cleansing": Develop a habit of confessing sins and receiving forgiveness and cleansing on a daily basis knowing that you will fail at times when following the flesh instead of walking in the Spirit. Sin, left unconfessed will cause a breach of communication and intimacy with the Lord.

"Knowing Timing": Trust God so completely that you are willing to wait on His timing while you continue to remain faithful wherever He has placed you. Your fulfillment will come as you follow His timing and not your own.

"Open and Closed Doors": Carefully evaluate and follow the opened and closed doors of opportunity in conjunction with the peace or unrest in your heart and the confirmation of God's Word.

"Peace or Unrest in Your Heart": Learn to listen to God's voice in your heart as you evaluate the opened and closed doors of opportunity and look for the confirmation of God's Word.

"The Confirmation of God's Word": Consistently study the precious Word of God and seek God's answers for your life out of its pages. As you follow the answers the Holy Spirit reveals to you out of His Word, in conjunction with the opened and closed doors and the peace or unrest in your heart you will stay on track.

"Putting the Three Keys Together": As you are sensitive to the leading of the Holy Spirit, you can watch His direction in fulfilling and combining these three keys and giving you the spiritual confidence for following His will.

"Discouragement the Great Defeater": Stay close to the Lord in your intimate walk with Him and remain spiritually aware of the devil's devices which he tries to use to overcome you. Find your joy, peace, assurance, and fulfillment through your love relationship with Christ. Remember to look at things from God's perspective found in the truth principles of His Word, and not a false perspective you have set up yourself.

"Prayer the Great Ingredient": Develop an intimate lifestyle of loving, consistent prayer. Seek to have a balanced prayer life that is pleasing to God and that knows how to get answers.

"Lordship the Great Issue": Follow Jesus Christ as the Lord and Master of your life. Follow His direction. Live your life out of love and devotion to Him as your top priority according to His desires and goals rather than your own.

"You the Great Champion": Realize that God's plan for you is to use your life in a great way. Throw off the lies of the adversary and live through the Holy Spirit's power to become all He intends for you to be. You have an unlimited scope of possibilities with an unlimited source of strength in Jesus Christ. Live your dreams in Christ.

Sweet friend, I know you can do it. God has something special for you that no one else can do exactly as you would do it. You are unique and one-of-a-kind and that means you are special to God. There is not another "you" on the planet. He has gifted you in order to make a lasting impact on the world. Don't allow anything or anyone to keep you from God's perfect will. If you want it summed up in a few words, "You shall love the LORD your God with all your heart, with all your soul, and with all your mind. This is the first and great commandment. And the second is like it: You shall love your neighbor as yourself" (Matt. 22:37–39), so "Go therefore and make disciples of all nations, baptizing them in the name of the Father and of the Son and of the Holy Spirit, teaching them to observe all things that I (Christ) have commanded you; and lo, I am with you always, even to the end of the age. Amen" (Matt. 28:19–20).

"Love God Supremely! Love Others Sacrificially! Go And Make Disciples Of All Nations!"

"You can do all things through Christ who strengthens you."
"You can make a spiritual impact on this world."
"Go for it!"
"Leave a legacy!"
"Live to impact eternity!"

In Christ, I can do it!

In Christ, I WILL DO IT!

ENDNOTES

I. Preparations For Knowing God's Will

Chapter 1

1 Spurgeon, C. H. *Lectures To My Students*. p. 11. Copyright 2017. Peabody, Mass.: Hendrickson Publishers.
2 Hyskell, Mark D. *I Want It All*. pp. 167–169. Copyright 2014. Collierville, TN: Innovo Publications.
3 Spurgeon, C. H. *All Of Grace*. p. 93. Copyright 1894. Chicago, Illinois: Moody Press.
4 Chafer, Lewis Sperry. *Grace*. p. vii. Copyright 1950. Grand Rapids, Michigan: Zondervan Publications.
5 Packer, J. I. *Knowing God*. p. 29. Copyright 1973. Downers Grove, Illinois: Inter Varsity Press.
6 Swindoll, Charles R. *Laugh Again*. p. 120. Copyright 1991. Dallas, Texas: Word Publishing.

Chapter 2

1 Keller, Timothy. *The Prodigal God*. pp. 65–66. Copyright 2008. New York, NY: Riverhead Books.
2 Ibid. p. 133.
3 Ibid. p. 128.
4 Federer, William J. *America's God And Country*. p. 383. Copyright 1996. Coppell, Texas: FAME Publishing.
5 Federer, William J. *America's God And Country*. p. 22. Copyright 1996. Coppell, Texas: FAME Publishing.
6 Ravenhill, Leonard. *Why Revival Tarries*. p. 25. Copyright 1987. Bloomington, Minn.: Bethany House Publishers.
7 Torrey, R. A. *How To Pray*. p. 9. Copyright 1988. Chicago, Illinois: Moody Press.
8 Bruce, F. F. *The Gospel of John*. p. 294. Copyright 1983. Grand Rapids, Michigan: William B. Eerdmans Publishing.
9 Swindoll, Charles R. *From Personal Testimony*. Copyright 1988. Houston, TX: Congress on Biblical Exposition.

Chapter 3

1 Hyskell, Mark D. *"Conviction Grace" (Poem)*. Unpublished.
2. Dennis, Lane T., Exec. Ed. *The ESV Study Bible.* p. 2430. Copyright 2008. Wheaton, IL: Crossway.
3. MacArthur, John. *The MacArthur Study Bible.* p. 1964. Copyright 1997. Nashville, TN: Word Publishing, a Division of Thomas Nelson Inc.
4 Lee, Richard. *Issues Of The Heart.* pp. 45–46. Copyright 1990. Dallas, Texas: Word Publications.
5 Blackaby, Henry & Richard; King, Claude. *Experiencing God.* p. 56. Copyright 2008. Nashville, Tennessee: B & H Publishing Group.
6 MacArthur, John. *The MacArthur Study Bible.* p. 875. Copyright 1997. Nashville, TN: Word Publishing, a Division of Thomas Nelson Inc.
7 Dennis, Lane T., Exec. Ed. *The ESV Study Bible.* p. 2435. Copyright 2008. Wheaton, IL: Crossway.
8 MacArthur, John. *The MacArthur Study Bible.* p. 877. Copyright 1997. Nashville, Tennessee: Word Publishing, a Division of Thomas Nelson Inc.
9 Packer, J. I. *Knowing God.* p. 91. Copyright 1973. Downers Grove, IL: Inter-Varsity Press.

Chapter 4

1 Cowman, Mrs. Charles. *Streams In The Desert.* p. 124. Copyright 1965. Grand Rapids, MI: Zondervan Publications.
2 Blackaby, Henry & Richard; King, Claude. *Experiencing God.* p. 71. Copyright 2008. Nashville, TN: B & H Publishing Group.
3 Rogers, Adrian. *Mastering Your Emotions.* pp. 61–62. Copyright 1988. Nashville, Tennessee: Broadman Press.

II. Provisions for Knowing God's Will

1 Blackaby, Henry & Richard; King, Claude. *Experiencing God.* p. 115. Copyright 2008. Nashville, TN: B & H Publishing Group.

Chapter 5

1 Platt, David. *Radical.* p. 13. Copyright 2010. Colorado Springs, CO: Multnomah Books.
2 Woolf, Henry Bosley, Chief Ed. *Webster's New Collegiate Dictionary.* p. 396. Copyright 1981. Springfield, MA: G & C Merriam Company.
3 Ibid. p. 361.

4 Shaeffer, Francis A. *The Great Evangelical Disaster*. p. 37. Copyright 1984. Westchester, IL: Crossway Books.

Chapter 6

1 Criswell, W. A. *Standing On The Promises*. pp. 128–129. Copyright 1990. Dallas, TX: Word Publications.

2 Hyskell, Mark D. *I Want It All*. pp. 156–157. Copyright 2014. Collierville, TN: Innovo Publishers.

3 Ibid. p. 158.

4 Lee, Richard. *Issues Of The Heart*. p. 109. Copyright 1990. Dallas, TX: Word Publications.

5 Twain, Mark. Quote. *Web Dictionary*.

6 Swindoll, Charles, R. *Laugh Again*. p. 40. Copyright 1991. Dallas, TX: Word Publications.

7 Moule, H. C. G. *Studies In Philippians*. p. 113. Copyright 1977. Grand Rapids, MI: Kregel Publications.

8 Ross, Allen P. *The Bible Knowledge Commentary (Psalms)*. p. 842. Copyright 1985. USA: Victor Books, a Division of Scripture Press Publications.

9 Radmacher, Earl D., Gen. Ed. *The Nelson Study Bible*. p. 944. Copyright 1997. Nashville, TN: Thomas Nelson Publishers.

10 Wiersbe, Warren. *Expository Outlines-New Testament*. p. 451. Copyright 1965. Covington, KY: Calvary Book Room.

11 MacArthur, John Jr. *The MacArthur New Testament Commentary (Ephesians)*. p. 34. Copyright 1986. Winona Lake, IN: BMH Books.

12 Hyskell, Joseph F. *Who's On Board*. p. 4. Copyright 2010. Lulu.com

13 Radmacher, Earl D., Gen. Ed. *The Nelson Study Bible*. p. 1953. Copyright 1997. Nashville, TN: Thomas Nelson Publishers.

14 Smith, Oswald J. *The Man God Uses*. p. 24. Copyright 1981. Burlington, ON: G. R. Welch Company.

15 Keller, Timothy. *The Prodigal God*. p. 137. Copyright 2008. New York, NY: Riverhead Books.

16 Hyskell, Mark D. *I Want It All*. p. 29. Copyright 2014. Collierville, TN: Innovo Publishing.

Chapter 7

1 Zodhiates, Spiros. *Pulpit Helps*. p. 6. Feb. 1992 Issue. Chattanooga, TN: AMG International.

2 MacArthur, John Jr. *Our Sufficiency In Christ*. p. 241. Copyright 1991. Dallas, TX: Word Publications.

3 Tozer, A. W. *The Pursuit of God*. p. 56. Copyright 1993. Camp Hill, PA: Christian Publications.

4 Hendricks, Howard G. & William D. *Living By The Book*. p. 233. Copyright 2007. Chicago, IL: Moody Publishers.

5 Hyskell, Mark D. *I Want It All*. p. 41. Copyright 2014. Collierville, TN: Innovo Publishers.

6 Spurgeon C. H. *Lectures To My Students*. p. 18. Copyright 2017. Peabody, Mass.: Hendrickson Publishers.

Chapter 8

III. Progressions Toward Knowing God's Will

Chapter 9

1 Tozer, A. W. *The Pursuit of God*. p. 71. Copyright 1993. Camp Hill, PA: Christian Publications.

2 Wiersbe, Warren. *Walking With The Giants*. p. 25. Copyright 1976. Grand Rapids, MI: Baker Book House.

3 Ibid. p. 38.

4 Ibid. p. 45.

5 Ibid. p. 55.

6 Ibid. p. 65.

7 Ibid. p. 173.

8 Hyskell, Mark D. *Personal Journal*. Unpublished.

9 Hyskell, Mark D. *"Desperately Trusting"* (Poem). Unpublished.

10 Schaeffer, Francis. *The Great Evangelical Disaster*. pp. 38–39. Copyright 1984. Westchester, IL: Crossway Books.

11 Woolf, Henry Bosley, Chief Ed. *Webster's New Collegiate Dictionary*. p. 708. Copyright 1981. Springfield, MA: G & C Merriam Company.

12 Lightner, Robert P. *The Bible Knowledge Commentary (Philippians)*. p. 664. Copyright 1985. USA: Victor Books, a Division of Scripture Press Publications.

13 Moule, H. C. G. *Studies In Philippians*. p. 114. Copyright 1977. Grand Rapids, MI: Kregel Publications.

14 Hendricks, Howard G. & William D. *Living By The Book*. p. 13. Copyright 2007. Chicago, IL: Moody Publishers.

15 Hyskell, Mark D. *"My Anchor"* (Poem). Unpublished.

Chapter 10

1 Ravenhill, Leonard. *Why Revival Tarries*. p. 25. Copyright 1987. Bloomington, Minnesota: Bethany House Publishers.

2 Federer, William J. *America's God And Country*. pp. 383-384. Copyright 1996. Coppell, Texas: FAME Publishing.
3 MacArthur, John Jr. *The MacArthur New Testament Commentary (Ephesians)*. p. 189. Copyright 1986. Winona Lake, IN: BMH Books.
4 MacArthur, John Jr. *Our Sufficiency In Christ*. p. 256. Copyright 1991. Dallas, TX: Word Publications.
5 Hyskell, Mark D. *I Want It All*. pp. 163–164. Copyright 2014. Collierville, TN: Innovo Publishers.

Chapter 11

1 Woolf, Henry Bosley, Chief Ed. *Webster's New Collegiate Dictionary*. p. 674. Copyright 1981. Springfield, MA: G & C Merriam Company.
2 Ravenhill, Leonard. *Why Revival Tarries*. p. 74. Copyright 1987. Bloomington, Minnesota: Bethany House Publishers.
3 Blackaby, Henry & Richard; King, Claude. *Experiencing God*. p. 102. Copyright 2008. Nashville, TN: B & H Publishing Group.
4 Barbieri, Louis A. Jr. *The Bible Knowledge Commentary (Matthew)*. p. 34. Copyright 1983. Wheaton, IL: Victor Books a Division of SP Publications Inc.
5 Spurgeon, C. H. *The King Has Come*. p. 130. Copyright 1987. Old Tappan, NJ: Fleming H. Revell Company.
6 Blackaby, Henry & Richard; King, Claude. *Experiencing God*. p. 82. Copyright 2008. Nashville, TN: B & H Publishing Group.
7 Lee, Richard. *Issues Of The Heart*. p. 48. Copyright 1990. Dallas, TX: Word Publications.
8 Patterson, Paige. *The Troubled Triumphant Church*. p. 108. Copyright 1983. Dallas, TX: Criswell Publications.

Chapter 12

1 Swindoll, Charles, R. *Laugh Again*. p. 57. Copyright 1991. Dallas, TX: Word Publications.
2 Unger, Merrill F. *The New Unger's Bible Handbook*. p. 538. Copyright 1984. Chicago, IL: Moody Press.

BIBLIOGRAPHY

1. Barbieri, Louis A. Jr. *The Bible Knowledge Commentary (Matthew)*. Wheaton, IL: Victor Books a Division of SP Publications Inc, 1983.
2. Blackaby, Henry & Richard; King, Claude. *Experiencing God*. Nashville, TN: B & H Publishing Group, 2008.
3. Bruce, F. F. *The Gospel of John*. Grand Rapids, MI: William B. Eerdman's Publishing Company, 1983.
4. Chafer, Lewis Sperry. *Grace*. Grand Rapids, MI: Zondervan Publications, 1953.
5. Cowman, Mrs. Charles. *Streams In The Desert*. Grand Rapids, MI: Zondervan Publications, 1965.
6. Criswell, W. A. *Standing On The Promises*. Dallas, TX: Word Publications, 1990.
7. Dennis, Lane T., Exec. Ed. *The ESV Study Bible*. Wheaton, IL: Crossway, 2008.
8. Federer, William J. *America's God And Country*. Coppell, Texas: FAME Publishing, 1996.
9. Hendricks, Howard G. & William D. *Living By The Book*. Chicago, IL: Moody Publishers, 2007.
10. Hyskell, Joseph F. *Who's On Board*. Lulu.com, 2010.
11. Hyskell, Mark D. *"Conviction Grace" (Poem)*. Unpublished.
12. Hyskell, Mark D. *"Desperately Trusting" (Poem)*. Unpublished.
13. Hyskell, Mark D. *I Want It All*. Collierville, TN: Innovo Publishing, 2014.
14. Hyskell, Mark D. *"My Anchor" (Poem)*. Unpublished.
15. Hyskell, Mark D. *"Personal Journal."* Unpublished.
16. Keller, Timothy. *The Prodigal God*. New York, NY: Riverhead Books, 2008.

17. Lee, Richard. *Issues Of The Heart.* Dallas, TX: Word Publications, 1990.

18. Lightner, Robert P. *The Bible Knowledge Commentary (Philippians).* Wheaton, IL: Victor Books, a Division of Scripture Press Publications, 1985.

19. MacArthur, John Jr. *Our Sufficiency in Christ.* Dallas, TX: Word Publications, 1991.

20. MacArthur, John Jr. *The MacArthur New Testament Commentary (Ephesians).* Winona Lake, IN: BMH Books, 1986.

21. MacArthur, John. *The MacArthur Study Bible.* Nashville, TN: Word Publishing, a division of Thomas Nelson Inc., 1997.

22. Moule, H. C. G. *Studies In Philippians.* Grand Rapids, MI: Kregel Publications, 1977.

23. Packer, J. I. *Knowing God.* Downers Grove, IL: Inter Varsity Press, 1973.

24. Patterson, Paige. *The Troubled Triumphant Church.* Dallas, TX: Criswell Press, 1983.

25. Platt, David. *Radical.* Colorado Springs, CO: Multnomah Books, 2010.

26. Radmacher, Earl D., Gen. Ed. *The Nelson Study Bible.* Nashville, TN: Thomas Nelson Publishers, 1997.

27. Ravenhill, Leonard. *Why Revival Tarries.* Bloomington, Minnesota: Bethany House Publishers, 1987.

28. Rogers, Adrian. *Mastering Your Emotions.* Nashville, TN: Broadman Press, 1988.

29. Ross, Allen P. *The Bible Knowledge Commentary (Psalms).* Wheaton, IL: Victor Books, a Division of Scripture Press Publications, 1985.

30. Schaeffer, Francis. *The Great Evangelical Disaster.* Westchester, IL: Crossway Books, 1984.

31. Smith, Oswald J. *The Man God Uses.* Burlington, ON: G. R. Welch Company, 1981.

32. Spurgeon, Charles H. *All Of Grace.* Chicago, IL: Moody Press, 1894.

33. Spurgeon, Charles H. *Lectures to My Students*. Peabody, Mass.: Hendrickson Publishers, 2017.

34. Spurgeon, Charles H. *The King Has Come*. Old Tappan, NJ: Fleming H. Revell Company, 1987.

35. Swindoll, Charles R. *Laugh Again*. Dallas, TX: Word Publications, 1991.

36. Swindoll, Charles R. *From Personal Testimony*. Houston, TX: Congress On Biblical Exposition, 1988.

37. Torrey, R. A. *How To Pray*. Chicago, IL: Moody Press, 1988.

38. Tozer, A. W. *The Pursuit Of God*. Camp Hill, PA: Christian Publications, 1993.

39. Twain, Mark. Quote. *Web Dictionary*.

40. Unger, Merril. *The New Unger's Bible Handbook*. Chicago, IL: Moody Press, 1984.

41. Wiersbe, Warren. *Expository Outlines On The New Testament*. Covington, KY: Calvary Book Room, 1965.

42. Wiersbe, Warren. *Walking With The Giants*. Grand Rapids, MI: Baker Book House, 1976.

43. Woolf, Henry Bosley, Chief Ed. *Webster's New Collegiate Dictionary*. Springfield, MA: G & C Merriam Company, 1981.

44. Zodhiates, Spiros. *Pulpit Helps*. Chattanooga, TN: AMG International, July 1991, Feb. 1992.

ABOUT THE AUTHOR

*M*ark D. Hyskell is director of Philippine Missions Outreach. He received his BA and MA from Luther Rice Seminary and has done further graduate work at The Criswell College and Dallas Theological Seminary. After spending over thirty years in vocational ministry in Southern Baptist Churches he left his last pastorate to devote his time to leading international mission teams. He has led four mission teams to Port au Prince, Haiti, and has made twenty one mission trips to the Philippines over the last eighteen years. He and his wife Gretchen have two grown children that are married and they reside in Tulsa, Oklahoma.

CPSIA information can be obtained
at www.ICGtesting.com
Printed in the USA
FSHW012352140421
80397FS

9 781645 699217